Praise for *Co...* T0013992

"Dan Gearino offers a more compelling and complex place for the comic shop in popular culture by demonstrating how entrepreneurs and distribution channels have reshaped that commercial space over the last 50 years. . . . Gender issues feature heavily in the text, and this offers scholars . . . a point of consideration lacking from many other outlets. . . . Above all, this work personalizes the comic shop as a collection of people who, through emotion and personal desire, embrace an evolving and unstable place in the commercial world of pop culture."

—*PopMatters*

"[Gearino] has clearly done his homework. . . . *Comic Shop* is an essential read for anyone interested in the mechanics and money of the comic industry, but I was most amazed to learn that, beyond Carol Kalish, there was another woman behind the formation of the direct market. That's not a story that's often been told."

—Johanna Draper Carlson, *Comics Worth Reading*

"Gearino pulls back the curtain on the seldom-seen end of the business encompassing sales, distribution and retail. . . . Drawing from original documents and firsthand interviews with key participants, [he] gives the retail and distribution side of the industry an account as dramatic and lively as Sean Howe did for the creative side in his 2012 book on Marvel Comics. . . . The result is a readable, well-researched account that fills a gap in existing comics literature and provides a great reference for future work."

—ICv2

COMIC SHOP

COMIC SHOP

The Retail Mavericks Who Gave Us
a New Geek Culture

UPDATED AND EXPANDED EDITION

Dan Gearino

Foreword by Tom Spurgeon

SWALLOW PRESS / OHIO UNIVERSITY PRESS / ATHENS, OHIO

Swallow Press
An imprint of Ohio University Press, Athens, Ohio 45701
ohioswallow.com

Printed in the United States of America
Swallow Press / Ohio University Press books are printed on acid-free paper ⊗ ™

First paperback edition, expanded and updated, published 2019
ISBN 978-0-8040-1213-3

29 28 27 26 25 24 23 22 21 20 19   5 4 3 2 1

The Library of Congress has cataloged the hardcover edition as follows:
Names: Gearino, Dan, 1975- author.
Title: Comic shop : the retail mavericks who gave us a new geek culture / Dan
  Gearino ; foreword by Tom Spurgeon.
Description: Athens, Ohio : Swallow Press/Ohio University Press, [2017] |
  Includes bibliographical references and index.
Identifiers: LCCN 2017032096| ISBN 9780804011907 (hardback : acid-free paper)
  | ISBN 9780804040839 (pdf)
Subjects: LCSH: Comic-book stores--United States. | Comic-book
  stores--Canada. | Selling--Comic books, strips, etc.--United States. |
  Selling--Comic books, strips, etc.--Canada. | Comic books, strips,
  etc.--United States--Marketing. | Comic books, strips,
  etc.--Canada--Marketing. | Booksellers and bookselling--United
  States--Biography. | Booksellers and bookselling--Canada--Biography. |
  BISAC: LITERARY CRITICISM / Comics & Graphic Novels. | BUSINESS &
  ECONOMICS / Industries / Retailing.
Classification: LCC Z480.C64 G43 2017 | DDC 381/.4574106573--dc23
LC record available at https://lccn.loc.gov/2017032096

For Mom and Dad

Contents

Foreword

Almost nothing about the existence of comic shops makes sense.

There is very little money in comics, period. There is less money than that in comic shops. Bookstores carry much of the same material. Nearly everything that you can read in a comic shop can be bought online.

There are no national chain stores that specialize in comic books. In a century defined by giant retail, comic shops stagger forward as a collective of sole proprietorships. They do a job that used to be performed—quite ably—by thousands of steel spinner racks sitting in the dusty corners of drugstores and supermarkets, shouting "Hey, kids! Comics!" When comics faded from mass-market outlets, comic shops rose to help fill the void, a shift that was not by design and far from ideal.

Comic shops are frequently and accurately parodied as bastions of high nerdity: monasteries of geekdom, inscrutable and inaccessible to all but a few true believers. They are historically for boys in a way that has ignored or even been hostile to half of their potential audience. They are few folks' idea of cool and almost no one's conception of a sound business decision.

And yet: here they are.

Comic shops were present for the birth and the death of video stores. They lived through the fall and gradual revival of record stores. Their market continues its unlikely growth across the board and is currently the dominant first medium for cross-platform exploitation. Several top-rated TV shows were once something you could buy only in a comic shop. Many top movies can be traced to a collectible back issue. There are even comics taken seriously as art, a notion that at one time seemed more quixotic than any superhero's quest. Comic shops have been there for those comics, too.

How is any of this possible?

In *Comic Shop,* Dan Gearino provides a patient, sane, and rigorously examined answer. When did our particular nation of shopkeepers grow ponytails and wrap things in Mylar and make every Wednesday a fantasist's holiday? What combination of luck and grit allowed some of them to survive? And now, how are the best comic shops evolving to appeal to new audiences? If America's castle on a hill rests on a foundation of how we buy and sell things, Dan Gearino shows us what's in the basement. Keep your eyes straight ahead. This isn't a library. You touch it, you buy it.

Tom Spurgeon

Tom Spurgeon is editor of the Comics Reporter, *an Eisner Award–winning website, and author of, most recently,* We Told You So: Comics as Art, *an oral history of Fantagraphics Books that he wrote with Michael Dean. He also is director of Cartoon Crossroads Columbus, or CXC, a festival of comics and cartoon culture in Columbus, Ohio.*

Part 1

The Cockroaches
of Pop Culture

We are the cockroaches of pop culture.

We will survive a nuclear fallout.

—Joe Field, owner of Flying Colors Comics
& Other Cool Stuff in Concord, California

1

Magical Powers

ON A Saturday, Gib Bickel sees a woman step into the children's section of his shop. He approaches and gives his usual opener: "Canwehelpyoufind-something?" The woman, with tattoos down both arms, is shopping for a graphic novel for her daughter. She has no idea what to get, although a book called *Hero Cats* has caught her eye. He points her toward something else, a favorite of his, *Princeless.*

"This girl, she's a princess," he says. "Her dad puts her there in a tower with all her sisters until a prince will rescue her, and there's a dragon guarding her. And then she's like, 'Why am I going to wait around for some dumb boy?' So she teams up with her dragon and they have adventures." Sold.

Bickel has hand-sold more than one hundred copies of *Princeless,* a small-press graphic novel that has become a cult hit and been followed by several sequels. This is what he does. It is what makes him happy.

He is in his midfifties, with a graying goatee and a wardrobe that is an array of T-shirts, shorts, and jeans. And he is an essential part of the Columbus, Ohio, comics scene. In 1994, with two friends, he founded The Laughing Ogre, a comic shop that shows up on lists of the best in the country. Though he sold his ownership stake years ago, he still manages the shop and can be found there most days.

Laughing Ogre is one of about 3,200 comic shops in the United States and Canada, mostly small businesses whose cultural significance far exceeds the footprint of their revenue.[1] They are gathering places and tastemakers, having helped develop an audience for *Teenage Mutant Ninja Turtles* in the 1980s, *Bone* in the 1990s, and *The Walking Dead* in the 2000s. And yet, for all the value that comic shops provide to their communities and to the culture, their business model has a degree of difficulty that can resemble Murderworld, the deathtrap-filled amusement park from Marvel Comics. Publishers sell most of their material to comic shops on a nonreturnable basis. By contrast, bookstores and other media retailers—some of which sell the same products as comic stores do—can return unsold goods for at least partial credit. The result is that comic shops bear a disproportionately high level of risk when a would-be hit series turns out to be a dud. And there are plenty of duds.

This book is a biography of a business model, showing comic shops today and how they got here. I come at this as a reporter who covers business, and as a lifelong comics fan.

Before going on, I need to define one important term: "direct market." The current comic shop model was born in the 1970s, and it came to be known as the direct market because store owners received comics straight from the printers. Before that time, nearly all material had to be bought from newspaper and magazine distributors. Today, the network of comics specialty shops are still called the direct market, although the "direct" part has not been accurate for a long time. More on that later.

The staff at Laughing Ogre, and at shops across the country, let me into their worlds for what turned out to be a tumultuous year, from the summer of 2015 to the summer of 2016. The two major comics publishers, Marvel and DC, did most of the damage, with many new series that did not catch on, relaunches of existing series that often failed to energize sales, and a months-long delay for one of the top-selling titles, Marvel's *Secret Wars*. The notable failures were almost all tied to periodical comics, single issues of which cost $3 to $5 apiece and are sold mainly to people who shop as a weekly habit. In other words, the leading publishers spent the year pissing off some of their most loyal customers and undermining their retailers. And yet, much of the sales slide was offset by growth of independent publishers and by small hits such as *Princeless*, big hits such as the sci-fi epic *Saga*, and many in between.

Amid the ups and downs, comic shops have a knack for launching ideas into the broader culture. Few do this as well as The Beguiling in Toronto. One example was in 2004, when a recent former employee had a book coming out from a small publisher. The store's owners had a launch party at a nearby bar, and about fifty people came. There was no reason to think the book would be a sales success, but the people at The Beguiling wanted to support their guy, and they loved the book: *Scott Pilgrim Vol. 1: Scott Pilgrim's Precious Little Life* by Bryan Lee O'Malley. That night, the entertainment was provided by O'Malley's garage band.

"It was going to be a blip as far as I could tell," O'Malley said. His publisher, Oni Press, had told him that preorders of the book were about six hundred copies, which was respectable but not great. He had no plans to quit his day job at a Toronto restaurant.

In the weeks that followed, The Beguiling sold the book with an evangelistic passion. Selling *Scott Pilgrim* was easy because the book was great, said the store's owner, Peter Birkemoe. Grounded in the real Toronto and sprinkled with bits of fantasy, it told the story of a young man getting his life together and falling in love. The artwork was strongly influenced by Japanese comics and the aesthetics of 1990s video games. *Scott Pilgrim* became a sales success at a few stores across North America, which built word of mouth and turned the book into a sensation at other comic shops and then in the bookstore market.

As of 2010, *Scott Pilgrim* had completed its seven-volume run and had more than one million copies in print in North America, according to Oni Press. That was the year the movie adaptation, *Scott Pilgrim versus the World*, was released. "I'm convinced that Scott Pilgrim will go down as one of those series that changed comics forever," said Joe Nozemack, Oni's publisher, in a 2010 news release. "When I'm out and see someone wearing a *Scott Pilgrim* T-shirt or sitting in a cafe reading one of the books, I get so excited about comics entering the mainstream and to know that Oni Press's books are helping lead the way, it's an indescribable feeling."[2]

By the time the movie was released, O'Malley had long since quit his day job to be a full-time comics creator. He remains grateful and a bit baffled that his book, of all books, was the one that made it big when many great ones do not. "There's no way it was going to be a success without this kind of network of people who were going to be enthusiastic about it. I didn't see it coming at all," he said.

The best comic shops have a connection with their customers that leads, repeatedly, to some artists and series bubbling up to prominence. This dynamic also plays out at the best independent bookstores and record stores. The difference is the way that many comic shop customers make weekly trips, allowing shop owners to get to know their clients and what they want to read.

"We're bartenders," said Brian Hibbs, owner of Comix Experience and Comix Experience Outpost, both in San Francisco. "We're the friend that you come to and go, 'What's on tap this week?'" He is one of the leading comics retailers of his generation, and played a role in the rise of several creators, such as Neil Gaiman, whose *Sandman,* from DC Comics, began in 1989, the same year Hibbs opened his store. "We're selling to alcoholics, essentially. We're there to solve their problems and take the burden of their lives away for a few minutes."

At first, I thought this book would be about comic shops facing an existential challenge as the country shifts away from print media and as Amazon and other mega-retailers continue to take market share. I learned, however, that the industry has had a nausea-inducing level of volatility almost since it began in its modern form in the 1970s. So yes, comic shops are at a crossroads, but they find themselves in a similar situation every few years. What is interesting is how this crossroads is different from the others.

To begin to answer this question, I went to Milton Griepp, an industry veteran and chief executive of ICv2.com, a website that covers the business of comics and pop culture. "The biggest force affecting comic stores right now is the demographic diversification and taste diversification of the audience," he said. "You've got women in sort of unprecedented numbers reading comics. We haven't seen this gender mix, I think, since the early fifties."

He also has seen a growth in sales of comics for children, and a resulting increase in material aimed at elementary school and middle school audiences. Among the superstars in this set is cartoonist Raina Telgemeier, whose books have sold in the millions to mainly middle-grade readers. But comic shops are not guaranteed this business, Griepp said. If shops do not work hard to accommodate all audiences, there are plenty of other places to buy the same stuff.

These new readers are in addition to what he calls the "core audience," a term that evokes the image of a certain type of fan, a white man in his thirties and older. However, the core group is defined more by its buying habits than by age, race, or gender. These fans make weekly or near-weekly visits to the shop, often on Wednesday, which is when new comics go on sale.

These are some of the same people who were an untapped audience before shops proliferated in the 1980s. And now they are a tapped audience, relentlessly and ridiculously tapped, as Marvel and DC narrowed their focus in the 1990s with products that enticed a shrinking fan base to spend more money per capita, as opposed to broadening the audience. There are no reliable data available to help define the size of the core audience or see trends in its spending. But store owners told me repeatedly that this audience continues to suffer attrition. Many stores, and the industry as a whole, are growing because new types of customers are coming in to fill the gap.

Griepp got into the comics business while a graduate student at the University of Wisconsin. In 1980, he cofounded Capital City Distribution, which grew from two employees to become the country's largest wholesaler serving comic shops. He got caught on the wrong end of a massive industry consolidation in 1995 and sold the business to his main competitor. Since then, he has reinvented himself as one of the leading analysts and writers about the comics industry.

"I think the story of comic stores is really the story of community," he said. "That community is a shared interest and a shared passion for these characters. Not just superheroes. Communities around manga and many other genres and subgenres and creators. It's just reinforcing community. 'Oh, yeah, that's really cool.' 'I think that's really cool too.'"

In Philadelphia, Ariell Johnson has managed to build community in short order. She opened Amalgam Comics & Coffeehouse there in late 2015, with the goal of creating a hub for all types of readers.

"I thought it would be cool to have a place where you could buy your comics and stay there and read them and hang out," she said. The space is split about 50–50 between a comic shop and a coffee shop.

Johnson, who is in her early thirties, got a flurry of media coverage when she opened because she is one of very few black female comic shop owners in the country. Her success has come from appealing to everyone. Her message, to staff and customers, is that all are welcome.

"I have gone into shops, especially when I was just getting into comics, and I was afraid somebody would question my geek cred," she said. "You feel scrutinized being the only person who looks like you."

The challenging part for her has been to learn the business side. She has an abundance of coffee-fueled energy and works sixteen hours most days, but only sometimes does she feel that she is getting on top of things. As generations of store owners could tell her, the key to success is learning how to read a chaotic market and manage risk. It also means controlling costs. Long-term retailers need to either have a reservoir of money to call upon or become masters of these practical issues.

The comics business is unlike almost any other. Consider:

- The country's comic shops are almost all single-site, independent stores. There are some regional chains, such as Newbury Comics in New England and Graham Crackers Comics in the Chicago area, but nobody with physical locations on a national scale. The closest thing to a national chain was Hastings Entertainment, based in Amarillo, Texas, which had more than 120 stores before closing in 2016 following a bankruptcy filing.[3] Hastings stocked new comics and back issues as part of a larger selection of electronics, books, and other media. For veterans of the comics business, Hastings was just the latest in a line of would-be national chains that found comics to be a tricky business.

- The comics industry has almost no verifiable sales data. The figures that do exist are estimates based on orders made by comic shops from the largest comics distributor. There are no data about the number of comics sold to actual customers. So whenever I refer to sales estimates, there needs to be this giant caveat. The lack of data is because the comics industry, with about a billion dollars in sales per year, is too small to attract more independent reporting. And so when I say the industry has about a billion dollars in sales, I don't really know, although that is the number cited by top analysts.[4]

- The move toward digital media has not affected comics the way it has other forms of entertainment, at least not yet. Digital comics sales were down in 2015, following several years of growth, according to estimates from ICv2.com.[5] Comic shop owners had high anxiety about digital comics a few years ago, especially when publishers began offering material digitally on the same day it was available in stores. But the growth of digital has been slow, and there is little evidence that it is taking away sales from print comics. In interviews with shop owners and readers, I heard over and over that digital comics provide a poor reading experience and that the current tablet hardware is not well suited to comics. A somewhat related issue is online comics piracy. Scans of comics get shared on torrent sites alongside music and video. I have seen no reliable estimate of the effects of piracy on comics sales, and few people in the business list it as a top concern.

The Laughing Ogre has lasted, with the same name and address it's had since it opened in 1994. All that time, the sign has had a goofy illustration of a portly ogre rubbing his belly and laughing so hard his eyes are closed. The store is in a 1950s-era strip mall in a quiet neighborhood about three miles north of Ohio State University. As you enter, the children's section is to your left, guarded by a five-foot-high Phoney Bone, the scheming antihero from the best-selling *Bone* comics. The statue is not something Bickel ordered out of a catalogue. It is one of a kind, loaned by Jeff Smith, the Columbus resident and *Bone* cartoonist, who had the statue built for a book tour. In the local comics scene, no name is bigger than Smith's. The Scholastic editions of his work have sold millions of copies. If you haven't heard of *Bone,* ask a kid about it.

The children's section is mostly books, from the wordless *Owly* by Andy Runton to the kid-friendly versions of DC superheroes by Art Baltazar. *Princeless*'s first volume is by writer Jeremy Whitley and artist M. Goodwin. The children's periodical comics are along the front wall, in a spinner rack and a wall rack with copies of *Scooby-Do, Steven Universe,* and many others.

Beyond the children's section, the focal point is the left wall, along which recent comics and books are racked. This is a near-overwhelming array of products, with precisely 1,008 slots, most of which are periodical comics. Each week about 150 new titles come in, so there is a constant churn, with old items selling out or being relegated to the back room or the back-issue bins.

"People say, 'You get paid to read comics,' but I'm so busy," Bickel says. "My job is never done."

Most of the rest of the floor space is taken up by bookcases, holding thousands of titles. The prices start at about $10 and go up to more than

$100. There are archival editions of classic newspaper strips, graphic novels, and graphic memoirs, among many others.

As comic shops go, Laughing Ogre is on the large side, with about thirty-five hundred square feet open to the public. It has seven employees, and at least three of them are there most open hours. Annual sales are more than $1 million, which again puts the store on the large side.

To understand the business, a few numbers are helpful. Sales of printed material are split about 55–45 between periodical comics and books. For the periodical comics, sales are split about 90–10 between new material and material that is more than a month old. For books, years-old titles are almost as likely to sell as new ones. One of the top-selling books is *Watchmen,* a collection of a comic book series that began publication in 1986. A strong seller will move about fifty copies per year, and the store keeps multiple copies on the shelf.

Meanwhile, the store has thousands of books with just one copy each. If, for example, you want to buy *Welcome to Alflolol,* the fourth volume of Valérian and Laureline, a French sci-fi series, it is there and probably not on the shelf at any other retail outlet in the city. But it may sit there for a year or two waiting for a buyer.

Laughing Ogre is now on its third owner, a businessman who lives in Virginia and also owns two shops there. Even Bickel was gone for a while. After the first sale in 2006, he stayed on as an employee but found he didn't get along with the new management. He left for five years to sell cars. That job paid better and offered more stability, but he missed the people at the store. He came back in 2011, welcomed as a returning hero by employees and longtime customers.

The store's most recent big change was in the summer of 2015, when several long-term employees left for other jobs or for school. This left Bickel with only one remaining full-time coworker, Lauren McCallister. She was twenty-two at the time and a recent graduate of the Columbus College of Art and Design. She also does autobiographical comics, which she sells on her website, at shows, and at the store.

During the time I spent at Laughing Ogre, it was the Bickel and McCallister show. They served as manager and assistant manager, respectively, and worked with a group of mostly new hires. McCallister likes to call her boss "Old Man," as in, "I just sorted that shelf, Old Man."

(*Top*) Lauren McCallister and Gib Bickel behind the counter at
The Laughing Ogre; (*bottom*) out front, the sign is the same from
when the store opened in 1994.

But when he's not around, she talks about him like this:

"I think he has magical powers," she said. "I don't even know how to de-scribe it. He's like a master salesman, really. He has a way with every single person who comes through the door. Even like the craziest person, he can deal with them so effortlessly. It's absolutely mind-boggling. Still to this day, after working with him for three years, I can't tell you what kind of weird voodoo he's working."

The owners and managers of the best shops are a collection small enough that most of them know each other. They have seen some of the best in the business fail. They have failed themselves, or at least come close. Much of this is because of the unique risks of selling comics, a set of dangers that exceed the substantial challenges confronted in running many other types of small businesses.

Almost nothing about this model makes sense if you look at it purely in terms of profit and loss. You are much better off opening a Subway fran-chise. The best comic shops can mitigate the risk with smart ordering, loyal customers, and a few lucky breaks. But why is the model so intrinsically challenging? How did it get to be this way? That story begins decades ago, and it involves a collection of hippies and geeks and a Brooklyn high school English teacher named Phil Seuling.

2

This Bold Guy (1968–73)

THE BOYS were in their early teens in the summer of 1968, a month away from starting high school, and this was an adventure. They got on the train in Manhattan and took it all the way out to Woodside, Queens. They had heard, but did not completely believe, that there was such a thing as a comic book store.

At that time, new comics could be bought in almost every neighborhood at newsstands, drugstores, and candy stores. Old comics could be found in dusty stacks in used bookstores and flea markets. But there were almost no places where a serious fan could look through an organized selection of back issues.

That was the novelty of Victory Thrift Shop in Woodside, and that was why Jim Hanley's life changed the day he and his friends entered the place. Hanley would grow up to become one of the most successful comics retailers on the East Coast.

"It was the most amazing thing we'd ever seen," he said. "We went there in the elevated train to the store, and as we get there, there's a window, a display window, floor-to-ceiling comics. There was *Action Comics* 1, 2, 3, 4, 5. *Superman* 1, 2, 3, 4, 5. *Marvel Mystery* 1, 2, 3, 4, 5."

There is some debate about where and when the first comics specialty shop opened, often turning on how you define "comic shop." The store in Woodside, starting in 1961, was one of the first to publicly display comics as collectibles and sell them for more than cover price. The comics were protected with clear plastic bags, another innovation of the store's owner, a pioneer of comics retail: Robert Bell.

Many fans from the 1960s to the 1980s know the name Robert Bell because of his ads in comics and fanzines, selling his products through mail order. Fewer people know that before the eponymous mail order business, he had the Queens storefront, which he opened when he was just eighteen.

There is a tall-tale quality to what old retailers and fans say about Bell, but I have yet to find one of those stories that doesn't check out. Yes, Bell hoarded copies of *Fantastic Four* #1 when it came out in 1961, acquiring them for as little as a dime apiece and then holding onto them as their resale value soared. Yes, he had at least a single copy of every Marvel comic from 1961 to about 1980. Yes, he had a prominent ad on the first *Overstreet Comic Book Price Guide* and remained a key advertiser in later years as the guide became an industry standard. The stories end with Bell selling his collection in the mid-1980s and vanishing from the comics scene.

"I bought my first property, real estate, when I was thirteen," said Bell, speaking from his oceanfront condo in Pompano Beach, Florida, where he is semiretired. His success in comics gave him the money to invest in commercial real estate, and that was the focus of his professional life in the thirty years since he stopped selling comics. "I had a vending route with gumball machines. I had mail-order drop shipping for multiple different products. And then, at eighteen, the bookstore."

The store was a successor to the thrift store that had been run by his parents in a separate part of the neighborhood. He grew up in that store, and, when his parents decided to get out of retail, he took the name of their business, Victory Thrift, and put it on a new location that would be his to run. The name referred to the Allies' victory in World War II.

At the start, his top-selling items were paperback books, which he bought for one-fourth of cover price and resold for half of cover price. But he could see rising interest in his small selection of comics. New titles, such as *Amazing Spider-Man* and *Fantastic Four*, were attracting an older reader and a more devoted fan. He found that he could resell back issues of those comics and others for more than cover price.

To protect the most valuable issues, he cut and folded clear plastic from a dry cleaner and then taped it shut in the back. Finding that some customers wanted to buy these makeshift bags, he decided to mass-produce them. He shopped around for contract manufacturers and selected one that would make him tens of thousands of clear bags. Unlike the dry-cleaner bags, the "Bell bags" were the perfect size for comics.

Comics were about 10 percent of his sales in 1961 and grew to half of his sales near the end of the decade, when he left the storefront and focused on selling comics through mail order. (After he left, his mother took over the space and turned it into more of a thrift shop, buying and selling household items.) He built his comics sales by making connections with suppliers, following leads toward private collections, and advertising on the radio.

He tells the story of a woman who phoned him and said, "I have a box of books and I was on the way to the dump to throw them out. My son said they might be worth some money." Her collection included the first three issues of *Walt Disney's Comics and Stories* and the first issue of *Batman,* all in near-perfect condition, among many others. He paid her $3,000, which was "a lot of money back then," Bell said.

The most valuable comics, then and now, were from the early days of superheroes in the 1930s. Among the first publishers of periodical comics was the company that would become DC Comics, which began with *New Fun* in 1935, an anthology series. Three years later, the company published *Action Comics* #1, the debut of Superman, and kickstarted the era of the superhero.[1]

Almost immediately, comic books were a mass medium, sold through grocery stores, candy stores, newsstands, and about anywhere else newspapers could be found. As with almost any printed material, some readers saved the old issues and some retailers resold them, providing a glimmer of a secondary market.

One of the earliest known comics specialty retailers was Harvey T. "Pop" Hollinger in Concordia, Kansas, a small city about a three-hour drive northwest of Topeka. Starting in the late 1930s, he opened a store selling used comics and other items, according to a profile in the 1981 edition of the *Overstreet* guide. He found that one of the big problems with comics was durability, so he developed modifications that included brown tape and extra staples along the spines. The results, which would horrify collectors seeking "mint" condition, can still be found on the secondary market, often described as Hollinger-rebuilt comics.[2]

Another early comics retailer was Claude Held in Buffalo, New York, who had a well-stocked comics section in his used bookstore and sold comics through mail order beginning in the 1960s. On the West Coast, one of the important early retailers was Cherokee Books in Los Angeles, which opened in 1949 and by the mid-1960s had a comics section on the second floor.[3]

In the New York City area, Bell was one of the big players in a small world of comics dealers. His contemporaries included Passaic Books in New Jersey, a giant used bookstore with a comics section, and Howard Rogofsky, who ran a mail-order business out of his home. The dealers knew each other and shopped each others' inventory, maintaining a polite rivalry.

The early dealers were a mix of adults and teenagers. In Texas, Buddy Saunders began to collect comics in earnest in 1961, when he was in his early teens. "When *Fantastic Four* #1 came out, I was pretty impressed with it, so I bought two copies, one for my collection, and one I sold a month later. Doubled my money at 25 cents," Saunders said. "I can make the claim that I am probably the only comics retailer around today that has sold a mint copy of *Fantastic Four* #1 for a quarter. Probably would have been better then if I had kept it, but I was doubling my money, and impressed with myself." Today, that comic would sell for hundreds of thousands of dollars.

He was a key player in some of the early fan-produced publications, including *Rocket's Blast Comicollector,* which started in 1964. He contributed illustrations, and also placed ads in which he sold his own comics, generating money that he used to buy more comics. More than a decade later, he would found Lone Star Comics in the Dallas area. It would grow into a chain of stores, and exists today as MyComicShop.com, a large online retailer of classic comics.

Most of the early dealers knew of Bell because of his ads and his mail-order business, but his Queens store was not as well known. The store is notable in hindsight because it looked so much like the shops that would follow. He turned out to have near-perfect timing, opening the business right on the cusp of a boom in fan culture and a growing interest in collecting comics.

As Bell sees it, everything changed in 1968. He got a table that year at the Convention of Comic Book Art, held at the Statler Hilton in Manhattan. The event was a leap up from its predecessors in terms of the level of organization and the size of the crowd. "People came in with money in their hands, not their pockets, they were so eager to buy comics," he said.

This is where Bell's story crosses over with a much bigger one. The convention had been organized by a high school English teacher from Brooklyn, a tough guy with a goofball smile who would turn out to be the instigator of an explosion of new comic shops. His name was Phil Seuling, and much of today's retail model, the good and the terrible, can be traced back to what he soon would start.

The New York convention got much bigger in the following year, 1969. At a Saturday luncheon, the guests, a group of mostly young men, turned to look at a camera. A few smiled. The resulting black-and-white photograph is a jolt of nostalgia, showing a time when comics fandom was so small that many of the country's best-known comics creators, and their fans, could fit into a room and have a meal together.[4]

Along the back wall are the guests of honor, including the one most likely to have been known to the general public: Hal Foster, creator of the *Prince Valiant* newspaper strip. He has white hair and dark-rimmed glasses, and is among the oldest people there. To his left is Gil Kane, the artist known for his work on DC's *Green Lantern* and *The Atom*, dapper in a jacket and tie and looking, as he often did, like the coolest professor on campus. Standing by the side wall are some of the Marvel guys, such as the boyish writer and editor Roy Thomas, whose glasses are white from the reflected flash, and his frequent collaborator, artist John Buscema, big and tall with a bushy goatee. In the foreground are tables for the paying guests, mostly young men in jackets and ties.

For Irene Vartanoff, it was the summer between high school and college. In the photo, she is dressed in a serape; she remembers that the room was chilly and that she wished she had brought a coat. To her right sits her younger sister, Ellen; they are some of the only women unaccompanied by a boyfriend or husband. Irene would go on to work on the editorial staff at Marvel and DC, and Ellen would become an artist and arts educator in Washington, D.C. Also at their table are friends they had met through the Illegitimate Sons of Superman, a fan-organized club for young DC readers. Among them are Marv Wolfman, Len Wein, and Dick Giordano, all of whom were already, or would become, prolific comics creators and editors.

"Everybody knew everybody," Irene said. "We'd all troop out to Tad's Steakhouse, where you could get dinner for less than $2. We'd talk about comics or James Bond or *The Prisoner* or *Modesty Blaise,* a bunch of the things that were related."

Among the overwhelmingly white crowd, the photo shows three black men: Richard "Grass" Green, a cartoonist from Indiana who was known for his work in fan publications; Arvell Jones, who would go on to draw comics for DC and Marvel; and a man dressed in a suit whom I have not been able to identify.

In all, there are more than one hundred people shown. But I want to draw your attention to someone in the back, next to the guests of honor. He is dressed in a jacket and tie and has slicked-back hair. He has a blank expression, choosing not to show his goofy smile. This is Phil Seuling.

He had organized the Saturday luncheon, a small part of his convention, a better follow-up to the convention he had done the year before. A few years later, he would help develop a new way of distributing comics. He was, in many ways, the father of modern comics retail.

"He was this bold guy," said Jim Hanley, who went to his first Seuling convention as a teenager the following year. "He didn't walk into the room, he stormed into the room. He jumped onto the stage and grabbed the microphone and captivated the audience instantly. He had spent probably ten years at that point teaching school, so he was used to being in front of an audience every day, and he was good at it. He always had the loudest voice in the room, and he knew us."

The "us" part was important. Hanley and the other mostly younger fans at the conventions saw themselves as a tribe, a group whose loyalty was hardened by the outside perception that comics were a kids' medium. "I was the reticent kid, which was pretty common among comics fans," he said.

Seuling had a way of welcoming strangers. For the 1968 convention, a young comics fan from San Jose, California, drove across the country to stay with Seuling and his family and serve as an assistant at the show. That was Michelle Nolan, who was twenty, and would go on to be prolific writer and editor on comics history.

"I stayed in his comic book room," Nolan said. "He had a nice apartment in Brooklyn near Coney Island. You could see the Wonder Wheel and Cyclone from his window."

Nolan would turn out to be a crucial connection. Back in California, she was part of a close-knit group of comics fans. Among them was a high school kid named Francis Plant, who went by his nickname, Bud. He would go on to

(*Top*) Phil Seuling on stage at the 1971 Comic Art Convention, held at the Statler Hilton in Manhattan; (*bottom*) outside the ballroom was the dealers' room, where dealers set up to sell to fans and collectors. *Credit: Mike Zeck.*

co-own what may have been the first comic shop chain, Comics & Comix, and would have a separate business selling comics and books through the mail.

For the 1970 convention, Nolan, Plant, and others loaded up a van and made the drive east to stay with Seuling and help at his convention. Other than Nolan, who had worked at the two previous shows, Seuling didn't know any of them.

The van rolled into Brooklyn at about 11:30 p.m. The visitors found parking and then arrived at Seuling's apartment door. With some reluctance, considering the hour, they knocked. The door swung open, and there was Seuling, dressed only in a pair of white briefs.

"It's New York and it's July and it's hot as shit," Plant said. Instead of being upset or embarrassed, Seuling waved everyone in and showed them to his living room, where they would sleep.

Plant was meeting a man who would become his most important business mentor and an even better friend.

"When there was a group of people, he would always be the center of attention," Plant said. "He told the stories. He flirted with the cute waitresses. He always picked up the dinner tabs. He was older than us, but he was a high school teacher, so he was used to dealing with lots of kids."

And yet there was another side to Seuling. He could go from a smiling pal to a red-faced fury. For out-of-towners, he fit the image of a tough New Yorker, tall and broad-shouldered, with a Brooklyn accent and a short fuse. "Phil was a streetwise guy," Plant said. "He was from Brooklyn, and they grow up a lot faster than little neophytes from California. We went back there and our eyes were opened. It was just a different world."

The Bay Area had its own burgeoning comics scene. Despite his youth, Plant had been a part of it for years. He grew up reading Disney comics and moved on to DC and Marvel. In his early teens, he shopped at Twice Read Books, a used bookstore in downtown San Jose. There was a stack of old comics by the door for a nickel each. Then one day he saw another customer ask to see the dollar comics.

"I was aghast. I never heard of a dollar comic," he said.

From behind the counter the store clerk pulled out a box of comics from the 1940s and early 1950s. Plant was fascinated by the idea that comics had a rich history of characters he had never seen. He bought *Thrills of Tomorrow* #19, cover dated February 1955 and published by Harvey

Comics, which was itself a reprint of a Harvey comic from 1946 called *Stuntman,* written and drawn by the cocreators of Captain America, Jack Kirby and Joe Simon.

From his visits to the dollar box, he met other fans of old comics, and they became friends, a mix of adults and teens that included Nolan. "If anything, I was probably very shy in high school," Plant said. "I just wasn't one of the hip guys. I had glasses. I had acne. I wasn't that good at sports." With comics, he felt like he was part of something.

In March 1968, when he was sixteen, several of the group pooled their comics, books, and cash and opened a small store, Seven Sons Comic Shop. Less than a year later, the partners sold the business to one of the co-owners. Some of the same people, including Plant, soon opened an even smaller store in San Jose called Comic World. It lasted about a year before the co-owners moved on to other things. For Plant, this meant enrolling at San Jose State. He would study business, having already been a co-owner of two businesses.

Meanwhile, an hour's drive north, Gary Arlington opened San Francisco Comic Book Co. in that city's Mission District. He was starting in April 1968, a few weeks after Seven Sons, although the people involved did not know of each other's stores at the time. His business became closely associated with underground comics, the irreverent and boundary-pushing publications that nobody would confuse with DC or Marvel. One of the key underground titles, *Zap Comix,* was published in San Francisco that same year, with stories by Robert Crumb, Spain Rodriguez, and others. The undergrounds developed their own retail networks of head shops and record stores as opposed to pharmacies and candy stores.[5]

"A buddy of mine turned me on to *Zap* and said, 'You've got to read this underground comic,' and I read it and I couldn't really understand quite what was going on," Plant said. "I was not smoking dope. I didn't have a kind of stoned attitude. I was a high school kid reading *Spider-Man.* The undergrounds sort of blossomed from there over the next two or three years, and I sort of grew into that."

All of this was part of the context when Plant and friends got in their van in 1970 to go to New York. The Bay Area guys were bringing their own bustling comics culture. As they made connections with Seuling, they would help create a national framework for comic shops to do business.

Some of the people and places of the Bay Area comics scene. (*Top*) A young Bud Plant in the 1970s; (*middle*) one of the only photos in existence of Comic World, the San Jose shop briefly co-owned by Plant and several others, including Dick Swan, pictured, who was fifteen at the time; (*bottom*) Gary Arlington at his store, San Francisco Comic Book Co. *Credits: Clay Geerdes, except for Comic World, which is courtesy of Dick Swan.*

Seuling's convention took off at a time when comics had begun to attract a broader audience that included older readers. The new fans didn't want to miss an issue. "There were more creators beginning to do work that presumed the audience was older or more intelligent," said Paul Levitz, who was a young fan in New York and would go on to be a writer and executive at DC Comics. "It's really in the early sixties when you get to Stan [Lee]'s work at Marvel, particularly Julie Schwartz's work on the superhero revival at DC, that it begins to be inviting to an older, brighter audience." He published his first fanzine in the late 1960s and became one of the leading writers in the fan community, years before he worked at DC.

At the same time, many readers found it difficult to obtain the comics they wanted. The major publishers sold through a network of independent distributors. The distributors were entrenched businesses that had hard-earned territories of newsstands, grocery stores, and drugstores. They sold a wide array of printed material, of which comics were a small and not particularly profitable part.

"There was no way for me to get a comic if I missed it on the stands," said Irene Vartanoff. She was part of a generation of fans who developed their own system for finding back issues, trading and selling comics through the mail with other fans. Some comics publishers helped facilitate this by printing letters from fans who wanted to buy or trade specific issues. Vartanoff became known in the fan community for how often her letters appeared in comics.

Fans in this new generation were willing to pay more than cover price to get an issue they missed. In turn, the idea of comics as collectibles began to gain currency, a concept that got a boost from news coverage of rare comics selling for hundreds of dollars.

In this environment, a time of rising interest in comics but an unreliable distribution system, Seuling came into prominence. He was a Brooklyn guy, born and raised. He got drafted during the Korean War, and did all of his service in the United States, mostly in Texas. From there, he went to City College in New York.[6]

He met a woman named Carole in an introduction to geology class, and they hit it off. They got married in 1954, while both were still students. "City College was a place where people let it all hang out," said Carole Seuling, who is now retired and living in Connecticut. The campus had a bustling political scene, an early glimmering of the protest movements that would later arrive on campuses across the country.

Phil and Carole both studied to be English teachers. After college, they got jobs in the city's public school system and settled in Bensonhurst in Brooklyn. They had two daughters, Gwen and Heather. Contrary to what Phil would later say in interviews, he was not a regular comics reader during his early adult years. His interest in comics was rekindled in the early 1960s when he and a friend, Doug Berman, came upon a stack of Golden Age comics for sale in a thrift shop, Carole said.

"He and his friend Doug decided there's money to be made here," she said. "They started scouring these junk stores and bought up all the comics they could find."

The couple's apartment became a warehouse for the growing collection. One memorable purchase was in 1963, which Carole remembers because it was the same day as President Kennedy's funeral. "They came back with the mother lode," she said. "I mean, there were six copies of *Life* #1 and three copies of *Action* #1. Three. And then that was the tip of the iceberg. . . . People didn't really know what they were selling. They wised up in the seventies and started asking for more money."

While Phil depended on teaching for his main income, he developed a bustling side business in comics. He bought and sold through ads in early fanzines. At some of the very first comics conventions in the mid-1960s, he was among the few dozen people there. He was part-owner of After Hours Bookstore in Brooklyn, which sold used books and comics.[7] Then, in 1968, he took over as lead organizer for an existing New York convention. The event, held on Fourth of July weekend, grew to become a destination for comics fans, dealers, and professionals from across the country.

The conventions mainly dealt with the sales of old comics, but Phil saw an opportunity in selling new comics. He later spoke about this in an interview with the cartoonist Will Eisner.[8]

"A friend of mine in the sixties owned a little candy store, so I got an inside view of distribution there," Seuling said. "Tony Fibbio was his name, lovely guy, passed away. He collected and he knew what kids wanted, but he couldn't get the books he wanted. The distributors would not give him the titles."

A store could not order specific numbers of each title and did not know when the titles would arrive. Instead, retailers received an assortment selected by the distributor, sometimes bound in ties that damaged the comics. One of the fundamentals of this system was returnability. If comics, magazines, or other printed material didn't sell, the distributor would pick them up and return them for a credit. So, while the service was often lousy for comics fans, the financial risk was low for the newsstands and pharmacies that sold them.

"I said and I repeated it: 'There is another way of doing this,'" Seuling said to Eisner. "You could sell them directly and not even take returns. That was considered so far out, so ludicrous, that it was greeted with laughter, a friendly pat on the back."

The people laughing were the comics publishers. Seuling was in a unique position to propose his idea because the publishers knew him from his conventions. He could connect on a personal level with people such as Carmine Infantino, DC's top editor and a longtime comics artist, because they were both New Yorkers and they had a love for the medium and a respect for its history. Despite those connections, Seuling could not immediately persuade the executives to make major changes to their distribution system. But he was persistent, and he was going to keep making his case.

In the convention's early years, Carole Seuling was there as a confidante and counterpoint. Many of the comics fans and creators who were part of the early shows were friends with both of them. In one photo from the era, Phil is dressed as Captain Marvel, with a sewed-on lightning bolt across the chest, and Carole is next to him dressed as Mary Marvel. They both look clean-cut, him with a smile and her with a grin.

But the couple was growing apart. She didn't go into specifics other than to say that he had become more interested in the hippie culture of the time. "I changed. He changed," she said. "He never got over Woodstock, the fact that he didn't get there," she said. "He didn't know a damn thing about it until he saw it on TV. He couldn't believe he hadn't heard about it and didn't get there." They separated in 1971 and later divorced.

Phil, who was still a full-time teacher, had to adapt to the financial strain of paying child support.[9] Their daughters would split time between the parents, who now had two apartments in Brooklyn. The younger daughter, Heather, whose last name is now Antonelli, was nine when her parents separated. "We knew we were safe and we were going to see both of them and it was not the end of the world," she said. "They did their best to make it palatable and acceptable."

Carole kept the name Seuling, which she says was to not confuse her children. "He and I remained friendly but not friends," she said. "His family never stopped considering me part of the family."

Phil's conventions remained strong, with the big one each July, and later monthly conventions at smaller venues. He supported all types of comics, and he allowed underground material to be sold at his shows. Among them was the infamous *Zap Comix* #4, which had a story by Robert Crumb called "Joe Blow." In a cartoony style reminiscent of children's comics, the story shows a smiling suburban family whose evening descends into an incestuous orgy. The story became a flashpoint with church-sponsored groups, used in campaigns to ban comics.[10]

On March 11, 1973, the campaign hit Seuling's monthly show. Police officers entered and asked to speak with the organizers. When they met Seuling, he was told, "This is an arrest." He and three of his workers were handcuffed and taken in a squad car to jail. They stood accused of selling indecent material to a minor, the kind of charges that Seuling knew could cost him his job and his reputation. He stood to lose everything.

Strong Silent Type

Mike Zeck was a star artist for Marvel, known for his dynamic covers and his knack for action sequences. He drew Captain America, The Punisher, and "Kraven's Last Hunt," a critically lauded Spider-Man story, among many others. Before he broke into the business, he was a young fan in Florida with a fondness for Black Bolt, the Marvel character who is often silent because his voice releases a devastating shockwave. Here, Zeck tells the story:

I was a rabid comics fan throughout my childhood and always dreamed of being a comics artist someday. In 1970, after art college, I went home to Hollywood, Florida, and I started connecting with the fan community there. I was well aware of Phil Seuling's Fourth of July shows in New York City and decided that 1971 would be the year I would realize the dream of attending one.

I started saving money to buy some titles I needed to fill in my Marvel collection. Most of my time, though, was spent preparing for the show's costume contest. I was inspired by Neal Adams's version of Black Bolt, so that was my character choice.

Never doing things in half measures, I mail-ordered stretch satin material, had a tailor help with the basic bodysuit, sewed all details of the costume myself (including the collapsible underarm glider wings), and shopped for or made all accessories. Even with my perfectionism, I liked the end product, so I knew I wouldn't be embarrassed in New York.

The drive from South Florida to Manhattan was a long one, but I was too excited to be tired. When I got to the show, it lived up to its billing. I saw many of the artists, writers, and editors I idolized as a fan. This went beyond the advertised guests because so many comics professionals lived in the city and attended the convention. One highlight: Frank Frazetta set up a gallery room at the hotel and let fans come in and browse his paintings.

As awesome as all that was, the best was yet to come, the costume contest. I suited up and made my way to the contestant holding room next to the auditorium. When I walked in, all faces collectively sank and there were mutterings about a professional showing up. I took that as a good sign.

I walked on stage to a roaring crowd. News crews were there as well. The judges, Jim Steranko, Gardner Fox, and Kirk Alyn, picked me as the winner. No doubt the best moment was accepting the first-place award and hearing the crowd start yelling "Speech!" "Speech!" I stayed in character and remained tight-lipped, just like the Black Bolt would do.

I didn't know much about Phil Seuling at that time other than he was a fan, a comics dealer, and he ran the biggest comics convention in the land. That made him something of a celebrity in my eyes. I had the chance to meet him and speak with him during and around the costume contest, and he was incredibly nice. I got the impression he was enjoying the show as much or more than the other attendees. He was always on stage or present, whether it be panel discussions, auctions, awards, contests, or dinners. Almost as if he was running the show entirely by himself.

While at the convention, Zeck took photos that now stand as some of the best records of the event. The photos in this section are all by him.

(*Top*) Mike Zeck in the home-made outfit that won him first place at the convention's costume contest. Black Bolt © Marvel Entertainment. *Credit: Mike Zeck.*

(*Bottom*) On the sales floor, a fan looks through old comics stored in a box labeled for egg noodles. *Credit: Mike Zeck.*

Some of the comics creators who were stars of the show: (*left to right*) Frank Frazetta, known for his fantasy paperback covers and paintings; Harvey Kurtzman, the cartoonist and editor who helped launch *Mad*; and Gil Kane, a star artist best known for his work on *Green Lantern*. Credit: Mike Zeck.

Phil Seuling auctions a page of original art from DC's *Showcase* #29, "The Last Dive of the Sea Devils." *Credit: Mike Zeck.*

3

Nonreturnable (1973–80)

"ON MARCH 11, 1973, at 4 p.m., I was told by a tall man with a firm angry voice that 'this is an arrest.' Then, within a few bewildered minutes, I was taken away from my friends and my business, put into handcuffs and led away to a waiting patrol car."

So begins a guest editorial written by Phil Seuling in the June 1973 issue of *Vampirella,* a magazine-sized comic from Warren Publishing.[1] Jim Warren, the publisher, said in an introductory note that he had provided the space for his friend, "one of the most respected dealers in the comics market."

Much of the comics industry stood to lose from this wave of censorship that had hit Seuling, including outfits such as Warren, whose publications were aimed at an older audience and had more sex and violence than a major publisher would ever put in a superhero comic.

Vampirella was pure pulp. In the lead story that month, the scantily clad title character was drugged by a band of street toughs. She got her revenge with a blood-sucking rampage. The letter column was dominated by a debate among readers about whether Vampi, as she was nicknamed, had an unrealistically large cup size. The editorial was an oddly sober counterpoint.

"I can't easily express the feelings of being led in handcuffs from the show. Or being questioned, fingerprinted, mugged [photographed], placed in a cell overnight, and left till morning. Or knowing that the animal pens procedure was being inflicted on two teenage girls who were working at my tables and were miserably frightened at this cold, heavy treatment."

One of those teenage girls was Jonni Levas, age seventeen. She had met Seuling when he was her teacher. At some point before the arrest, she and Seuling became a couple, something she said she instigated. "Of course people raised eyebrows," she said. "After a while, when people saw we were still together, they stopped raising their eyebrows." Other people in their circle, including Bud Plant, remember her as hip but not a hippie. The day of the arrest was one of the worst of her life.

"All I knew of New York City detectives was Kojak," she said, speaking from Palmyra, New Jersey, where she now lives. "We were taken away in handcuffs and we were told it was a felony and that meant they could shoot us if we ran away."

Seuling, Levas, and the others spent more than twenty hours in separate cells without food or water before they were allowed to see a lawyer. During that time, news of the arrest appeared in the local media, Seuling said in the editorial. The reports named a church-sponsored group that had a campaign against so-called obscene comics, which he saw as evidence that the arrest and the immediate coverage were all a publicity stunt at his expense.

Stunt or not, he faced life-changing consequences. His employer, the New York public school system, forced him to leave the classroom and report for nonteaching duty while school officials investigated the charges. Instead of going to work, he went to a place nicknamed the "rubber room," where teachers who had run afoul of the system sat at desks and waited out the days while their cases worked through the system.

A few months after the arrest, a court dropped the charges. Seuling agreed to refrain from selling potentially obscene material. He continued with his monthly shows and his big show in July. "Since then, only the tamest titles have appeared at the Second Sunday shows," said a report that summer in *The Buyer's Guide for Comic Fandom*. "Unfortunately, that leaves out much of Richard Corben's work and many of the better-written titles, like *Skull*."[2]

Even with the charges dropped, Seuling's bosses would not let him return to the classroom. He was on an indefinite hiatus.

As this was happening, the comics industry had gone into one of its periodic downturns. Sales at newsstands had plummeted. The retail world was shifting away from independent grocers and pharmacies and toward large chains. While many older retailers stocked comics out of habit, the chains were deliberate in deciding how to allocate rack space. In this type of assessment, comics did not fare well. They had low cover prices, about 20 cents each, which meant the retailer stood to make only a few pennies of profit from each sale.[3]

Another factor was fraud by some of the news distributors. Since comics and other printed materials were sold on a returnable basis, the distributors could return unsold items for credit toward other purchases. At one time, returns meant sending whole comics, or at least the covers, to receive credit. This evolved into a system in which publishers allowed distributors to file an affidavit saying that a list of items was unsold and had been destroyed. Some distributors would sell the books out the back door, often to comics dealers, and still report them as unsold.

"You'd send them ten thousand copies and they would send you an affidavit that said they only sold two thousand," said Jim Shooter, who started writing for DC Comics as a teenager in the mid-1960s and went on to be editor in chief of Marvel from 1978 to 1987. "Well, maybe they sold four thousand. With the affidavits, they only had to pay for two thousand."

He remembers that one particularly audacious news distributor sent an affidavit claiming that the number of unsold copies was greater than the number of copies that had been shipped. Instead of rejecting it out of hand, Marvel trod carefully. News distributors were gatekeepers to doing business in their territories, and some of the companies had reputations for ties to organized crime. Shooter remembers that Marvel's circulation managers warned that specific distributors were not to be trifled with.

In 1973, the news distributors were the only option for getting comics into the hands of customers. Sales were way down, which probably was tied to a decline in consumer interest, exacerbated by fraud by news vendors. Now Seuling found an audience that was more receptive to his idea of selling directly to specialty shops.

In August, he was at the San Diego Comic-Con, where he scheduled a breakfast with Sol Harrison, a vice president at DC. The San Diego convention would grow to become the largest in the world, but at that time it was smaller than Seuling's annual event in New York. Also at the breakfast was Levas, whose role was business partner in addition to girlfriend.

Seuling and Harrison knew each other because of the New York show. Harrison "was an older gentlemen, a dapper New York gentleman," Levas said. "He was funny and kind."

By the end of the meal, they had a handshake deal. They agreed to meet soon in New York to set the details. In the months to follow, Seuling would make similar agreements with Marvel, Archie, and Warren, which were other major publishers. In that moment, however, the new venture didn't seem big, Levas said. It was one of several side businesses involving comics, along with the conventions and mail-order sales of old comics.

"Did he think it was something monumental? No," Levas said. "But it turned out to be monumental."

Here was the new business model: retailers could order comics from Seuling and get shipments straight from the printing plants, bypassing the old-line distributors. This meant the comics would arrive sooner than at other outlets, and in precise quantities.

The system would come to be called the "direct market," because comics were skipping the middleman and going directly to the retailers. This was possible because the major publishers did their printing with the same company in Sparta, Illinois. The printer would collate the orders and ship them to Seuling's customers, just as they did for hundreds of news distributors.

The new system had benefits and risks. Orders from Seuling had a greater wholesale discount than those from the old distributors, but also were nonreturnable. This meant that if a store ordered twenty-five copies of *Superman* and sold only five, it was stuck with the surplus. Also, Seuling required up-front payment with each order, even though the comics didn't ship until months later.

At that time, there were few retail outlets that could be called comic shops. If you broadly define "comic shop" to include used bookstores with large comics sections, there were fewer than two hundred stores nation-wide, according to retailers from that time.[4] Within this total were only a few dozen of the kind of comics specialty stores that would come to dominate the industry.

Seuling was able to get orders from many of the store owners because the business model made sense to them, and because he had built up trust from his years in fandom and his conventions.[5] His new idea was an immediate success, exceeding his expectations.[6] The new venture was later incorporated as Sea Gate Distributors.

Within months of Seuling starting the distribution business, Marvel made a similar deal with another vendor, Donahoe Brothers, in Ann Arbor, Michigan.[7] Other distributors would soon open, such as Pacific Comics in San Diego and Irjax Enterprises in Maryland, but they mostly sold comics-related goods and did not have contracts with the major publishers.[8]

Seuling was king, with the best retailer accounts and the best terms with the companies that produced comics. But those other players, at least the ones that lasted more than a year or two, would have important roles near the end of the decade, when the industry got much bigger and more complicated.

Of all the non-Seuling upstarts, Donahoe Brothers, also known as Comic Center Enterprises and by its nickname, Donahoe Brudders, was notable for the swiftness and audacity of its rise and its equally rapid fall. The man in charge was Tim Donahoe, a smooth talker in his midtwenties.

"Some people distrusted him on sight, including my wife," said Jim Friel, who had built a business selling publishers' new comics at conventions, and also drew his own comics. "I just thought of him as a smooth guy who was probably okay. Her perception was more accurate than mine."

Friel was one of the first people hired by Donahoe Brothers who was not a member of the family. He had grown up in North Carolina and came north to attend Michigan State University. His employment with Donahoe Brothers would turn out to be a small blemish on what would become a long and successful run working for some of the key players in comics retail.

Donahoe Brothers' ambition was to be a regional comics distributor serving Michigan, Ohio, and the other Great Lakes states. The company signed up a roster of accounts that included longtime bookstores and newly opened comic shops. The retailers could order precise quantities of specific comics on a nonreturnable basis and receive a larger discount than what was offered by news distributors on a returnable basis. It was almost the same as Seuling's model.

The first shipment was in early 1974. Friel remembers that one of the comics from the first batch was *Marvel Super Stars* #1, which had a cover date of May.[9] Comics publishers typically set the cover date three months ahead, which means that first shipment likely was in February. Soon after, Donahoe Brothers added DC Comics to their offerings, along with other publishers.

About a year after that first shipment, Friel was by himself in the warehouse when the phone rang. It was Carmine Infantino, DC's president and one of the most popular artists in the business, known for *Batman* and *The Flash*. He asked to speak with Tim, who was not there.

"Well, you tell that son of a bitch I'm going to come out there and padlock his fucking warehouse," Infantino said, according to Friel.

Donahoe Brothers had been receiving merchandise and reselling it, without paying the publishers. Friel had suspected that something was amiss, but did not know the scale of it.

"It was a deal Carmine had made personally, and he felt betrayed personally," Friel said. "It feels terrible to have one of your artistic idols yelling at you like that. It was Carmine Infantino, for God's sake."

Later that day, Friel confronted Tim Donahoe, who matter-of-factly confirmed that many bills had gone unpaid. Within a month or so, the company ceased operation, a little more than a year after it had gotten into comics.

Donahoe Brothers was more than just a curiosity. It turned out to be the first in a succession of midwestern distributors that helped develop comic shops in that part of the country while Seuling's business was in its infancy. Donahoe Brothers' fall was followed by the rise of Big Rapids Distribution of Detroit, whose demise in 1980 was followed by the rise of Capital City Distribution of Madison, Wisconsin. These were some of the first few steps that would lead to explosive growth in the number of comic shops, along with turf wars between distributors.[10]

By early 1974, Seuling and Levas were living together in a house in Sea Gate, a gated community on the western end of Coney Island. From there, they ran the comics distribution business, planned the conventions, and presided over a gathering place for comics professionals and fans.

Jonni Levas during a 1978 trip to London with Phil Seuling, who is seated to the left. *Courtesy of Jonni Levas.*

After his arrest, Seuling never returned to the classroom. He did non-teaching duties for a few months and then applied for early retirement. He likely could have been reinstated as a teacher, because the criminal charges had been dropped, but he didn't bother, Levas said. He was ready to move on to something else.

Several people told me that there was a kind of cause and effect with Seuling's arrest and the founding of the distribution business. In other words, if not for the arrest, Seuling would have kept teaching and not been able to devote himself full-time to comics. Based on interviews with some of the other people closest to Seuling, however, this doesn't seem to be true. When I asked Levas if Seuling wanted to continue teaching, she said, "No way." He loved teaching, but he loved comics more.

"And he was always teaching, even if he wasn't in an actual classroom," she said. "He would teach whatever silly thing there might be. He would teach what Italian food you should eat, or what movie you should see, or why you should like the Mets more than the Yankees."

Heather Antonelli, Seuling's younger daughter, agrees that her father wanted to leave teaching and was not pushed. She was with him the day he went to the administrative offices to file paperwork to leave his job.

"The lady who was processing the paperwork was like, 'Are you kidding me, because you only have like a year and ten months left to get the pension?' And he was like, 'I can't. I can't come away from what I'm doing,'" Antonelli said.

Unlike most new businesses, the venture that would become Sea Gate had no cash before its first orders. Seuling and Levas worked for no income. Their operating money came from retailers' prepayments, most of which was used for prepayments to the comics publishers. There was no credit for anyone.

"It's insane to think this could work," Levas said. "I'm amazed we were able to pull this off, with no capital."

The first accounts included some established and reliable retailers, such as Collectors Book Store in Los Angeles. Among the newer stores was Comics & Comix in Berkeley, California, co-owned by Bud Plant, which would go on to become one of the first, if not the first, comic shop chain, with other locations in Northern California.

Other new stores soon followed. In 1974, Chuck Rozanski used his savings to open a comic shop in the back room of Lois Newman Books, a science fiction bookstore in Boulder, Colorado. He was nineteen and had been buying and selling old comics for years at conventions. The shop was in a basement room with a single lightbulb hanging from the ceiling. He spent most of his $800 budget on a counter and new lights. Mile High Comics was in business.

"The original shop had to be diversified because in those days you were buying new comics for 14 cents and selling them for 20 cents, so you were making a whopping 6 cents per comic book," he said. "It's very hard to pay rent or utilities with 6 cents, no matter how much volume you're doing."

His big-ticket items were posters by fantasy artists such as Frank Frazetta. He also sold *Playboy* and *Penthouse,* and had a selection of bongs and other drug paraphernalia. He had short hair because he had just been in Reserve Officers' Training Corps in college. His ponytail, the one he would have for decades, braided down to the small of his back, was still in his future.

Seuling's distribution business had started by the time Mile High opened, but Rozanski got his comics from a local news distributor. Rozanski had worked out a deal with the distributor to get new comics a few days earlier than most other outlets in Boulder. "Instantaneously, every collector in town came to me to get their books," he said. "It was awesome."

For small shops, it often didn't make much sense to do business with Seuling. He required up-front payment for orders of comics that would not be delivered for two months. He also set minimum order limits, meaning shops could not order just one or two copies of low-selling titles. In fairness to Seuling, many of these conditions had been imposed on him by the publishers. Rozanski would come to see Seuling's rules as an impediment to growth for the industry. "I loved Phil, but Phil could have his head up his ass for no reason," he said.

But first Rozanski had to learn to run a business and deal with the public. "I was very obnoxious, kind of like a chipmunk on speed," he said. "I was so enthusiastic and I couldn't understand why other people didn't instantly share my enthusiasm. It took me a while to moderate my own enthusiasm. I was also extremely dismissive of other people if they didn't agree with me. I was kind of an obnoxious little peckerhead. That's the God's honest truth."

A year after he opened, he met the woman he would marry—she'd gotten a job in the adjacent bookstore. He mellowed. Chuck and Nanette Rozanski would soon move Mile High out of the coal closet, and would go on to have a chain of stores that extended down into Denver. The more experience he got, the more he could see the shortcomings of Seuling's model. Things needed to change, he thought.

Sea Gate was growing about as fast as Seuling and Levas could handle, but it and its customers remained less than 10 percent of sales by major publishers. Shops continued to open, and existing ones grew. In 1977, there were about two hundred comics specialty shops in the United States, a figure that excluded used bookstores that did not sell new comics, according to Melchior Thompson, an economist who studied the market as a consultant for Marvel. Seuling was the den leader for a small industry that was about to get much bigger.

Meanwhile, Seuling maintained his convention business. In 1977 and 1978, he relocated his July show to Philadelphia, before a return to New York. To publicize the 1977 show, he got a booking to appear on *The Mike Douglas Show*, a nationally syndicated daytime talk show that was filmed in Philadelphia. The cohost was Jamie Farr, the actor who played Corporal Max Klinger on *M*A*S*H*. The other guests included General William

Westmoreland, who had commanded the U.S. forces in Vietnam; and Fabian, the singer, actor, and former teen idol.

"A grown man with a handful of comic books," said the host, Douglas. He had just introduced Seuling in what was likely the latter's only national television appearance. There Seuling sat, with bushy sideburns and a stack of vintage comics in his lap. His plastic-rim glasses looked a few sizes too small.

"I didn't know you were my mother," Seuling replied, smile in place, his accent turning the last word into "mutha."

Douglas asked how this comics habit got started.

"I read thousands of them as a kid," Seuling said. "The interest never died. It's a love. It's something that you just can't do unless you really love it, unless you're devoted to it."

Douglas told the audience that Seuling had brought along a superhero. Then out from behind a curtain came a woman dressed in a chain-mail bikini with a prop sword, in the character of Red Sonja. She walked up to Farr and pointed the tip of the sword at his face.

"No nose jobs," the actor said, laughing. He was known for his oversized schnozz. Seuling was laughing uproariously.

The whole scene epitomizes the late 1970s almost to the point of parody. But the biggest shock for a present-day viewer is the woman playing Red Sonja, not because of the costume, which she wore with aplomb, but because of what she later would do.

Her name was Wendy Pini. She had been performing at comic conventions and other events as Red Sonja for about two years, doing a stage show in which a well-known comics artist, Frank Thorne, played a wizard.

Fewer people knew that Pini wrote and drew comics of her own. She and her husband Richard had created a fantasy story called *Elfquest,* and they were about to start self-publishing it. Unlike Marvel, DC, and other major publishers, the Pinis did not operate on a scale large enough to get their product into grocery stores and drugstores. They would depend on alternative channels, such as the burgeoning network of comic shops. In turn, comics such as *Elfquest* would help define the shops as places where fans could find things that were not available through mainstream sources. *Elfquest* was one of the first big commercial successes of the early comic shop era, inspiring many imitators.

As the show began to cut to commercial, Farr said about Pini, "Now that's a superhero."

"The audience loved it," she said. "But we heard later on that Mike Douglas was quite upset by my racy costume, which didn't fit in with the tone of his show. C'est la vie."

Westmoreland was no longer on the set when she made her appearance, but the two did meet backstage. When she arrived, the military man noted her battle armor and said, "I didn't know we were still at war."

The first *Elfquest* story appeared in early 1978 in *Fantasy Quarterly* #1, published by IPS, a new company controlled in part by Tim Donahoe, the Michigan businessman who had already tried and failed at comics distribution. The Pinis, who felt burned by the poor production values and by some of the business practices of Donahoe, decided to become their own publisher.

The first self-published issue was *Elfquest* #2, released later in 1978 with a print run of twenty thousand copies. The Pinis called their company WaRP Graphics (WaRP stood for Wendy and Richard Pini). To pay the printing bill, Richard Pini borrowed about $2,000 from his parents.

Self-publishing would have been a highly risky venture if not for the help of Phil Seuling and his network of friends and customers. He knew the Pinis and wanted to support their work. Seuling and Bud Plant pooled their resources to buy the entire print run of twenty thousand copies. They would sell *Elfquest* through their respective distribution businesses.

"What both Bud and Phil saw, I think, was a new kind of ground-level comic storytelling, heavily influenced by Japanese manga, that had not been seen before," Wendy Pini said. "They trusted me and my ability to deliver because of my prior experience as an illustrator. And I think, after they sold out the first ten-thousand-copy run of the first issue in under a couple of months, they realized these weird, elfin characters could appeal and catch on. Also we did cliffhangers very well."

Seuling and Plant sold every copy, giving the Pinis confidence to continue the work. "That took all the pressure off of us," Richard Pini said. "It was bing, bang, boom."

There is little doubt that Phil Seuling saw himself as the hero of his story. So who was his archenemy? There are many candidates, but my vote goes to a

pugnacious young man named Hal Shuster. As of 1978, Seuling was the biggest player in comics distribution, with the top accounts and the best terms
from publishers. Shuster had a small business in Maryland, distributing
comics and other material for his family-owned company, Irjax Enterprises.

Irjax had been started in 1973 by Irwin Shuster and his sons Jack and
Hal. The name was combination of Irwin and Jack. Although he wasn't in
the name, Hal gave the impression that he ran things. The business was set
up to act as a wholesaler of comics and related materials to comic shops. It
also was a publisher of magazines about geeky interests, such as *Star Trek*
fandom.[11]

"I never really felt comfortable talking to him," said Mike Friedrich, who
was on staff at Marvel, serving as the first sales director for the comic shop
market from 1980 to 1982. He describes Shuster as an in-your-face kind of
guy, with a wardrobe that favored white shirts and thin black ties.

"He was intelligent and confident, but arguably, in my view, overconfi-
dent. He was kind of driven by the idea that he was smarter than everybody
else and had realized things that the rest of the business had not realized.
And, given that he had proven himself to be litigious, I was very careful
around him."

Before coming to Marvel's sales department, Friedrich was a writer for
Marvel and DC and publisher of a comics anthology called *Star*Reach*. Although barely thirty years old, he had been around the business long enough
not to be impressed by Shuster.

Irjax grew from its base in Rockville, Maryland, in the Washington, D.C.,
suburbs. It wanted to be the dominant wholesaler in the state and neighboring
states, and then build from there. This put the company on a collision course
with Phil Seuling and Sea Gate. Seuling had started with a few accounts in
places such as New York, Buffalo, and the Bay Area. By 1977, he had worked
out many of his own organizational problems and was in an expansion mode.
He was looking to sign up new retail clients, including in Maryland.

He came into Irjax's backyard and formed an alliance with retailer Mark
Feldman, owner of Maryland Funnybook Shop in Silver Spring. Feldman
would serve as a subdistributor for Seuling, obtaining products for his store
and then acting as a wholesaler for other stores in the area.[12]

Examples of this model had already happened in other metro areas. Seuling found retailers to serve as his middlemen. These coveted roles often

Hal Shuster of Irjax / New Media (*left*); Mike Friedrich (*below right*) speaking with Dean Mullaney, who was then an editor at Eclipse Comics. Both photos from the 1982 San Diego Comic-Con. *Credit: Alan Light.*

went to friends and associates he had met through his conventions. In almost every market, competing retailers found themselves in the awkward position of having to buy from their local rivals if they wanted to have the advantages of Seuling's services.[13] At that time, several small comics distribution companies were trying to build and sustain regional territories. Some of them, such as Irjax, saw Seuling's expansion as an existential threat.

Irjax and Seuling started to trash each other in conversations with potential clients. Seuling would say that Irjax was a small-time operator that didn't know what it was doing. Irjax would say that Seuling was secretly bleeding money and about to go out of business. The comments, made in private, were not unusual for the rough-and-tumble world of comics distribution. Then Seuling kicked it up a notch with this note in his November 1977 newsletter to customers:

> A notice I think is probably unnecessary: For a few months, an off-the-wall pseudo "distributor" on the middle of the East Coast has been telling everyone that "Seuling is out. He won't be able to deliver books any more." This nut has also suggested returning unsold books (bought from him) through the local distributor as "returns," a policy which would automatically get you cut off from *all* supplies from *all* publishers. . . .
>
> Additionally, this sickie made threatening and harassing phone calls, and has used the mails fraudulently. He is inches away from deep (Federal) trouble. And yes, I intend to prosecute.[14]

Hal Shuster saw this and was livid, according to Levas. The part that most incensed Shuster was the use of the word "sickie," which he took as a reference to his father. Irwin Shuster used a wheelchair, and his sons were sensitive about anything that seemed to be making fun of this.

"That's certainly not cool to have written that, but that was Phil, impetuous and headstrong," Levas said. She thinks the newsletter, as much as any business disagreement, is what made the conflict escalate into what would turn into a legal quagmire.

On October 2, 1978, Irjax Enterprises filed suit in Maryland federal court against Seuling and just about every major comics publisher, accusing them of violating antitrust laws. At its heart, the case was about how Seuling and Sea Gate had more favorable terms with publishers than Irjax did. The most glaring example may have been the way Seuling could get his customers' orders collated and shipped directly from the printer, which meant his clients received items sooner than his competitors' clients did.

What Irjax was doing was audacious. The company was a small business, and it was suing some corporate giants. Among the nine defendants were Warner Communications Inc., the parent company of DC, and Cadence Industries Corp., the parent of Marvel. Other retailers and distributors had talked about suing Seuling and the publishers, but only Irjax was willing to take the risk to its finances and reputation.

In the lawsuit, Irjax claimed that the defendants "have engaged in an unlawful combination and conspiracy in restraint of interstate trade and commerce" and have "endeavored to force Irjax out of business of wholesale distribution of comics books and related items."

Along with the antitrust claim, Irjax also made a libel claim against Seuling for the comments in the newsletter. The court filing says Seuling's letter had been mailed to many of Irjax's customers, contained statements that Seuling knew were untrue, and was "clearly intended to, and did, hold plaintiffs up to contempt and ridicule."

Two months later, in an amended complaint, Irjax provided some additional details about how all the defendants fit into the larger comics business. The filing said that Marvel accounted for 70 percent to 75 percent of sales to comic shops; DC was 20 percent to 25 percent of sales; and Warren Publishing, known for *Vampirella* and other horror titles, had 4 percent. Marvel was dominating the industry, while DC, the former industry leader, was struggling. Warren would go out of business a few years later.

Seuling was not the type to walk away from a fight. He responded to the lawsuit by denying the allegations and then making claims of his own against Irjax and the publishers. He also added a claim against Big Rapids Distribution of Detroit, a company that had not been named in the Irjax lawsuit but was a competitor of Seuling's. His argument, in essence, was that Irjax and Big Rapids were the ones getting favorable terms of service from the publishers.

From there, many lawyers expended many billable hours. Filings piled up at U.S. District Court in Baltimore. Beyond the nuts and bolts of the case itself, the publishers came to the realization that distribution to comic shops was becoming a big business, and it needed to be handled in a more organized way. No more handshake deals. From then on, Marvel and DC would seek to have uniform terms of service.[15]

By the summer of 1979, less than a year after the Irjax complaint had been filed, the major issues had been resolved in a series of settlements. The upshot for Seuling was that he would no longer receive terms of service that were different from what other distributors got. His time as king of the business was waning. Meanwhile, the number of comic shops continued to grow. Irjax, Big Rapids, and others had a wide-open playing field in which to sign up customers, leading to the next era, one marked by chaotic competition, rapid rises, and even more rapid falls.

This was about the time that the "direct market" stopped being quite so direct. The term had come from the fact that Seuling's retailer customers were getting orders shipped directly from the printers, bypassing news distributors. In part because of the lawsuit, the system shifted to one in which comics distributors set up warehouses to receive material from printers, collate it, and then ship it. This was still better than the old system with news distributors, retailers said, but the straight line from printers to stores was gone.

It would be easy to say the Irjax lawsuit is what knocked Seuling from the top of the industry, but there were many other factors. Among them was that Seuling and Sea Gate continued to require prepayment and other terms that made it difficult for customers. And now some comic shops had been around long enough and become large enough that their owners felt comfortable making their case for change.

Among the outspoken retailers was Chuck Rozanski. He had gained a national profile in the industry for having acquired the Edgar Church collection, one of the largest and best-preserved troves of Golden Age comic

books that had ever changed hands. He gradually sold the collection and used the proceeds to build Mile High Comics into what remains one of the country's largest mail-order dealers of back-issue comics.

In the spring of 1979, while the Seuling-Irjax lawsuit was still active, Rozanski decided to write Marvel Comics to raise his concerns about

Chuck Rozanski in his original Boulder, Colorado, store in the late 1970s.
Courtesy of Chuck Rozanski.

the ways that the comics market was falling short of its potential. The letter
was sent to Robert Maiello, Marvel's manager of sales administration.
Here it is in its entirety:[16]

> Dear Mr. Maiello:
>
> My name is Charles Rozanski, and I own Mile High Comics. I
> am one of the largest comic book retailers in America (sales 1979
> about $400,000), and thus a customer of yours. I am also a small
> advertiser in your comic books. This letter is an attempt on my part
> to bring to your attention some suggestions which I believe will be
> relevant, if your job truly encompasses sales and promotion.
>
> To begin with, I have been an active retailer of your products
> for over four years. Starting with no more than 15 of any comic
> title, I am now purchasing over 10,000 Marvel comics a month on a
> nonreturnable basis. I get these books through Seagate Distributing
> (Jonni Levas, Phil Seuling). It is my latest order with them that has
> especially prompted this letter.
>
> My order (of which a photocopy is enclosed) for your products
> is just under $4,000 for this month. These are books that will arrive
> between June 10 and July 10. Under your existing policies you have
> just lost at least $1,000 in sales. The reason: After putting my order
> together I cut my list to the bone in order not to have to lay out any
> more up-front cash than was absolutely necessary during May, a
> slower month for my business. So, we both lose: you lose my busi-
> ness, and I lose those sales that I could have gotten by having a reserve
> instead of ordering just barely enough for my guaranteed sales.
>
> Why is this foolishness still necessary? In November of last year
> an "outside consultant" who supposedly was representing Cadence
> Industries / Marvel Comics approached us about direct contact
> with your office and the possibility of some mutually beneficial
> programs. He told us he would get back to us in December. We
> have heard nothing. Did you send out a representative? If so, did he
> present you with a breakdown of what is happening? I am going
> to take your silence of the past six months as evidence that either
> the "consultant" in question did not really work for you or else did
> his job very poorly. Or, there is one other possibility. Did he tell
> you that you would be better off without us? Is this why rumors

of a lawsuit on predatory pricing are circulating? For your sake and mine, I hope not.

Whatever the case may be, I think it is about time you heard from a retailer directly. Ours is a dying industry and if we don't get together and cooperate there will be no comic books at all. If you don't believe me, check with John Goldwater, the president of the Comic Magazine Association of America. According to him, circulation from 1959 to 1978 dropped from 600,000,000 to 250,000,000. This alone should be enough for your office to be highly interested in actively seeking to expand our business as much as possible.

Well this has not been the case. The policies currently in force are restricting severely the ability of comic book retailers to grow or even in some cases to stay even. How can you justify continuing to require advance payment for all comic deliveries? Do you realize the cost in lost sales of this policy? As I pointed out earlier, I would have spent another $1,000, this month alone, on your products. Multiply my business by the hundreds of independent retailers, large and small, across the nation, and you come up with a staggering sum that is being wasted. Stop and think, what is the variable cost of a 40 cent comic? When you have already paid all your costs except paper and shipping, how much does it cost to leave the presses running for another 10,000 copies? My guess is between 3 and 5 cents a copy. In a business with razor thin margins, you can't afford not to get every bit of profit available.

And don't be misled, we do not siphon off business from existing distributor accounts. Quite to the contrary, we salvage thousands of customers who otherwise would have left the field in disgust at the poor distribution. When you print continued stories, it is imperative that the customer who wants the next issue should be able to find it easily. This is not currently the case. Comic books are among the lowest items on a normal distributor's priority list. And thus the whole point of continued stories (i.e. creating customer demand for future issues) is lost, and instead the opposite occurs as customers quit buying from frustration. Pardon me for being the one to say it, but that is stupid.

Another point is that we do not just salvage customers you otherwise would have lost, we also create new ones. At 40 cents and up, comics are no longer able to sell themselves. You have made the product so thin and unattractive with advertising that it takes salesmanship to get them to sell, even to collectors. How much salesmanship do you get in a 7–11? We go out of our way to sell comics, they are our main business. (For example, the *Superman the Movie* book from DC . . . I set up a stand in a local theater and sold over 1200.) Isn't it about time we got some help and support?

Well enough of generalities. After four years I have some concrete suggestions that will make you money and make me money. Here they are:

1. Give us billing, or at least COD purchases.

2. Start a cooperative advertising program to promote comics.

3. Pay for artists and writers to do promotional tours.

4. Give us better information about what is coming out. We will buy many more books if the uncertainty about artists, etc. is alleviated.

5. Start up a listing (on one of the ad pages) where comic book retailers could list themselves at cost.

6. Make it an editorial policy to support us. Present policy never even mentions we exist.

7. Ask us for feedback. When you do something, we hear about it, believe me.

8. Set up a remainder sales division. Since I, and many other retailers, also sell back issues, we would buy thousands more comics if they were available at a remainder price instead of normal cost.

While I realize that not all of the above suggestions are currently viable, at this point anything would be better than the situation as it exists. I sincerely believe that I am echoing the sentiments of other independent dealers when I say I am tired of not getting any help from you, the people who benefit from my efforts. Right now, comics are my life. I work seven days a week, ten to twelve hours a day, to make my business exist and your business better. And you have been no damn help at all.

So please give me some feedback. We are both in the same business and cooperation between us can do nothing but make our mutual jobs easier and business more profitable. I'll be awaiting your reply.

Sincerely,
Charles W. Rozanski

P.S. I am going to distribute this letter as widely as I can and ask my fellow dealers to send you signed copies to indicate their agreement with most of my points. Without an official organization to support us (we are all very independent) this is the best I can do to prove that other dealers are in agreement with my opinions.

Rozanski received a reply from Ed Shukin, Marvel's vice president for sales, who invited him to come to the company's offices in New York to discuss the matter further. Soon after, when Marvel was setting its terms of service following Seuling's lawsuit, the publisher threw the door open to businesses that wanted to become Marvel distributors. The standard of entry was a certain monthly order threshold. According to Mike Friedrich, who soon would be working in Marvel's sales department, the level was intentionally set so that Rozanski would be just above what was needed to become a distributor. More than a dozen businesses set up distribution deals with Marvel.

The dominance of Seuling was done, replaced by a much messier and more complicated mix.

Indie-Minded Elves

Wendy Pini, cocreator of Elfquest, became one of the first star artists to reach fans mainly through comic shops. In hindsight, she is a pioneer for independent publishing and for women in comics. At the time, she was just a young creator trying to find an audience. The following are excerpts from our interview.

Becoming an Indie Publisher

After being turned down by Marvel and DC and several others, we knew we pretty much had to *Little Red Hen* it. The story and characters were in my blood and I was passionate—obsessed, really—with getting it out there any way we could. We'd discussed writing it as a prose novel or as a screenplay. But in the end we both decided that the art was just as important as the words. So the comic format was ideal.

At the time we were impressed with indie publications such as *Star*Reach* and *First Kingdom* (our actual role model for the magazine-sized format). Richard taught himself from scratch how to be an indie publisher. I dove blind into the deep end of writing and drawing a series. Had no idea how much work it was going to be or how hard.

Therefore I blush to admit the issue of my being a woman pioneer in the male-dominated comic scene didn't loom very large for me at the time. I just wanted to push ahead on the strength of my work. Also I soon became so consumed by deadlines that I didn't have any energy to devote to the political side of things. I'm honored to be regarded as an innovator, now. But I was completely naïve, stubbornly single-minded, and driven back then. What we were—underground, indie or mainstream—never mattered as much as "Can I get the damn thing done close enough to deadline so Richard won't kill me?"

The Role of Comic Shops

Without comics specialty shops I'm certain we would not have been the overnight success we were. What we owed, back then, to the positive word of mouth of comic shop owners—plus exposure at early comic conventions, particularly San Diego—is incalculable. It was all word of mouth in the late 1970s and early 1980s. But it spread damn near as fast as the Internet does now.

Elfquest grew up right along with the burgeoning of comic shops all over the country.

What *Elfquest* did was bring in a new kind of readership to the comics market. It brought in fantasy and sci-fi readers, a lot of them fans of my prior work, who weren't all that familiar with the comics medium. But they were eager to get to know the elves.

Most important, *Elfquest* brought in an unheard-of female audience. Girls were haunting comic shops like never before. *Elfquest* was responsible for opening up a new dialogue about who comics were really for. All at once women could say, "Keep your superheroes and your Archies! We've got this now!" As a result, and as more eclectic indie titles started to come out, comic shops had to clean up their act a bit and become more female-friendly.

Being Red Sonja

On a more serious note, despite those who have occasionally claimed that my Red Sonja cosplay has haunted me all these years and caused me to be taken less than seriously as a creator, I say the notoriety gained from portraying Sonja opened very important professional doors for me in the comics industry back then. It got my name and certainly my picture out there. . . .

Rather than hinder me, my association with the Red Sonja character brought me attention and, oddly, a certain amount of respect. I took my performances seriously. This was far from just T&A to me. And there were some—not everyone, but some—who seemed to get that. There had never been, and there hasn't really been since, a multimedia presentation like "The Red Sonja and The Wizard Show" at comic cons. It was unique in how it delivered a powerful feminist message with a spoonful of ale-soaked sugar. I will always remember it fondly and proudly.

(*Top*) Wendy and Richard Pini posing in the late 1970s.

(*Left*) Wendy Pini as Red Sonja.

(*Bottom*) With the success of *Elfquest* came merchandising. *Photos courtesy of Richard Pini.*

4

An Ogre's Story

ON A Saturday in May, a line extended out the door. This was Free Comic Book Day 2015 at The Laughing Ogre. The store would give away thousands of comics. It also would ring up more sales, by far, than any other day of the year. Near the front door was a face-painting station for the kids, some of whom came dressed as superheroes. Across the aisle was a table for the Hero Initiative, a national charity that sells prints and books to raise money for comics creators in financial need.

The annual event takes place at thousands of shops around the world. Publishers produce special titles that they sell at a deep discount to retailers, who in turn give the comics away to customers. Started in 2002, it is by far the largest promotion in the industry. Customers come for the free stuff, but almost nobody leaves without buying something else.

"On Free Comic Book Day, 90 percent of the people through are not your usual crowd," Gib Bickel said.

He saw the day as an opportunity to turn casual fans into regulars. At the same time, he knew that the first-time customers that day were walking into a store so crowded that it could feel uninviting. The cool air escaping because of the constant opening of the front door, along with the roomful of warm bodies, made the whole place feel sticky, especially for the employees.

Laughing Ogre was going through a rough patch. The previous February, the store had been sold for the second time in its history. It was not a happy transaction. Bickel was there for both sales, first as the owner and then as an employee. Each sale was stunning in its own way. He had reason to feel shell-shocked, except that he was accustomed to upheaval. Indeed, the history of the store could be seen as a series of rough patches.

Way before Laughing Ogre, Bickel was an up-and-coming manager for Wendy's restaurants. He had started with the company while a student at Ohio State University and soon dropped out because he liked the idea of getting a decent paycheck rather than paying for classes. Still in his midtwenties, he was a Wendy's veteran by the time he got assigned to manage a store on Columbus's west side in the mid-1980s.

In his first week there, he told the employees that the store had an unusually small number of comment cards from customers. A few days later, he looked at a bulletin board for the cards and saw three had been received, a veritable avalanche. "They were very complimentary," he said. Then he saw the names on each card: Peter Parker, Reed Richards, and Anthony Stark, the secret identities of Spider-Man, Mr. Fantastic, and Iron Man, respectively. "I realized, holy cow, these are all fake and someone in here is a comic fan."

Bickel had been a comics reader ever since high school, when he picked up *Amazing Spider-Man* #149 off of a spinner rack. It was at a pharmacy in his hometown, Greenville, Ohio, a county seat near the border with Indiana. The issue's cover had the title character fighting his clone, so there were two Spider-Men. He was hooked.

By the time he got to the west side Wendy's, he had thousands of comics and had branched off into ancillary geeky pursuits, such as role-playing games. He was excited at the idea that someone at the store was also a fan. The author of the comment cards turned out to be Rod Phillips, an employee who was in high school. When Bickel asked about the cards, Phillips burst out laughing.

"Back then, nobody knew who Anthony Stark was," Phillips said. This was long before the *Iron Man* movies made Tony Stark more of a household name. "We formed a really fast friendship."

Gib Bickel in high school in 1979. *Courtesy of Gib Bickel.*

A year or so later, another comics fan came to work there, Daryn Guarino. He had moved from Connecticut for college and lived in an apartment across the street from the restaurant. The three of them became close friends and stayed that way after they all moved on to other jobs. About ten years later, they co-founded The Laughing Ogre.

Bickel was the oldest of the three, in his early thirties when they opened the store. He had been married and divorced, and had two children. He had experience from years of managing employees and maintaining the books for his Wendy's stores. He also had worked as a manager for Wizard of Comics, a small local chain of shops.

"Gib was very much the heart of what we wanted to do," Phillips said. "He was always the one [for whom] this is what you're born to do. It's what makes you happy. It's your niche in life."

For the other two, it was more of a lark. Phillips had worked part-time at Wizard of Comics with Bickel, and he liked the idea of running his own shop. He was young and single, with nobody to talk him out of doing a crazy thing like opening a small business.

Guarino was a freelance computer programmer, and was putting up all of the cash, about $30,000. "Daryn was always the wheeler-dealer guy," Phillips said. "He just wanted to have a business, and he had only a middling interest in standing behind a counter and stuff. The classic description of Daryn is the guy who owns a restaurant and doesn't like to cook or anything, but loves to walk around and ask, 'Hey, how are you doing? Are you enjoying your meal?'"

In terms of temperament, Bickel and Guarino were near-opposites. Phillips likes to use a *Star Trek* analogy, saying Bickel was the analytical Spock, while Guarino was the passionate Dr. McCoy. And yes, Phillips concedes, he cast himself at Captain Kirk, the ruggedly handsome adventurer and natural leader.

The friends began to talk seriously about opening a store in spring of 1994. By the summer, they were scouting locations. They wanted to be close to a residential area, preferably near a high school, and not too far from Ohio State. The spot they ended up renting was a familiar one, a recent former home of Wizard of Comics. The search took almost no time at all.

"It went from notion to reality in an incredibly short span of time," Phillips said.

As he remembers it, they were able to move forward with abandon because only one of them, Bickel, had any serious commitments at home. He had two children and was dating the woman who would become, and still is, his wife, and she had a child of her own. Phillips and Guarino were single and could throw themselves wholeheartedly into this new pursuit.

Not everything was working out, however. The friends had planned to sell comics and role-playing games, but the former Wizard location sat next door to The Soldiery, a role-playing game store. In hindsight, Bickel thinks the presence of The Soldiery was a boon for his store. He and his friends decided to focus exclusively on comics, aiming to have the most diverse selection in town. They did this while still benefiting from foot traffic for The Soldiery, an audience that was likely to be interested in comics.

Laughing Ogre had a mission. It wanted to be a store that gave you no reason not to shop there. It would be open longer hours each day than any competitor, and seven days per week, and most holidays. While some stores favored Marvel or DC or independent titles, Laughing Ogre would have everything.

On top of all that, the store would have a name you couldn't forget. Where did it come from? The friends had a long been players of Warhammer, the tabletop role-playing game. Guarino ran the game, and he had invented a tavern that was a recurring setting for the characters. It was called The Laughing Ogre.

"We wanted a character," Bickel said. "We wanted something people would remember." The ogre logo was designed by an acquaintance, Gary Thomas Washington, who was a commercial artist. The original sign remains in place, more than twenty years later.

(*Top*) The original counter at The Laughing Ogre when it was still a work in progress. *Courtesy of Gib Bickel;* (*right*) The ogre himself, designed by Gary Thomas Washington. *Courtesy of Gib Bickel.*

The store opened on October 28, 1994, a Friday. The co-owners had built the counter and fixtures themselves. On that first day, many of the shelves were empty, and long boxes of comics were stacked along the wall.

"A guy walks in and says, 'I thought you were open today,'" Bickel said. "We said, 'We are open.' He said, 'I'll come back when you're more open.'"

At first, the co-owners were the only employees, and they received no income. They worked all of the store's hours themselves, and each of them maintained a full-time, or close to full-time, job on the side, just in case the store flopped.

In the history of the comics business, 1994 was a significant year, the beginning of the deepest downturn since the creation of the direct market two decades earlier. The bust followed an early 1990s boom in which many retailers overextended themselves. Laughing Ogre was coming onto the scene with no debt, low costs, and an abundance of enthusiasm, right as many of its local competitors were being whipsawed by the downturn. So, while 1994 looked like a terrible year to open a comic book shop, it turned out to be fortuitous timing.

But any new business has its problems, and the first one for Laughing Ogre had to do with staffing, or the lack thereof. The co-owners found that details got missed because the store was nobody's full-time job. They needed one of them to quit his other job and become a day-to-day manager. That person turned out to be Bickel, in the spring of 1995. His pay was the store's first salary, and its largest expense other than inventory.

The store had a full selection of comics from Marvel and DC and other big publishers, and made a point of having an extensive selection of material from smaller publishers. There were competitors in town that specialized in mainstream superhero comics or small-press comics, but none that tried to do both, Bickel said. As a result, many of Laughing Ogre's first customers would pick up a few items they couldn't get at their main store, while still doing the bulk of their buying somewhere else.

"We were everybody's second store," he said. As some of the other shops went out of business, Laughing Ogre was poised to pick up the customers.

Within four years, the store was the largest in the region, by Bickel's estimate. Some of the gains were by conquest, with people switching from other stores. And some were by expanding the market into underserved groups, such as women.

"Pretty early on we had a large female clientele that we were really proud of," Phillips said. This was in contrast to shops that had a boys' club mentality, where women would "get treated like a Martian, if not outright harassed," he said.

The store became one of the social centers of the Columbus comics scene. It hosted regular signings for comics creators and had parties on the nights before major conventions, such as Mid-Ohio Con and the Small Press and Alternative Comics Expo. In doing this, the owners got to know many of the creators who were coming up during that time.

One year, the convention guests included Tony Moore, the cocreator and artist on a new horror series called *The Walking Dead*. Bickel bought the original cover art for issue #15, showing the protagonist, Rick Grimes, riding his motorcycle. The price was $200, and it helped Moore recoup the costs of the trip, he would later say. Years later, *The Walking Dead* has been adapted into a hit television series, and the cover likely is the most valuable comics-related item that Bickel owns, worth thousands of dollars, but he's not selling.

Bickel was eager to buy the cover because he was a fan of the series, long before it was a commercial success. "We pushed it really hard from day one," he said. *The Walking Dead* was one of the titles that had a sign by it saying, "Recommended by Gib." This meant that customers who tried the book could bring it back and exchange it if they didn't like it.

Among the other titles that won the status of "Recommended by Gib": *Ultimate Spider-Man, Stray Bullets,* and *Strangers in Paradise.* His favorites tended to come from a select few creators, such as Terry Moore, the writer and artist behind *Rachel Rising* and *Strangers in Paradise,* and Brian Michael Bendis, the writer of *Ultimate Spider-Man, Powers,* and *Daredevil.*

And yet all those creators were secondary to the hometown favorite, Jeff Smith. He had launched *Bone,* his self-published comic, in 1991 from his Columbus studio. He and his wife, Vijaya Iyer, lived in California from 1991 to 1994, before returning to Columbus. When they got back, Smith became a regular customer.

The store's sales grew in each of its first eight years, and it was profitable that entire time. "A lot of the mistakes we were making were getting eaten up by sales increases," Bickel said. The mistakes were almost all related to runaway costs, much of it for inventory that was poorly tracked and got lost in the back room.

This was about when the trio of owners became a duo. Phillips decided he wanted to get a more traditional job, and went back to information-technology work. He sold his share to Bickel and Guarino, and the three remained friends.

The store's fortunes began to turn during what Bickel calls the "Bush recession" of 2002 and 2003. The country's economy was sluggish, and the store found that its expenses had grown to exceed its income. By 2005, a business that had once known nothing but profit was $150,000 in debt, and the co-owners had no idea how to reverse course.

Bickel worked nearly every hour the store was open. He found he was too tired to give proper attention to ordering and organizing the back room.

He staggered through the days. One of the most upbeat people you ever will meet was tired and depressed. In the middle of this, his family dog, Charlie, died.

"I remember being devastated. I don't deal well with that kind of loss," he said.

Bickel began to see that there was no way forward for the store. He and Guarino would need to close. It was just a matter of when.

Bickel reached out to Gary Dills, owner of Phoenix Comics & Games, a two-store chain in Virginia. Bickel had met Dills a few years earlier through a comics retailer group, and they had kept in touch to trade ideas. This time Bickel had a plea. He asked Dills to consider buying Laughing Ogre's excess inventory.

"The more we talked, [Dills] said, 'Have you ever thought about selling the business?'" Bickel said. He knew of nobody in the Columbus area who had the desire and the money to buy the store. And he hadn't considered that somebody outside Columbus would want to own it.

Dills visited the store and was astounded by what he saw as a great business that was being run poorly. "That was probably one of the top forty stores in the country in terms of volume, and they had one guy doing everything," Dills said, referring to Bickel. "He's running ragged and he has no time to get anything done."

He saw big problems in the way Bickel and Guarino related to each other. Bickel worked most of the retail hours and interacted with customers, while Guarino was largely behind the scenes. "It was kind of this left hand not talking to the right hand," Dills said.

In February 2006, Dills bought the store. Bickel would remain as an employee, and Guarino would leave the business. I was unable to reach Guarino for an interview. He still lives in the Columbus area, and is not in regular touch with Bickel.

The fix for Laughing Ogre turned out to be easy. Dills emptied the store of more than fourteen hundred storage boxes of unsorted comics and books that had accumulated in the back room. He sold them in bulk to another comics dealer and had them trucked away. He followed this with a remodel, taking down walls so that there was more space open to the public and less storage space. Then he started using inventory-management software so that he could better align his ordering with sales.

Less than a year after the sale, Laughing Ogre was profitable again, and monthly sales were up $10,000 from the prior year, Dills said. But this was not a happy time for Bickel. Dills, who spent most of his time in Virginia, had hired a friend of his to be the store manager. The new manager turned out to be one of the few people on earth who couldn't get along with Bickel.

"I chose the wrong person is what the reality was," Dills said. "I take as much of the blame as there is in that situation."

Bickel quit his job at the store in December 2006, less than a year after the sale. Customers received this note with their comics:

Dear Ogre shoppers,

"I believe it's time for me to fly." OK that was REO, but it also sums up what I need to tell all of you. When I leave on December 21st, I will no longer be working at The Laughing Ogre. It's a very tough thing to do, but it is time. I can't express how much I will miss you all. The hardest thing about leaving is realizing that so many friends won't be visiting me anymore. Your friendship and loyalty as customers is greatly appreciated, and I do mean greatly. . . .

I'll still buy my comics at The Ogre, so I may see some of you from time to time. I encourage everyone to treat the new store as wonderfully as you did the old one. Thanks again, you have all been absolutely great to work for.

Take care,

Gib

He went to CarMax, a national chain of used-car dealerships, and worked on the sales staff. He liked it, but he missed comics. During Bickel's time selling cars, Dills went through two store managers before promoting Jeff Stang to the job, an employee Bickel had hired back in the day. Stang had moved to Columbus for college and was a customer at Laughing Ogre before he was an employee. He had, and has, a memorable look, with a bald head and a clear fondness for the weight room.

In August 2011, Stang posted online that he had a big surprise for long-time customers. That Monday, Bickel returned to Laughing Ogre, and he's been there ever since. "Anyone who had been shopping there for any amount of time was just ecstatic," Stang said.

He and Bickel found that they easily fell into complementary roles, with Stang doing the paperwork and hiring and Bickel doing most of the work with customers. One of Stang's hires was Lauren McCallister, who was on the young side but had experience working at a smaller shop near her hometown.

"She's a very matter-of-fact woman and she doesn't take any shit," he said.

Even before buying Laughing Ogre, Dills had made a name for himself among comics retailers for the rapid growth of his business. He had been a comics fan his entire life. In 1994, when he was in his early twenties, he got a job at Galaxy Comics in Herndon, Virginia, on the outskirts of the Washington, D.C., metro area. Three years later, the store's owner ran into problems paying taxes and abruptly closed.

Dills and a partner made a deal to open a new store in the same space in 1997, using many of the same fixtures and inventory. They called it Phoenix Comics because it was rising from the ashes. The new business had the good fortune to be near the corporate headquarters of America Online, a company whose growth was fueling an economic boom throughout that part of the D.C. suburbs.

"It was a case of right place, right time," Dills said.

His business grew and he became known among the top store owners in the country. When several top retailers formed ComicsPro, a trade organization, in 2004, Dills was one of the founding board members. But he was not a jacket-and-tie kind of guy. In group photos of the board, Dills often looks like he just woke up, with stubble and an untucked shirt.

It was no secret to people who knew Dills that he liked to gamble. He had been a risk-taker as long as he could remember, and gravitated toward games of chance. In elementary school, he got suspended for running a poker game during recess, he said. He thought he could control his desire to gamble. Then, in the early 2010s, he fell into depression and began to gamble more than ever before.

"I'm really good at juggling problems and not letting anybody know," he said.

He lost large sums of money, and tried to cover by shifting money around. Near the end of 2014, he had run out of ways to hide the problem. He was broke, and his businesses were too.

In December 2014, ComicsPro announced it had discovered financial irregularities related to a board member. Several outlets reported the board member was Dills. "Professionally I burned every single bridge I could," he said. "It wasn't on purpose." He never faced criminal charges, but several ComicsPro members have said that lawyers had to get involved to try to recover the lost money. Nobody would specify how much money was mishandled or whether all the issues have been resolved.

Dills was in a financial tailspin, and about to be cut off from receiving new comics. He needed to find someone to buy his businesses while there still was something to sell. Through it all, the stores continued to operate.

"The electricity would occasionally get turned off," said Christopher Lloyd, the Virginia retailer who would soon buy the stores' assets. "They were getting books days or a week late. [Employees] were in that unfortunate position of having to cover for the fact that they were not getting bills paid, which is so awkward."

Just as Bickel had once reached out to Dills, Dills now reached out to Lloyd, whose main store was Painted Visions Comics in Woodbridge, Virginia. The asset sale happened with no public announcement in February 2015. Lloyd bought fixtures and inventory of two stores, and negotiated leases with the landlords. He did not assume any of Dills's debts.

"It was a huge decision, probably the biggest decision I made in my life other than marriage," Lloyd said.

The sale came together so quickly that the deal had largely been negotiated before Lloyd visited Laughing Ogre. He walked through the door for the first time and met Stang, Bickel, and the other employees. "I was full of butterflies," he said.

Within a few months, Stang had left for a job in California, doing retailer outreach for Image Comics. Lloyd made Bickel the store manager, back in charge for the first time since 2006.

"I'm extremely lucky to have him," Lloyd said. "He runs the place as if it's his own, but he really respects me as the owner."

The two bonded over their shared affection for *Usagi Yojimbo*, the long-running comic series by Stan Sakai about an anthropomorphic rabbit samurai. Lloyd found that Bickel could describe a good comic in a way that would make anyone want to read it.

"I've seen really good salesmen, and Gib is one of the best because he's not a salesman; he's an educator."

And that, with all the twists, was how Laughing Ogre went from that first day in 1994 to Free Comic Book Day 2015.

McCallister spent most of Free Comic Book Day at one of the two cash registers, ringing up the seemingly unending succession of customers. Every once in a while she got a respite. "My favorite job is when I get to stand by the line and yell to get people to form the line," she said.

She viewed Lloyd's purchase of the store's assets as an almost entirely positive development. The new owner, unlike his predecessor, was willing to replace old equipment. "Can we have a new shelf? Yes. Can we have new computers? Yes," she said. "It was amazing."

Among the new purchases was a red metal cart that employees used to carry stacks of comics to the shelves. Bickel had asked Dills to buy one for years. The presence of the cart, as much as anything, typified what the employees hoped would be a less anxious era. Lloyd could afford to make the purchases because his stores were making money and the comics market had been growing for years.

And yet the pace of growth was about to slow almost to a halt. As people waited in line for free comics, the shelves containing that month's new releases were filled with special issues from DC's *Convergence* event. Marvel had its own event, called *Secret Wars,* which made its debut on that day with a #0 preview issue. In different ways, *Convergence* and *Secret Wars* would do damage to their publishers and the retailers.

Bickel was back in charge, just in time for what was shaping up to be a chaotic year in the comics business. He had seen booms and busts, and this looked like the early stages of a bust.

But that was yet to come. For now, all that mattered was ringing people up and managing the line. At closing time, the employees were sweaty and tired. They took two hours to count the drawers and restock the shelves. When they finished, the numbers were stunning: that day was the best in the store's history, with the most dollar sales, the most transactions. They would have celebrated, but everyone just wanted to go home.

5

Secret Convergence

GIB BICKEL sits in the back room of The Laughing Ogre after closing on a Tuesday. It's September 2015, four months after Free Comic Book Day. He opens the phone-book-sized tome that contains almost all of the new products the store will be selling in two months. The monthly catalogue, called *Previews,* is published by Diamond Comics Distributors. This month there are 2,657 items available for order. To an untrained eye, and sometimes even to a trained one, the choices are overwhelming.

For each item, Bickel needs to decide how many to order. His store's success or failure will largely be determined by how close his order comes to the actual sales to customers. "There are very few things we order zero of," he said.

He has some rules of thumb for ordering. With each new series, he tries to peg it to some other series with a sales history, often based on the lead character or the creators. For example, when ordering *Joe Golem: Occult Detective,* a book cowritten by Mike Mignola, he looks at others that Mignola has cowritten.

"You've got a book that Mignola's writing, you're not going to roll *Hellboy* numbers into it," he said, naming the creator's top-selling series. "Not everybody that gets *Hellboy* is going to get *Joe.* You take one of his other characters, maybe Lobster Johnson, maybe Lord Baltimore."

Once he has figured out how many to order of the first issue, he knows that most of the time sales will fall by half for the second issue, and then fall by an additional one-third. This is important because he is sometimes ordering the second and third issues of a title before he knows how the first one sold.

Retailers grumble about Diamond. They complain about errors in the shipments, damaged books, and any number of other things. At the same time, Diamond has made a number of changes in response to retailers' concerns. The best example may be something called "final order cutoff," a policy that allows retailers to change their orders for major publishers within three weeks of the shipping date. So, while orders are still two months in advance, store managers have time to change their minds. Marvel was the first publisher to adopt final order cutoff in the 2000s, followed by DC and others. "It's a game-changer," Bickel said.

The monthly ordering process is about putting numbers next to thousands of line items, a tedious process. The larger market is difficult to conceptualize when you're bleary-eyed and trying to decide whether to order one or two of *Ivar, Timewalker* #11.

At that moment, the comics market had taken a turn south. Comics sales had been growing for more than a decade. Now a downturn had arrived, and the main culprits were the biggest publishers, DC and Marvel.[1]

Of the two, DC had the more acute problem. The company had reeled off a series of creative and sales flops, often born from the competing desires to appeal to longtime fans and to attract new readers. One of the greatest misfires was *Convergence,* published in April and May 2015. Too few people read it, leading to boxes full of unsold copies for many retailers. People who did read it were likely to come away confused by the nonsensical plot and wishing that they had spent their money on something else.

"*Convergence,* for DC, really hurt them, and they never really have gotten that market back," Bickel said. "They basically told their fans to take two months off, and people were like, 'You know what, I didn't miss you that much.'"

Here, in the interest of understanding the fiasco that was *Convergence,* is my attempt to explain why DC did the project, and the plot of the comics themselves. Brace yourself.

DC has long been part of the entertainment conglomerate Time Warner, part of Warner Entertainment. In 2014, executives at Warner decided
to relocate DC's offices from New York, where they had been since their
inception in the 1930s, to the Los Angeles area. The move would put DC
next to the film and television divisions, which often use DC characters.
Also, some DC employees already were based in Los Angeles, so the move
would put everyone in the same place.[2]

However, the logistics of a cross-country move were not compatible with
the weekly deadlines for publishing comics. To deal with this, DC's editorial
leadership came up with a special event that would cover the two months
of the move. Nearly every DC title would go on hiatus for the two months,
replaced by a weekly limited series called *Convergence* and twenty different
tie-in series. In all, the project would cover nine issues of *Convergence* and
about forty issues of tie-ins.

Most of DC's top creators were busy with other projects or with the
relocation. In their place was a hastily assembled group of writers and artists. The main *Convergence* storyline was written by a committee and drawn
in shifts by various artists. The story begins with an issue that serves as a
prologue to the entire event. In it, a disoriented Superman wakes up in a
place outside space and time and finds himself face to face with various versions of one of his top villains, the green-skinned scientist Brainiac. There
is some punching and exposition. Brainiac has long been collecting cities
from doomed planets and storing them on his ship in bottles. It's kind of
his thing. He decides to take dozens of the cities and plop them onto an
otherwise unoccupied planet, where he will pit pairs of cities against each
other. Superman is displeased.

The remaining eight issues follow the inhabitants of one of the worlds,
Earth 2, a cast of characters that you wouldn't know unless you had been
reading their series, called *Earth 2,* and a follow-up series, *Earth 2: World's
End.* The heroes include some familiar names with unfamiliar faces, such as
a black Superman and a Batman whose secret identity is Thomas Wayne,
father of Bruce Wayne. Among the villains is a kind of Brainiac-lite named
Telos, a henchman of Brainiac, who wields godlike power over the planet
that houses the domed cities.

The plot takes a turn when the heroes meet a goateed wizard named
Deimos, who offers to help them defeat Telos. He points the way to a

safe haven in an underground fantasy realm called Skartaris. Longtime DC readers may have recognized Deimos as the villain from *Warlord,* a sword-and-sorcery comic that ran from 1976 to 1988, and in several shorter-lived series since then.

From there, the characters from *Earth 2,* a recent series with middling sales, throw themselves into the conflicts of characters from *Warlord,* a series whose heyday was during the Carter administration. Later on, the action shifts back to the surface, Deimos is defeated, and the story wraps up with an near-incomprehensible plot point that reverses some of the effects of a 1985 story, *Crisis on Infinite Earths.*

"In one sense, *Convergence* confirms, yet again, what long-time fans already know: For the most part, the arc of superhero comics always bends back to where it began," said Laura Hudson, writing for *Wired.* Her comments were in response to marketing materials before *Convergence* was released, but pretty much nailed what the series would be.

"But *Convergence* also illustrates one of the great marketing dilemmas of modern comics, which are often torn between catering to their aging hardcore fans and trying to welcome new readers. The latter is a difficult proposition, as demonstrated by the fact that as superhero movies make billions of dollars at the box office, superhero comics remain an incredibly niche industry where the #1 best-selling comic moves 150,000 copies in a given month—if it's lucky."[3]

While DC was wrapping up *Convergence,* Marvel was just beginning its big event of the year, *Secret Wars.* On the surface, the two series have similar concepts. *Secret Wars* takes place on Battleworld, a planet ruled by a godlike Doctor Doom in which various timelines and storylines in the history of the Marvel Universe exist as countries and fight against each other.

And yet, Marvel's execution was much different from DC's, with the same writer and artist for the whole story and much more coherence. This is not to say that *Secret Wars* was a success. The desire to use the same creators throughout became a problem when the artist, Esad Ribic, fell behind schedule. The final issue of *Secret Wars* would be published in January 2016, months later than originally planned. But that wasn't the worst part. Marvel was using the series to relaunch its entire superhero line, and had a slate of debut issues that had already been scheduled for the last few months of 2015.[4] The new series were taking place in the world established at the climax of *Secret Wars,* only readers wouldn't get a chance to see that part of the story for another few months. Retailers say the scheduling problems meant that fewer readers picked up the series debuts, which they say was a shame because several good titles got too little notice.

While lamenting the shortcomings of *Convergence* and *Secret Wars,* retailers could take comfort that a surefire hit was coming in November: *Dark Knight III: The Master Race.* The miniseries was the latest sequel to Frank Miller's 1986 series *Batman: The Dark Knight Returns.* Only this time Miller was not the writer-artist, as he had been before. He served as a cowriter, and his only art contributions were alternate covers and backup stories.[5] The fact that DC's salvation was a sequel to a sequel, and that the original creator was much less involved, provided fodder for critics who said the company was losing its way.

Somewhere in there, from summer into fall of 2015, comic shops went into a quiet panic. "I remember a lot of [retailers] were saying, 'I don't think I'll still be here in six months,'" said Brian Hibbs in San Francisco. The problem was that a rare event had occurred: DC and Marvel had made major mistakes at about the same time. "Usually it's just one at a time that's screwing up," he said. "We need at least one of the main publishers to be functioning properly just to keep cash flow going."

Many retailers cut their orders to account for the decrease in customer interest. "It was a little scary," said Shelton Drum, owner of Heroes Aren't Hard to Find in Charlotte. "*Convergence* and *Secret Wars* really let people know that they didn't have to come to the comic shop. They got out of the habit of buying comics. You have to give it to them on a regular basis. That regular traffic is so important to our business."

Drum had been selling comics since the 1970s, and had lived through a few downturns. He knew his business well enough that he could sense shifts in the market. While he wasn't the type to panic, he knew there was an uncomfortably high probability that things could get ugly.

I reached out to DC and Marvel, but neither company provided an official for an interview.

At The Laughing Ogre, the drop in sales meant Bickel would get no honeymoon in his return as store manager. He faced a deteriorating market and

Shelton Drum, owner of Heroes Aren't Hard to Find, interviewed at the
Gem City Comic Con in Dayton, Ohio, in 2016.

would need to do it with a largely inexperienced staff. His chief advantage
was that he had seen downturns before. He had won some and lost some,
and knew life would go on no matter what happened.

"The comic market is always this series of disasters," he said. "It's always
coming or just left us. Well, here's another one."

He didn't know how long or how deep the downturn was going to be,
but he was unafraid.

6

The Valkyries

ON MOST Saturdays at The Laughing Ogre, the employees are all women. The trend started in the fall of 2015 with an influx of new workers, a quirk of scheduling. Lauren McCallister, the store's assistant manager, was in charge. The other Saturday regular was Sarah Edington, who started at the store in the summer of 2015, following some time at a T-shirt printer. For much of 2015 and 2016, the third slot was taken by Alissa Sallah, an art student who draws her own comics.

A decade ago, it would have been remarkable to see a comic shop staffed on a busy weekend day with no male employees. Comic book readers were overwhelmingly male, and so were the people who sold comics.

But the gender mix was changing. The number of female readers grew, which led to publishers putting out more titles aimed at women, or at least not aimed strictly at men. And more women started working at comic shops. This is according to interviews with shop owners and employees. Unfortunately, there are no reliable data about the gender mix of shop customers or employees.

"I'm glad that things are the way they are," McCallister said. "I'm glad we have a lot of ladies."

As the store struggled though a difficult stretch of sales, the role of women would be essential. Female customers are more likely than male ones to prefer comics from independent publishers and to buy comics in book form,

The Ogre's Valkyries: (*left to right*) Sarah Edington, Alissa Sallah, and Lauren McCallister.

employees said. The store's sales of those items were rising and helping offset some of the losses from periodical comics from Marvel and DC.

The three women at Laughing Ogre are members of a group called the Valkyries. To explain what this means, we need to go to Halifax, Nova Scotia, in 2013. An up-and-coming cartoonist named Kate Leth was an employee at a comic shop called Strange Adventures. She saw that the store's owner participated in an online message board for comics retailers, and got the idea to set up something like that, only for women. She started an online club called the Valkyries, with a members-only message board and meetups at comic conventions. The group had 150 members as of January 2014.[1]

Member number 147 was Annie Bulloch, co-owner of 8th Dimension Comics & Games in Houston. "I've never been much of a joiner," she said. "But I joined, and I loved it. It was great. It was nice to be able to talk to people who had similar experiences and insight."

Bulloch, who had experience doing social media for her shop and for outside clients, soon was helping run accounts for the Valkyries. She became one of six coadministrators of the group in 2015.

Meanwhile, Leth's comics career has taken off. She has written the *Hellcat* series for Marvel and continues with her *Kate or Die* webcomic. She moved from Nova Scotia to the Los Angeles area. She now works mainly as a screenwriter.

There is a public side of the Valkyries, such as a Twitter feed with book recommendations. There also is a private side on the message board, whose membership is open only to women who work at comic shops or are librarians.

"We try to make it positive and upbeat, because, you know, Twitter has so many problems," Bulloch said. "We're angry about harassment in the industry and poor treatment of women characters, but we don't want that to be 100 percent of the discussion."

The rise of the Valkyries is part of what has been a sometimes contentious shift in comics culture. Some of the fans don't like what they see as a proliferation of politically correct comics and shops. Gender is just a part of this, as Marvel introduced many new versions of characters that were previously best known as white men, such as a Korean American Hulk, a black Captain America, and a white female Thor.

In my interviews with shop employees, I tried to find other groups like the Valkyries. Were there, for example, groups for black workers, Latino workers, or LGBT workers? Some groups exist, but none are as large and well-known as the Valkyries.

The Valkyries are responding to what has been, and in many places remains, a male-dominated comics culture. Sexism permeates many parts of the industry, from the depiction of women in comics to the way that some store owners and employees treat female customers.

Bulloch bristled at this as a young comics fan. She recalls a visit to a shop in Austin in the 1990s when she was a recent college graduate.

"I walked in and they immediately asked me if I was looking for something for my boyfriend," she said. "They just acted like I didn't belong. They tried to talk over my head. They acted as though I had to be some kind of expert to shop there. That was common at a lot of shops, especially if you were a woman. It was like you were invading the clubhouse."

That shop ended up closing a few years later. Bulloch eventually found her way to Austin Books & Comics, a place where the staff greeted everyone and was eager to help. She became a regular customer, and used that store in many ways as a model when she and two co-owners opened 8th Dimension. Meanwhile, Austin Books remains open and has several Valkyries on staff.

If something like the Valkyries had existed in the early days of comic shops, it would have been a small but formidable club. The roster might have included Diana Schutz, who dropped out of graduate school in 1978 and got a job at her local shop in Vancouver, British Columbia. She would go on to a career as a writer and editor, much of it with Dark Horse Comics.

"It had a homey feel," she said about the store, called simply The Comicshop. "It wasn't dusty and scary like some of the early comic shops."

On her first day, the co-owners showed her how to "bag and tag"—to bag comics and put price tags on the bags. While she was doing that, a male friend of the owners walked in and, without saying anything to her, went up the stairs to the apartment above.

"The first words out his mouth were 'Who's the skirt?'" she said.

She would find that the owners treated her with respect, but the customers often didn't. "There were definitely male customers who would come into that store who simply would not talk to me, would not look at me,

would not engage with me in any way, shape, or form."

She did her job and learned the business. In 1981, she moved to the Bay Area to work at Comics & Comix. Even in a larger metro area, and at a chain of comic shops, she was one of only a few female employees, and the customers were overwhelmingly male.

Diana Schutz in 1982 at Comics & Comix. The store made buttons to sell, and she loaded up a sweatshirt with them. *Credit: Clay Geerdes.*

Some comic shops have felt like clubhouses for men, in part because of the content of the comics, with title after title that featured overmuscled men, busty women, and lots of fight scenes. In other words, the product went a long way toward determining the audience.

"It's kind of like, if you build it they will come," Schutz said. "If you give women something they want to read, they will read it. But if you only give them the typical male fantasy stuff, then it's kind of no wonder that women weren't comfortable in the industry for so long."

Suffice it to say, she is a fan of the Valkyries and what they stand for.

The product and the audience are both changing and diversifying, but it has been a long road to get here. When comic shops began to proliferate in the late 1970s, women customers tended to gravitate toward independent titles, such as *Elfquest* and *Cerebus,* according to shop owners from that era. In the early 1980s, women were a key part of the audiences for alternative publishers, with titles such as *Love and Rockets.* Among mainstream titles, women helped support some of the biggest hits, including Marvel's *X-Men* and DC's *New Teen Titans.* But women remained a tiny share of comics buyers.

All of this was prehistory to the title that many shop owners say was their first hit for which women were a key part of the audience: DC's *Sandman,* which debuted with a cover date of January 1989. Written by Neil Gaiman and drawn initially by Sam Keith and Mike Dringenberg, the series was about Morpheus, a godlike being with power over dreams. *Sandman* was one of the first series that had more readers of its paperback collected editions than of the original periodical comics. The paperback format became a regular feature at bookstores, which is where many readers encountered *Sandman* for the first time.

Gaiman has seemed to embrace his role as an advocate for his female fans, writing about how some shops are unfriendly to women:

> There are comics stores out there which are simply boys' clubs, owned or run by people who've never been much good at talking to or being in the presence of women, and for that matter, have never quite mastered basic women-friendly skills, like washing, changing their tee-shirts, or sweeping the floor. Women feel as uncomfortable

in these places as most men do when inexorable circumstances cause them, blushing, coughing and staring nervously at the floor, to spend any amount of time in the lingerie department of a large department store.[2]

The female comics audience, which was small but growing through the 1990s and into the 2000s, got a boost when publishers began to translate more Japanese comics, or manga. The manga boom of the 2000s is a story unto itself, as some comic shops were slow to embrace the trend, and customers got in the habit of shopping for manga titles at bookstore chains such as Barnes and Noble.

The 2000s were also when Brian K. Vaughan emerged as a creator whose sales success was due in large part to female readers. His breakthrough title was *Y: The Last Man,* started in 2002 by DC's Vertigo imprint. The story, drawn by Pia Guerra, was about Yorick Brown, who somehow survived a plague that had instantly killed every other man on earth.

Vaughan is cocreator of the current top-seller at many shops, *Saga,* which is a collaboration with artist Fiona Staples. Another of his titles, *Paper Girls,* cocreated with artist Cliff Chiang, was one of the most successful debuts of 2015.

Until recently, nearly all of the comics popular with women were written by men, reflecting an industry that had few female writers and artists. This has changed in the last few years with big names such as G. Willow Wilson, who writes *Ms. Marvel,* and Kelly Sue DeConnick, who helped revitalize Marvel's *Captain Marvel* character and now works on her own creations for Image Comics.

All of this means that comic shops have many options when a female customer walks in and is looking for suggestions. But the customer shouldn't just be pointed toward "girl books," as female employees are quick to point out. *Saga, Paper Girls,* and many others do well with men and women, and are indicative of a market that has broader appeal than the latest issue of *Wolverine.*

Back at The Laughing Ogre, the three Valkyries go about their business in a way barely distinguishable from male employees. The difference is in how some of the customers react. McCallister noticed when she was new at the store that some male customers would direct questions to the male employees rather than her and act as if she didn't know much about comics. Now she has been around long enough that most of the customers know better. And, on Saturdays, there are no male employees to ask.

The most blatant sexism she sees is in the comics themselves. "To me, honestly, I'm so desensitized to all of the ridiculous, absurd depictions of women," she said. One of the main offenders is the line of comics from Dynamite Entertainment featuring Dejah Thoris, a character from Edgar Rice Burroughs's fiction, who is drawn nearly naked, with enormous breasts.

"Ah, the golden nipples," McCallister said. And Dejah Thoris isn't the worst of it. Several other comics are more gratuitously sexist, with titles such as *Cavewoman* and *Tarot: Witch of the Black Rose*. "It's absolutely insane to me that this kind of stuff exists."

She thinks there will always be a small market for comics that edge toward pornography. At the same time, she is encouraged that those types of books are far outnumbered by new ones that she can hand to women and girls without embarrassment.

Sallah, the art student, left Columbus in 2016 and moved to Portland, Oregon, where she went to work in a newly opening comic shop, Books with Pictures, and be an intern at a studio for comics professionals. On her last day at Laughing Ogre, I asked her what she liked about the store and what she would miss about it.

"So many people are used to the Comic Book Guy, the *Simpsons* character," she said, referring the ponytailed, dismissive proprietor of the comic shop on the television show. "They'll come in on a Saturday and say, 'Well this is different.'"

The differences go beyond that the employees on Saturday are all women. "We try to hold ourselves to a higher standard," she said. "The Laughing Ogre appreciates what comics are becoming now, as opposed to what comics used to be. It's a bigger market with more literary content coming out."

7

Heyday (1980–84)

AT THE start of 1980, Greg Ketter's comic shop was operating in its third location and under its second name. He had a small space on the second floor of a Minneapolis pharmacy, maybe six hundred square feet. A neon sign in the window said, "BOOKS." He chose brevity because the full name, The Compleat Enchanter, was too long to fit. Down below was 14th Avenue Southeast, a few blocks from the University of Minnesota campus.

In many ways, he was just a kid messing around, not a serious business-man. He had opened his first store in 1977, barely out of high school. Now he was a student at the U, going to classes in the mornings and working the counter at the store in the afternoons and evenings. He had a part-time job on the side, taking tickets at the Uptown Theater. He did all this with long hair and a perpetual stubble. "I was pretty wild looking," he said.

The pioneers of the direct market had mostly gone into business in the early 1970s. Their growth was steady, but they remained a tiny segment of overall comics sales. Now a second generation was getting started right on the cusp of a boom in sales and a proliferation of shops. Ketter was about to get serious.

One driver of growth was competition between wholesale distributors. Ketter had been a customer of Phil Seuling's company, Sea Gate. Then he got a visit from a sales representative for Big Rapids, a Detroit-based distributor that was spreading across the Upper Midwest. Big Rapids was emboldened by recent legal settlements involving Sea Gate, which mandated that comics publishers needed to have the same terms of service for each distributor. In sales calls, Big Rapids made the case that it could provide the same products as Sea Gate, only in a way that was much more retailer-friendly.[1] For example, Big Rapids did not have strict prepayment rules.

A similar dynamic played out across the country, as regional distributors were winning Sea Gate accounts and also getting a large share of the newly opened stores. Irjax was doing this in Maryland and surrounding states. Pacific Comics was growing from a base in San Diego. Meanwhile, Sea Gate remained the key player but was taking hits from almost all sides.[2] Bud Plant Inc. in the Bay Area specialized in art books and foreign imports.

"I liked the competition because everybody had different things," Ketter said. "Each distributor seemed to have a specialty, along with comics."

Pacific had a series of art portfolios, some of which were big sellers for Ketter. Bud Plant Inc. had a deep selection of European and Japanese comics. And then there was a wholesaler whom Ketter remembers only as "Wild Bill," who walked a route in the Minneapolis area, often accompanied by an infant son he carried in a sling, and sold bundles of underground comics. At the same time, Big Rapids was Ketter's main supplier, including for Marvel, DC, and other mainstream comics.

His main contacts at Big Rapids were Milton Griepp and John Davis, who operated out of a Madison, Wisconsin, office. Griepp and Davis had backgrounds working for Wisconsin Independent News Distributors, or WIND, a cooperative that sold mainstream comics and magazines along with left-wing publications.

"It wasn't like I was joining the co-op as a political statement," said Griepp about WIND. He was in his twenties and working toward a masters degree in sociology from the University of Wisconsin. "It was just that I liked comics. They wanted an expert in the field, and I was the closest to it."

WIND ran into financial problems, and Big Rapids bought some of its assets, including the comics distribution business. At a surface level, Big Rapids had a lot in common with WIND. Both were officially cooperatives, which means that they were member-owned. Both had their roots in the late 1960s counterculture. Employees dressed in jeans and T-shirts and had long hair and beards.

"These were strange people," said Jim Friel, the former Donahoe Brothers employee, who had gone on to work for Big Rapids. "They were ideologically leftist in that kind of Detroit, urban way. They drove step vans with posters of Lenin in the back."

Big Rapids had started as the Keep on Truckin' Co-op. It was run by Jim Kennedy, a man jokingly described by former employees as the "first among equals." Despite the hippie trappings, many employees carried themselves with an air of menace. The business operated with a hunger to grow and acquire territory. It sold comics as part of a broader selection of printed material.[3]

"They weren't a straight-up criminal organization, but they sort of were adjacent, we'll say," Griepp said. "Magazine distribution was a tough business. They had territories carved out over years. They didn't want competition."

By that, he means Big Rapids was moving in on turf held by established news distributors that had reputations for tough tactics. He thinks the company adopted some of those approaches just to be able to survive and grow. "Once you understood what the magazine business was like, it wasn't shocking at all" to learn of how Big Rapids conducted itself, he said. "I never witnessed this with my own eyes, but I would hear stories. To go collect money, they would hang a guy out the window by his feet. I don't know if they ever hurt anybody, but they definitely scared people and made people think they would get hurt."

Friel wasn't sure if the tough talk was a pose or not. "Some of them carried guns," he said. "Some of them dealt dope. They were tough people, and they tried to project an image of being tougher than they really were. There was a lot of jocular talk of breaking people's legs and throwing them in the Detroit River."

In Wisconsin and adjacent states, Big Rapids had a different identity. Customers, such as Ketter's store, worked almost exclusively with the affable Griepp and Davis and had little idea that they were dealing with such a rough-and-tumble company.

Then, suddenly, Big Rapids went out of business. It was right near the start of 1980. The very things that fueled growth, such as generous credit terms and not requiring prepayment, meant there was not enough cash coming in to pay the bills. Griepp had been with the company less than two years and was not surprised to see the end had come. "It was an amateur business in the sense that it was entrepreneurs, a couple of guys who saw this opportunity and were taking advantage of it. There was nobody doing cash-flow projections," he said.

A month or two after Big Rapids' demise, Griepp got a visit as his apartment from Davis, who had an idea. Griepp was drawing unemployment insurance and was willing to listen to anything that might constitute a job. "Really it was John coming over and saying, 'I think we can do this,'" Griepp said.

So, at just twenty-six, Griepp became co-owner of a new company called Capital City Distribution, established in April 1980. Davis, who was nine years older, would hold the title of CEO, and they would each go out and try to sign up accounts. They started with about ten stores, mainly in Wisconsin. Ketter was not one of the first batch, but came soon after. The transition between Big Rapids and Capital City was so smooth that Ketter can't remember missing an order, although the gap was long enough that he and other former Big Rapids customers must have had to find other sources for comics for months.

The initial investment from Griepp and Davis was about $1,000, which mostly covered rent for the first headquarters. That space was part of a small warehouse, with a garage door and a loft office. The landlord was a company that manufactured concrete forms and occupied the rest of the building.

From this small beginning, Capital City would become the largest distributor in the country. And, with the possible exception of Bud Plant Inc., it would be the first run by people with the business acumen to manage expenses and set up a nationwide shipping network. The comics-distribution business was growing up.

Intense competition among distributors was happening at the same time publishers were beginning to see comic shops as a market that deserved special attention. Some of this was evident from the success of a few self-published comics. Among these was *Cerebus* by Dave Sim, started in 1977 and starring an anthropomorphic aardvark. It began as a parody of *Conan* and grew into a complex satire. *Elfquest,* the fantasy series by Richard and Wendy Pini, began in 1978 and became a steady seller. The creators of both titles did not have the resources to get their products into pharmacies and newsstands, but they were able to sell small press runs to distributors, which then had a ready market in comic shops.[4]

Soon the major publishers began to offer selected titles exclusively to the direct market of comic shops, with no availability through newsstands. Marvel released *Dazzler* #1 in 1981, featuring a disco-inspired heroine who had previously appeared in *X-Men*. That same year, DC published *Madame Xanadu* #1, which starred a sorceress who had been in several of the company's horror titles.[5]

The direct market steadily grew in importance at Marvel during the tenure of Jim Shooter, editor in chief from 1978 to 1987. The nonreturnable model helped reduce the company's financial risk. "Yes, it was a very deep discount, but it was a firm sale, so it worked out." When he started, the direct market was less than 10 percent of Marvel's sales. When he left the company, that number had soared to about 70 percent.[6]

"The trouble was that the direct market was kind of like shooting fish in a barrel," he said. Fewer pharmacies and grocery stores were stocking comics, and those that did were devoting less space. Marvel could withstand the loss of newsstand sales because of the growth of comic shops. This was trouble, as Shooter saw it, because the newsstand was the entry point for new readers, and now it was withering away.

Some of the upstart comics distributors also became publishers. Pacific Comics got the industry's attention in 1981 with the debut of *Captain Victory and the Galactic Rangers,* written and drawn by Jack Kirby, the cocreator of Marvel's *Fantastic Four* and DC's *New Gods,* among many others. Pacific would follow with other titles from star creators, including *Starslayer* by Mike Grell.[7]

Pacific was started in San Diego in 1971 by brothers Steve and Bill Schanes, who were seventeen and thirteen, respectively. They were comic fans and collectors who sold to their friends and began to have tables at conventions.

"We were kids," Bill Schanes said. "We didn't have a so-called business plan. We didn't have a document saying this is our plan for the future. . . . It was kind of a little bit of skill and little bit of luck and some help from some friends."

Their family's house became overrun with comic books, and their mother told them to get a separate space for the business. In 1974, they found an inexpensive storefront in the Pacific Beach neighborhood, about a mile from the ocean. They shared a retail center with a dog groomer, a real-estate agent, and a bar.

The business initially got its comics from the local news distributor. Then it switched to buying from Phil Seuling. Early in their relationship with Seuling's company, Bill Schanes got a visit at the store from Jim Kennedy, the executive from Big Rapids in Michigan. Kennedy was looking to poach customers from Seuling.

Kennedy "opened up his briefcase with a bottle of whiskey and a couple of shot glasses, and a gun," Schanes said. "He said, basically, 'We should talk about maybe you moving your business over to us.'"

Schanes, who was in high school, replied, "I don't know how to drink. I don't drink whiskey." Until then, Kennedy didn't know that this fast-growing store was run by teenagers. The meeting went on awkwardly for a few minutes, and then Kennedy closed his briefcase and headed out the door. Schanes laughs at it now, but it was scary at the time.

When Marvel opened itself up to working with new distributors, Pacific signed up, and became the regional player in Southern California. The brothers, unshaven and often dressed in flip-flops and shorts, were part of a laid-back California scene.

Much less laid back were the news distributors in the region, some of whom were rumored to have ties to organized crime. "My car had a series of unfortunate incidences where I was getting four flat tires every day, and you knew where that was coming from," Schanes said. But vandalism turned out to be the extent of the pushback. Evidently, comics were too small a business to warrant any actual violence.

Pacific Comics grew as a regional distributor and then as a national publisher. The two sides of the business seemed complementary, especially when *Captain Victory* caused a big sensation among longtime fans of Kirby. But soon one side of Pacific would run into trouble, and both sides would feel the pain.

In this chaotic and dynamic period, some of the new comics distributors wanted to look at ways to work together. It was a novel idea, considering the animosity that existed between many of the companies.

"The big thing then was competing with the old magazine-distribution network," Griepp said. "We felt like we needed our combined volume to compete with something that was huge and well-established."

This led to the formation of a trade group, the International Association of Direct Distributors, which held its first meeting in July 1981 in San Diego, concurrent with the San Diego Comic-Con. They met in a function room in the restaurant at the Westgate Hotel, across the street from the convention. Around the table were representatives of more than a dozen companies, including Phil Seuling, Hal Shuster, Bud Plant, Chuck Rozanski, and Griepp.[8]

Several of the group had gone into the meeting hoping to come up with a strategy for how to do business with DC, which had been slower than Marvel to open itself up to dealing with direct distributors. What followed was an embarrassment, according to Rozanski.

"They started screaming at each other," he said. The argument was between Shuster and a distributor from Kansas City. "I can't even remember what the hell they were arguing about, but it disturbed the other patrons at the restaurant."

"I think there was some yelling," said Griepp. "Someone walked out. I think people were standing up and looking threateningly at each other, so I think there was an implication that violence might result."

Shuster had managed to alienate just about everyone, whether by suing Sea Gate or by moving into competitors' territories. "The Irjax guys were really unreasonable, tough to negotiate with," Griepp said. "They were kind of sketchy characters."

Rozanski recalls that it was Seuling who had pushed for the group to form, even though the new distributors were carving up a market that once was his. "Phil could hold a grudge about as well as anyone I've ever known, but he was also remarkably pragmatic," Rozanski said in a column he wrote for *Comics Buyer's Guide*. "He stated to all of us quite unequivocally during that first meeting that the publishers were our enemies, and that they would plot endlessly to screw us without mercy. Many of us rolled our eyes as Phil ranted on and on about how it was only his dominance of the distribution system prior to 1980 that had held the evil plans of the comics publishers in check."[9]

The meeting took place in the middle of a period of great change in the industry. From roughly 1979 to 1982, comics distribution was thrown wide open and the number of comic shops grew tremendously, although numbers are difficult to verify. Melchior Thompson, the consultant to comic shops, estimates the number of outlets rose from about two hundred in 1977 to five hundred in 1987. In addition, many small shops became big shops.

Irjax was in many ways the instigator of the rapid changes, but its bad decisions would be a big part of the transition to a new era in about 1982. The company had led the way to opening up comics distribution with the Sea Gate lawsuit. In the disorder that followed, Irjax moved aggressively to expand. It had generous discounts and credit terms. Irjax had also expanded its publishing division, New Media. The combined company was then known as Irjax/New Media.

One of Irjax's largest customers was Geppi's Comic World, a Baltimore-area comic shop that had grown into a successful chain. The owner was Steve Geppi, a former letter carrier who had a passion for classic comics. Remember that name.

Despite gains in market share, Irjax was a mess. The company had relocated to Florida. Hal Shuster remained in charge. Irjax was bleeding financially, with margins as low as 2 percent, said Mike Friedrich, who was Marvel's director of sales to the comic shop market. In other words, Irjax bought products from publishers and then resold them to retail clients for just 2 percent more than cost, leaving almost no room for all the expenses of running the business.

"They were literally in their last months," Friedrich said, recalling his only visit to Irjax's Florida offices. "But on their wall was a map that was coded 'us' and 'them' that showed their warehouses and all the other warehouses. They wanted 100 percent of the business. They thought they deserved it because the publishers were stupid."

Irjax went out of business as a distributor in 1982. The publishing side continued for a while, but was done by the mid-1980s. (Hal, Jack, and Irwin Shuster are all deceased, so I could not get their versions of events. Jack died in 2015 in Las Vegas. He was fifty-six. His obituary says Hal and Irwin had died previously, but lists no dates.)[10]

So, by 1982, two of the leading upstarts, Irjax and Big Rapids, were done. Sea Gate was struggling because of the price competition. The pioneering distributors were on their way out, being replaced by companies better suited to do business in a market that had become much larger and more complex.

At the head of the class was Capital City, whose co-owners had seen the errors of Big Rapids and others and were determined not to repeat them.

Intense competition between distributors was mostly good for local comic shops. In Minneapolis, Ketter continued to get most of his products from Capital City and supplement with smaller orders from others. His sales were rising.

By 1983 he had changed his shop's name to DreamHaven Books and had outgrown his space above the pharmacy. That year he moved down to a street-level location that was about fifteen hundred square feet, which was triple what he had been used to. The space was split about 50–50 between comics and science fiction books. He was beginning what he, and many of his customers, consider the glory days of the business.

"A lot of it just had to do with the atmosphere, and the fact that he had or could get items I was interested in," said Steven Ward, who enrolled at the University of Minnesota in 1982 and has been one of Ketter's most faithful regulars ever since. "It was spacious. He had lots of product. He had friendly salespeople who knew what they were talking about."

When I asked if Ward ever was employed by DreamHaven, he gave a qualified answer. He was going to school to be an electrical engineer, and knew how to do basic electric repairs. So if there was a light out or some other problem at the store, he would volunteer to fix it.

The store had the good fortune to be expanding right as comics publishers were catering to an older and more sophisticated audience. The turning point for Ward, and for many other readers, was *The Saga of the Swamp Thing* #21 from DC Comics, released in 1984. It featured a relatively new writer, Alan Moore. He and artists Stephen R. Bissette and John Totleben were reimagining the horror character. The new version was revealed to be a living collection of plant matter that thought it had been a man, as opposed to a man transformed into a plant monster, as in the original.

"I was like, 'Wow,'" Ward said. "That did mark an era in comics when things started to get darker."

For Ketter's business, it was a time in which he made enough money to hire staff. He could take days off to go to comics or science fiction shows, and not have to worry about who would cover the store. At a show in Peoria,

Writers Chris Claremont (*left*) and Neil Gaiman (*center*) with Greg Ketter hanging out at DreamHaven Books in the early 1990s. The two writers were at the top of their profession, Claremont on *Uncanny X-Men* and Gaiman on *Sandman. Courtesy of Greg Ketter.*

Illinois, he met the woman he would later marry. About the mid-1980s, he said, "It was a very good time."

In the larger market, however, competition among distributors would continue to have casualties, and new players would spring up to fill the void. That was what happened in the Maryland territory that had been the core of Irjax's business. When the company went out of business, its largest customer stepped up to buy the warehouses and other assets.

The customer was Steve Geppi, who already had a reputation as one of the shrewdest retailers and collectors in the industry. He called his new business, opened in 1982, Diamond Comic Distributors. It started small, joining a crowded market in which there was a steady churn of arrivals and departures. It would not stay small for long.

Jim Hanley spent most of his twenties in the wrong business. He worked in supermarkets across New York City, and rarely stayed in one place for long. "I was not the type to complain if I was treated badly," he said. "I would let it build up to the point that, like Popeye, I'd had enough, and enough was too much, and I'd just quit."

He was unhappy, but he was learning the retail trade. At A&P, the supermarket chain, he saw how to set up displays at the ends of aisles and how to organize shelves. He got experience handling cash and supervising people. Through it all, he remained a comics fan. He continued to attend Phil Seuling's shows. He made friends with collectors and dealers, and worked to build his personal collection.

His turning point was the day in 1980 when he saw a comic shop had opened on Staten Island, near where he lived. He walked in the door and saw piles of merchandise instead of displays, and a disinterested clerk. The place had no cash register. Many items were not priced. Hanley had long wanted to own a comic shop, and he could see that, if this was the competition, he might have a chance to succeed.

"But I still didn't have a pot to piss in or a window to throw it out, so I spent essentially three years trying to work out the financing for a store," he said.

On June 11, 1983, he and a childhood friend opened a shop on Staten Island called The Merchant of Venus. It sold comics and science fiction books. The start-up financing was about $10,000, which was unusually large for shops at that time.

"Most comic stores that open up, open up with nothing," he said. "They had the money to pay the first month's rent. And they would open up and pay for next week's books with this week's sales. That wasn't sensible." He was a rarity in the comics business, someone who was coming in with knowledge of merchandising and managing budgets. He kept costs low where he could, and invested in having a large and diverse inventory.

"We always approached it as merchants, rather than thinking customers were lucky to buy their precious comic books from us," he said. "We wanted customers to buy their comics from us for the rest of their lives. When they asked for something, the next time they came in, we wanted to have it for them, so they had no reason to look anywhere else for it."

The partners stayed together for two years before Hanley left. He says it was an acrimonious parting at the time, the result of his frustration that he worked long hours while his partner was much less of a presence in the store's daily operations. Hanley moved on to the venture that he is known

(*Top*) The storefront of the original Jim Hanley's Universe in Staten Island in the mid-1980s, and (*bottom*) the man himself, photographed in his store. *Courtesy of Jim Hanley.*

for, Jim Hanley's Universe. He and a new partner began in 1985 with one shop in Staten Island and would grow to four, including one across the street from the Empire State Building.

He got into the business right as the entire comics market was shifting toward specialty shops and away from newsstands. And he became a notable figure in the maturing of the industry. His stores would be emulated, and several of his employees would go on to have stores of their own.

But he had help, some of it from high places. He says some of the credit for the success of his stores, and the industry as a whole, should go to a woman from Marvel Comics whose name is little known outside industry circles: Carol Kalish.

Kalish came to Marvel in 1982 because Mike Friedrich needed to hire an assistant. Until then, he had been a one-person department, overseeing sales to the direct market of distributors that supplied comic shops. His tenure at the publisher, starting in 1980, had been marked by chaos in the market. New distributors were opening. Others were failing. The number of comic shops was skyrocketing, and Marvel was trying to figure out how to deal with the new landscape.[11]

Friedrich found Kalish in the wreckage of one of the defunct distributors, Irjax/New Media. Still in her twenties, she had a degree from Radcliffe College and a lifelong love of comics. She had worked in a comic shop in the Boston area and became a writer and editor for fanzines, later getting a job at the magazines published by Irjax.

Her boyfriend was Richard Howell, an aspiring comics artist who had met her when he was a student at Harvard. This was before the schools merged, when Radcliffe was all women and Harvard was all men. Howell describes her as having a tremendous aptitude for just about anything. He thinks her decision to go into comics was largely because that was what he was doing. "It was like, 'Richard's in comics. I could be great in comics too,'" Howell said.

Friedrich invited her out to lunch to talk about coming to Marvel. "She was already feeling uncertain about whether she could pull this job off," he said. "I was certain she was about the smartest person in the field."

He knew, and he told her, that he was planning to leave Marvel to move back to California. He also knew there was a good chance his assistant would be his successor. And that is what happened. Months later, he left Marvel, and Kalish got promoted. It soon became apparent to retailers that she was an advocate for them in a way that had never before been seen from a major publisher.

In her first few months on the job, a freelance writer named Peter David came to the Marvel offices to interview her. He was writing an article about the origins and growth of the direct market for *Comics Scene* magazine.

"We talked for two to three hours, and we just really hit it off," he said. "We talked so long our throats were dry and our voices were raspy." The conversation turned into a job interview. She said she had an opening for an assistant and asked if he could come back in a week to talk about the job.

David was in his twenties and recently had lost his job as an editor for the paperback book division of Playboy. He needed full-time employment. He came back a week later, dressed in the only suit he owned. When he entered, Kalish was at her desk, working on a model kit of Rodan, the monster from Japanese movies.

"She reaches for something on the far side of her desk and she overbalances herself and the chair skids out from under her and she hits the floor," he said. "She climbs back into her chair and says, 'So, why do you want to work at Marvel Comics?'"

He got the job and began a career in comics, first in sales and then as a fan-favorite writer of *The Incredible Hulk* and other titles. For him, Kalish was a mentor and a friend. "She was insanely bright," he said. "If you were in a crowded room, she was easily the smartest person there. She had little tolerance for idiots. She was always extremely sure of herself, to the point that she got on the nerves of people in editorial."

Marvel's editor in chief was Jim Shooter, whose tenure was marked by a creative renaissance and a dominance of the market. "It wouldn't surprise me if she conflicted with Jim, because everyone conflicted with Jim," David said. "I'm not telling tales out of school here. It was obvious." Shooter also spoke of his constant battles with the sales and circulation side of Marvel over issues big and small.

Luckily for Kalish, Shooter was not her boss. She reported to Ed Shukin, the director of sales, who had been at the company long enough that he had negotiated Marvel's distribution deal with Phil Seuling in 1973.

While Kalish fought battles within Marvel, she made inroads with retailers. She could see the trends showing that sales were shifting toward comic shops. At the same time, she knew from visits to shops that many of them were poorly run, with no cash registers, little sense of merchandising, and almost no financial reserves. The direct market was nearly a decade old, but the majority of shops had been open less than five years.

She liked to say that most store owners were comic collectors who had little ambition to build successful businesses. She made this point by saying that a typical owner's financial goal was to be able to own a decent used car. There are different versions of this, depending on who's telling. She also would say that the owner's goal was to buy a Big Gulp at 7-Eleven, or a Big Mac meal at McDonald's.[12]

"I remember one guy who had a big tank with a long snake in the window," Howell said. "And Carol said, 'This is not going to encourage parents to drop their kids off to buy comics.'"

For Hanley, she was one of the first people to look at comic shops the way he did, and to take on the lack of professionalism that he saw as harmful to the entire industry. He didn't mind if his immediate competitors ran poor businesses, but he thought that comics were doomed if the average retailer did. "It was clear to me from the moment I met her that this was the brightest person I had seen by a wide margin," he said. "The cliché would be to say she didn't suffer fools gladly. She was an intellectual, extremely knowledgeable, extremely opinionated. You didn't dare say anything stupid around her because she would shove it down your throat."

Her official job was to act as Marvel's point person in dealing with comics distributors, which were the companies that bought comics from publishers and resold them to the shops. Over and over, she went beyond her narrow mandate, Hanley said.

One of her projects was to encourage stores to get cash registers. She found a register manufacturer that would provide a bulk discount, and then Marvel provided an additional discount. The result was that many stores got registers for the first time, which meant they had a much easier time tracking sales and staying on top of finances.

In Minneapolis, Greg Ketter got his first cash register through the program. This was right about the time that many retailers of his generation were starting to move away from their shaggy roots and adopt basic business practices. The trend was in motion before Kalish, but shop owners say she helped accelerate it.

Another of her big initiatives was a cooperative advertising program. If retailers in a certain region wanted to buy advertising or do some other promotions, the group could apply to have Marvel cover some of the cost. The result was that regions with well-organized retailer groups were able to invest much more in marketing.

The Bay Area Retailer Group in California was one of the most active, said Joe Field, owner of Flying Colors Comics & Other Cool Stuff in Concord, east of Oakland. The ads featured Marvel characters and directed customers to their local shops. This was notable because the shops sold much more than just Marvel product, so any advertising was going to provide benefits to other publishers too, Field said. Kalish believed, and Field agreed, that Marvel, as the top publisher in the industry, would benefit when shop owners thought more strategically about marketing.

The effect on sales was striking. Some of this was due to the high quality of Marvel comics at the time. Several titles had defining creative periods in the mid-1980s, such as Walt Simonson's work writing and drawing *Thor* and

Carol Kalish in 1982 at a convention in Minneapolis. *Credit: Alan Light.*

John Byrne's work on *Fantastic Four*. At the same time, retailers give Kalish much of the credit. Howell thinks the sales figures speak for themselves.

"Marvel became dominant during that period," he said. "They were already dominant on newsstands, but they became the profit center of the direct market."

By the mid-1980s, Bud Plant had become king of West Coast distributors. His portfolio was big and diverse. He remained a partner in Comics & Comix, the Bay Area retail chain, although he was not a day-to-day presence in the stores. He had a thriving mail-order catalogue business, specializing in art books, erotica, science fiction, and imported comics. He sold many of the same products as a distributor to comic shops. And then, almost by happenstance, he expanded to start selling mainstream comics such as Marvel and DC.

In 1982, Charles Abar was the top comics distributor in the Bay Area. He covered a territory that was small in terms of square miles but dense with comic shops, such as Gary Arlington's San Francisco Comic Book Company. Abar had a warehouse and about ten employees. In addition to comics themselves, he sold supplies for use with comics, such as protective bags and long boxes, and supplies for baseball card shops. The business had grown too large for Abar's liking, and he looked to sell the comics-distribution side to focus on the other products. Rather than go out to seek top bids, he reached out to Plant.

"Bud is really an incredible guy," said Abar, who now lives on a farm in Oregon. "I knew he would do a very good job of taking care of my customers, and that was a big concern of mine. These people are not just my customers, they're my friends. We've spent a lot of years together and I care about them."

Unlike many of the other distributors going out of business, Abar was making money. By taking over Abar's accounts, Plant had entered a larger and more cutthroat part of the comics industry. He did this from his home and offices in Grass Valley, California, a small town in the foothills of the Sierra Nevada Mountains, where he had lived since decamping from the Bay Area in 1975. His location, about a three-hour drive from San Francisco, helped him stay out of the rivalries that sometimes flared among his friends and colleagues back in the metro area.

Plant's business was growing right as Pacific Comics was running aground. Pacific had gotten the attention of the industry when it became a comics publisher in 1981, in addition to being a distributor. "We extended ourself too far with too many publishing programs," said Bill Schanes of Pacific. In some cases, the company gave advance payment to artists who did not complete the work or were late. Then the industry hit a mini-downturn, which led some shops to go out of business while owing Pacific money.

"All of those things added up to us being in a negative cash position, and we were unable to pull out," Schanes said. He thinks the distribution side could have survived if not for losses on the publishing side.

In 1984, Pacific was no longer able to pay the money it owed vendors. Among those vendors was Bud Plant Inc., which had sold Pacific books on a wholesale basis for Pacific to distribute to its retail clients. So, right as Pacific was about to stop operating, Schanes suggested that he settle his debt with Plant by handing over assets, such as two warehouses, inventory, and customer lists.

Plant was on his way to becoming the third-largest distributor in the country, behind the leader, Capital City in Wisconsin, and the fast-growing runner-up, Diamond in Maryland.

Meanwhile, in Brooklyn, the onetime biggest name in comics distribution was on the verge of insolvency. Sea Gate, still run by Phil Seuling and Jonni Levas, had seen its growth rate slow to almost zero, despite being in an industry that was in a steady expansion. The company had made changes to adapt to competition, such as offering credit and being willing to increase discounts. Those adjustments helped retain some longtime customers but cut profits to below a sustainable level. As with so many other distributors, Sea Gate found that when it gave credit to retailers, some of those clients went out of business or switched to other distributors without paying their bills.

"We ended up with people owing us outrageous amounts of money," said Levas, who was a 50–50 co-owner with Seuling. They stopped being a couple in 1978, but remained business partners. She had gotten married to someone else, the co-owner of Forbidden Planet, a Manhattan comic shop, and they had a newborn daughter.

The factors that hurt Sea Gate were affecting other distributors too. But, as Seuling would have been the first to say, his company wasn't like all those Johnny-come-lately bozos. He could claim to have invented the direct market, and he did not take well to being perceived as an also-ran. It didn't help that his convention business was also on a gradual decline.

"In many ways, his ego sabotaged them," said Ron Forman, who had worked closely with Seuling at conventions and as a subdistributor in the 1970s. Forman and his business partner, Walter Wang, started a rival distributor in 1977. "He would not recognize the fact that other people could do what he could do, perhaps better than he could."

Forman and Wang's company Comics Unlimited, based in Staten Island, was one of the first subdistributors for Seuling. That meant they bought comics from him and then resold to retail stores in the New York area, acting as middlemen.

Then Forman and Wang found that they could get a larger discount if they bought Marvel comics directly from the publisher. Seuling had been giving them a 50 percent discount, and Marvel would give 60 percent. This was during the chaotic period when Marvel was signing up many new distributors.

"We met with [Seuling] and said, 'If you give us 55 percent, we'll buy Marvels from you.' He said, 'No. Without me, you guys will drown,'" Forman said. They didn't drown. Comics Unlimited grew every year from its inception until the owners sold it in 1994. The company grabbed a big share of the New York market, as did another upstart distributor, Heroes World, which was based in New Jersey.

The business problems at Sea Gate were happening at the same time that Seuling's health took a sudden turn. He had noticed he was losing weight in the fall of 1982, Levas said. He saw several doctors before he got a diagnosis: sclerosing cholangitis, an inflammation of the bile ducts that leads to severe liver damage.

His treatment included a series of small tubes attached to his abdomen that drained some of the waste. Despite the inconvenience of this apparatus, he kept on working. His weight loss continued, to the point that he no longer looked like himself, and needed to rest for long periods. All of this was for a man who was not yet fifty and had been known for his limitless energy.

Levas and Seuling's sister, Barbara, met with his doctor to get an idea of his prognosis. The doctor said the damage was so great that there was almost no chance Seuling would recover. He had maybe a year left. Later that day, the two women went back to Seuling's house. They steeled themselves with a drink of Scotch and then went to Seuling's bedroom to tell him what the doctor had said.

"Of all things, Phil would certainly want to know the truth about everything, and would want to be aware of what was happening to him," Levas said.

Hanley remembers a 1983 visit to Sea Gate to pick up an order. He had heard that Seuling was back in the office after some medical treatment. "When I turned a corner, I was greeted with a 'Hi, Jim' by a shrunken, cadaverous Phil Seuling," Hanley said. "I said, 'Hello,' then headed for the basement, where I hid in the back aisle, and broke out crying."

As the illness progressed, Sea Gate's finances continued to deteriorate. Seuling suggested Levas look into selling the business, but a deal never came together. "Once Phil became ill, the vultures began settling in," she said. Competitors moved in to take customers, and customers were less likely to pay the money they owed.

While Seuling had slowed down, he did not stop doing the things he loved. He took a trip to France and Sweden to visit with some of the comics creators and dealers he had gotten to know there over the years. He traveled to Maine for his daughter's graduation from college. He went to a small comics convention, held in Manhattan for some European creators. "He still wanted to be a part of everything," Levas said.

He died on August 21, 1984, at age fifty. There was a wake at a funeral home on Madison Avenue. The seats were filled with comics professionals, retailers, friends, and family. Seuling had never been widely known outside the comics industry, but in that room it was like a head of state had died. The only thing that wasn't quite right was the setting.

"Phil on Madison Avenue? No, Phil would like to be in Brooklyn in some ornate Italian funeral home, not in Manhattan," Levas said. "He was really a Brooklyn kind of guy. So that was kind of incongruous, the whole thing."

Bud Plant made the trip from California. "I'd never been to a funeral or wake before, but when Jonni and the gang put together a wake, I think it was just four or five days later, I flew to NYC to attend," he said. "I'm so very glad I did, since it was the last time all the wonderful friends that Phil had introduced me to all got together in one place. It was actually a fun occasion, as Phil would have wanted it, just hanging out and swapping stories."

Plant's daughter was born the day before Seuling died. Whenever something big happened, Plant used to call Seuling, and that was one of his first calls following the birth. This time, his friend was too sick to come to the phone. Two years later, when Plant and his wife had a son, they named him Philip.

Hanley was one of many people in the comics business who felt he had lost something profound. I asked him to sum up his thoughts, and he wrote this:

> For me, he was 21 years older. So he was also a father figure. Not that we were ever really close. But I idolized him, sort of from afar. I was 15, at the 1970 Comic Art Convention, over July 4th weekend. In the midst of an amazing circus of old comics, comics creators, and more people interested in comics than I'd ever seen, there was Phil. A whirlwind, charging into rooms and storming stages. His years teaching school were evident in the way he dealt with the 1,500 people he was hosting that weekend. I remember him introducing panels and film shows and acting as an auctioneer. A slide show that introduced me to the pulp magazine heroes, by Bob Weinberg, was a highlight. But, when Phil was in the room, his booming voice always drew all the attention. . . .
>
> Phil was a visionary and a pain in the ass. While I often wondered about working for him, I was probably better off not. I'd hate my feelings for Phil to have been poisoned by memories of stupid arguments that would have inevitably arisen between two people who were always certain.
>
> He knew things, as anyone with varied experience does, but he believed he knew a bit too much. He invented the business of comics specialty wholesaling, but too often refused to learn from people who'd learned from him. And that always bothered me. So smart and so human, Phil did amazing things, but could have done much more. Then, so could I. We're all the product of our lives and experiences and, especially our personalities. And Phil's was capacious, but also, slightly limited.

Seuling was buried with his old Captain Marvel costume folded up next to him. Levas, who was in an unhappy marriage to someone else, was devastated. "Phil was without question the love of my life," she said. "It was more than just a friendship, more than just a romance, more than just a business partnership." She realized when he was ill that she had assumed they would

Phil Seuling (*left*) and Jonni Levas (*right*) at the Museum of Modern Art Sculpture Garden. Levas displays these two photographs together so that she and Seuling are looking at each other. *Courtesy of Jonni Levas.*

get back together someday, that no matter how bad things got with her marriage or the business, he would always be there. "That was where my head was. Unfortunately, he died too soon, and that never happened."

Sea Gate filed for bankruptcy a few months later, and soon would liquidate its operations. Levas had kept the business afloat in part so that Seuling would continue to have medical insurance. Once he was gone, it was just a matter of time until the company had no options other than to close.

In my interviews with people who were there at the beginning of the direct market, one of the recurring themes was that Levas was the backbone of the company. "She was the business brain in that operation," said Forman. And yet she rarely got much credit, even though she was a co-owner of the company from the day it started. Some of that may be because she used to be Seuling's girlfriend and she started so young. Some of it may be because there were almost no women on the business side of comics, and some people didn't know what to make of her.

After Sea Gate folded, Levas stepped back from comics. She raised her daughter and moved to New Jersey. She separated from her husband, and they later divorced. She had a succession of jobs: real-estate agent, cook in a health-food store, and making phone calls for a collection agency. If money got tight, she would sell some of her original comics art and other memorabilia from her Sea Gate days. When she looks back, she wishes she had done more to stay in comics.

"I regret not trying to get another job in the industry that I knew about, as opposed to becoming a hermit and exorcising myself from the whole situation," she said. "I miss what was a kind of incestuous family of people."

Chauffeur for the King

Years before comic shops had made it to most parts of the country, the Bay Area was a kind of parallel universe, in which some of the best shops were a few blocks from each other, and Comics & Comix ruled the roost as likely the country's first chain of comic stores. People who lived there were spoiled by all the options, while visitors recall feeling gobsmacked by what they saw.

"I thought I had gone to heaven," said Diana Schutz, recalling her visit to San Francisco in 1978 when she walked into Comics & Comix on Lombard Street.

It turned out to be a pivotal moment for her. She was growing disenchanted with her life as a graduate student in Vancouver. Soon she dropped out of school and got a job at a comic shop there.

In 1981, she wrote to Bud Plant, co-owner of Comics & Comix, and asked for a job. He put her in touch with John Barrett, a co-owner and the day-to-day manager. A job offer soon followed. She moved to the Bay Area to work at the Comics & Comix store on Telegraph Avenue in Berkeley. The sidewalks were dense with foot traffic and panhandlers, she said. People's Park, which was a frequent site for protests, was a short walk away.

She would go on to edit the company's newsletter, which helped her develop the skills that she later would use as an editor for comics publishers. But she did much more than the newsletter. Her responsibilities included driving special guests who had come to do signings. That is why she found herself serving as chauffeur for Jack "King" Kirby, an artist whose work for Marvel, DC, and others had made him a near-mythic figure for fans. He had cocreated Captain America, the Hulk, and the X-Men, among many others for Marvel. At DC in the 1970s, his work had a psychedelic edge on titles such as *New Gods* and *Kamandi*. Then, by the early 1980s, he helped legitimize independent publishers and was an advocate for the rights of comics creators to own their characters.

"I was so intimidated, so terrified," she said.

(*Top*) Diana Schutz at Comics & Comix in Berkeley in the early 1980s; (*right*) Jack Kirby at a Bay Area convention in 1977.
Credit: Clay Geerdes.

She drove Kirby and his wife Roz in a 1968 Volkswagen Beetle. "Jack, being the gentleman, gave his wife the front seat, and he scrolled himself into the back as I drove him from store to store."

At each store, Kirby gave a brief talk and then fans formed a line to speak with him and get autographs. He was short and old enough to be the fans' grandfather. He spoke with a Brooklyn accent, and often had a cigar.

What Schutz remembers was his gentleness and the sense that his mind was elsewhere. He had spent his career creating or cocreating some of the best-known characters in fiction, and now had a tendency to daydream. It was often up to Roz to keep up the conversation.

"He was friendly but on another planet," Schutz said.

Today, Schutz is known in the business as the editor for a generation's worth of critically lauded comics, most of them during her long stint at Dark Horse Comics. She says she owes her career to what she learned at Comics & Comix.

8

Turtles, Mice, and Fish (1984–88)

THE IDEA of collectibility had been part of comic shops since the beginning, but there also was an assumption that retailers and readers enjoyed the material. Highly sought-after back issues, such as Marvel's *Conan* #1 from 1970, were praised for their stories and art. And early retailers were some of the medium's most rabid promoters of the work they saw as high quality.

That was about to change. By the mid-1980s, the number of shops continued to grow, and some of the new crop of retailers saw comics mostly as an investment vehicle. Buy low, sell high.

Into this mix came a new black-and-white comic published by two guys in New Hampshire. *Teenage Mutant Ninja Turtles* #1, released in mid-1984, was a self-consciously ridiculous parody of other comics, such as Frank Miller's critically acclaimed run on *Daredevil* for Marvel. In *Daredevil*, the cabal of evil ninjas was called the Hand. In Turtles, it was called the Foot.[1]

The cocreators, Kevin Eastman and Peter Laird, called their company Mirage Studios, because there was no studio, just two guys in their twenties, goofing around. The first issue had a print run of less than four thousand, and the title might have been quickly forgotten except for two factors. One, a few retailers loved the book, and made it their mission to sell it. Two, Eastman and Laird kept publishing new issues and became better creators, to the point that *Turtles* began to sell in numbers large enough to gain notice with store owners across the country.

"Up until then, a comic in black and white was considered déclassé," said Jim Hanley. "*Elfquest* was successful. *Cerebus* was successful, and not much else."

Since *Turtles* #1 had such a small print run, that issue became highly collectible, selling for hundreds of dollars. The lesson from *Turtles* was that seemingly any self-published book could become a huge hit. This turned out to be a highly destructive idea.

"The success of the Turtles meant that everyone else came up with their own idea, the *Adolescent Radioactive Black Belt Hamsters* and all that crap," Hanley said. "You could print a black-and-white comic really cheaply." And yes, *Adolescent Radioactive Black Belt Hamsters* was real, and actually one of the best of the bunch.

For Hanley, the poster child for the excesses of the period was a title called *Miami Mice*, a parody of the television show *Miami Vice*, except with mice. The comic was created by Mark Bode, the son of underground comics artist Vaughn Bode, and it was published in 1986 by Last Gasp, a company that had started in the Bay Area underground scene.

Hanley had gotten to know a newer retailer on Long Island who wanted to specialize in collectible comics. The new guy had missed out on *Turtles* #1, and now he looked for opportunities to corner the market on the next new thing. He made a deal with Last Gasp to buy thousands of copies of *Miami Mice* #1. His plan was to hold on to them until they were valuable.

To Hanley, this looked like insanity. He would rarely order more of any comic than he thought he could sell to individual customers. But to his shock, the Long Island dealer almost immediately fielded an offer from an even larger dealer to buy every copy. As Hanley recalls, the offer was to buy half of the stock for $4 each, or buy all of the stock for $8 each. This was an immediate windfall, more than quadrupling the wholesale price of the comics.

"The most important thing was to get a corner [on the market] where you could set the price," Hanley said. "And this nonsense went on for a year or two years, getting crazier and crazier. And, as these things always do, it all fell apart."

The Long Island dealer had sold all those copies of *Miami Mice* to Steve Milo, a dealer in the Washington, D.C., area. Milo had gotten into the business a few years earlier when he was a college student. "On the weekends I would do comic book conventions," said Milo, who now lives in Florida. "I became fascinated by the exchange of money and goods and services." He, as much as any dealer, would come to be associated with a type of collecting that relied on the idea that any comic could become valuable.

He was an early buyer of *Teenage Mutant Ninja Turtles* and benefited handsomely when it became valuable. The same was not true of *Miami Mice,* whose first issue can be bought today for a few dollars. I asked Milo to confirm Hanley's details on *Miami Mice.* He said, "That was probably true," but he didn't remember the quantity or the price for the comics.

After the debut of *Turtles,* but before the black-and-white boom was fully underway, a young employee at Comics & Comix in Berkeley self-published his own black-and-white comic. Cartoonist Steve Moncuse named his creation *Fish Police,* a crime story about anthropomorphic fish. He sold about ten thousand copies of the first issue in 1985. Then the wider interest in black-and-white comics helped make his title a hit, with sales peaking in the fifty thousand range.

Unlike many of the titles that followed, Moncuse was not looking to make a quick buck. He had gone to art school, and had a twenty-five-part story mapped out for his characters. And yet a quick buck is what Moncuse got. He made about $100,000 from the first few issues.

"If I didn't know the [comics] world and work in it for years, I could have gotten really full of myself," said Moncuse, who now lives in Vallejo in the Bay Area. "I was dealing with collectors day and night," he said about his time at the store. "They wouldn't ask if there were any good new comics. They would ask, 'Is this going to be worth something someday?'"

He worked at Comics & Comix for about two years, ending when the success of *Fish Police* meant he could make a living from his art. Among his coworkers was Diana Schutz, who was about to begin her own career in comics as an editor. A few years later, she would be his editor when he stopped self-publishing *Fish Police* and began to work through Comico, the independent publisher for which she worked.

He could see that collectors, not readers, were fueling sales of *Fish Police* and of the many other black-and-white comics that soon came on the market. "It was all artificial," he said, a sentiment that collectors did not want to hear. "They wanted to hear that within ten years they could bring their comics back to a comic shop and retire to a wealthy lifestyle. Like, 'No. No, you can't.'"

At the end of the boom, *Fish Police* sales went back down to the ten-thousand-copy range. He thinks he had a stable core of readers who stayed with him the whole way, while the collectors came and went. He kept putting out the book until he finished the story in 1991. It ran for twenty-six issues.

He would go on to do work for major comics publishers. He also spent time as a stay-at-home parent, and later became an elementary school teacher. Most of the people in his life today don't know about his work in comics.

"It was a wonderful time," he said about the 1980s. "It was like high school. I don't know what your high school years were like, but mine were amazing."

Steve Moncuse holding a copy of *Superman* #1 when he was an employee at Comics & Comix in Berkeley. In his spare time, he was working on *Fish Police,* a black-and-white series he self-published starting in 1985. These are the covers of the first three issues. *Courtesy of Steve Moncuse.*

In many ways, the black-and-white boom was based on a flawed premise, said Milton Griepp, co-owner of Capital City. "The idea was that these black-and-white comics would be rare because they don't print many," he said. "Well, they'll print as many as there are orders for."

Turtles #1 was rare because almost nobody saw it coming. The same was not true of the imitators, but the idea persisted that black-and-white comics had tiny print runs. It didn't help that the imitators were almost all terrible comics, produced quickly and cheaply. The combination of plentiful supply and low quality meant that this trend was going to end as soon as the buyers, including retailers and their customers, realized they had been had.

The *Turtles*-fueled boom lasted about two years, followed by the most severe market downturn since the comic shop era began in the 1970s. And yet the damage was highly localized. Some stores and publishers went out of business, including many of the opportunistic players who were the most blatant about trying to exploit black-and-white mania. Others went on almost as if nothing had happened. Milo, for example, could see sales falling off. He slashed his purchases of black-and-white comics and survived the downturn.

Mile High Comics in Denver survived because it did not order large quantities of black-and-white comics to sell to the general public, said owner Chuck Rozanski. The orders were almost exclusively by customers who made preorders. Some of those customers vanished when the bust happened, leaving unpaid orders, but the store's exposure was small compared to many others'. At the same time, he saw competitors go out of business, which he suspects was because their owners had made some of their own bets on black-and-white comics.

"The ones that went hog wild and bought all that material are all gone. They went broke," he said.

The whole episode was troubling for many makers of independent comics. Since the underground days, black-and-white printing had been an inexpensive way for artists to get their ideas to the public. By the mid-1980s, this had grown into a lively alternative comics scene, with groundbreaking titles such as *Love and Rockets* from Fantagraphics. And now the greed of the black-and-white boom had been typified by products that seemed, to an untrained eye, similar to alternative comics.

"And the reason all of this happened, in a nutshell, is because mobs of amateurish, opportunistic publishers flooded the market with an avalanche of junk that, instead of being rejected out of hand by distributors and re-tailers who, one would presume, set certain minimal standards for what they sell, were embraced wholeheartedly," said Gary Groth, publisher of Fantagraphics, in a 1987 issue of the company's news magazine, the *Comics Journal*. His essay, "Black and White and Dead All Over," is one of the most scorching reviews of this period.

"Retailers may have been at fault for not exercising even the most mod-est degree of judgment in ordering these artistic travesties, but even worse were these publishers who schlepped into the direct-sales market with all the enthusiasm and integrity of purpose of a particularly seedy brothel greeting the debarkation of the fifth fleet."[2]

Bud Plant escaped the black-and-white bust with minimal damage. He was one of the few people from the dawn of the comic shop era who re-mained prominent. But he was getting uncomfortable with the cutthroat nature of the business. He wanted nothing more than to be a regional distributor, serving California and nearby states. He had succeeded, out-lasting and buying assets from his local competitors and becoming the biggest player in the region.

In doing so, he found himself in the crosshairs of some even larger play-ers. The wild market with dozens of distributors had consolidated, with Capital City of Wisconsin the largest, followed by the fast-growing Dia-mond of Maryland. Plant, following the acquisition of a Denver distributor in 1987, was third largest.

At the same time, Comics & Comix, the chain of comic shops Plant co-owned, had run into financial problems and owed money to Plant's distri-bution business. In part to settle the debt, Plant bought out his partners and then sold the chain to its then–chief financial officer in 1988. The deal ended up working out, and Comics & Comix continued its run as one of the country's longest-running shops. The end would come much later, in 2004, after yet another change in ownership.

But Plant wanted to sell much more than his retail shops. He also wanted to get out of comics distribution so that he could focus on his mail-order book business. The logical buyers for the distribution company were Capital or Diamond. But in reality, there was just one real candidate.

To understand Plant's eventual decision, let's go back a few years to an episode that was later called the "airfreight wars." In the woolly days of dozens of distributors, several of them began shipping by air and could deliver comics a day or two earlier than competitors. Other distributors began to follow suit to prevent the loss of business, even though airfreight was a big increase in cost.

Around the same time, Capital City had opened a warehouse in the Bay Area, providing a direct challenge to Plant's dominance of the region. Plant says he had a cordial relationship with Capital's Griepp, and thought they had a mutual understanding that neither would use airfreight in the region.

Soon after, Capital City began to offer airfreight, and used this to try to persuade Plant's customers to switch. Plant had to scramble to provide equivalent service. For a few months, he faced the fear that his distribution business could be destroyed because of what he saw as a double-cross.

"I felt very violated by that," Plant said. "At that point, I didn't trust [Capital City]. The last thing I wanted to do was ask them if they were interested in buying my business and have them go out to my accounts and say, 'Bud Plant is going out of business. You better go with us.' Distributors were all stealing each others' accounts as much as they could."

Milton Griepp, who by then had switched roles with his partner and become CEO, says he and Plant previously had a cordial relationship and had talked about how they both saw air freight as a waste of money. But Griepp says there was no agreement between the businesses, and he adds that such a deal would have been inappropriate collusion.

What changed for Capital City was that it found a way to do air freight in the Bay Area in an affordable way. "If we could get comics to our customers earlier at the same cost, we were going to do it," Griepp said. "It definitely created hard feelings with Bud, but we were competitors."

The distrust between Plant and Griepp left Diamond as the best candidate to buy Plant's business. And Diamond had a huge asset in dealing with Plant. The former co-owner of Pacific Comics, Bill Schanes, had become a vice president at Diamond. This was a guy who had known Plant since the Seuling Con days, and who had already done deals with Plant to sell assets when Pacific had gone out of business.

Plant and Schanes were both entrepreneurs who got into the comics business while still teenagers. They were not close friends, but each of them regarded the other as a decent guy who could be trusted.

Schanes began the conversations about buying Plant's distribution company. Soon after, Diamond owner Steve Geppi got involved in the talks. In 1988, Plant agreed to sell all of his distribution assets to Diamond. With that transaction, Diamond leapfrogged Capital City to became the largest distributor in the country, and joined Capital City as the only player with warehouses from coast to coast.

The business of selling comics to comic shops, started and once dominated by Phil Seuling, and followed by the chaos of dozens of competitors, had become a duopoly. A few smaller regional companies remained, but they would soon disappear.

"That changed the market forever," said Griepp. "I didn't realize it at the time because I thought we could catch up again, but we did not."

9

Collectors vs. Readers

ON THE rear wall at The Laughing Ogre are back issues. A customer can reach out and grab the comics in the bottom rows, but the top rows, the ones with the most valuable issues, are out of reach without the help of an employee. Each comic book is covered by a Mylar bag and backed by a thin, white piece of card stock. The oldest are from the 1950s and 1960s, although these are not key issues and are far from mint condition. The most expensive comic book in the store is Marvel's *New Mutants* #98, the first appearance of Deadpool from 1991, in near-mint condition for $275.

Below the wall display are waist-high metal shelves filled with white card-board boxes of back issues, arranged alphabetically. This part of the store is wedged into a back corner, almost like an afterthought. It tells you that back issues are not a major part of Laughing Ogre's business. This is a "readers" store much more than it is a "collectors" store. So, in the sales downturn of late 2015, back issues played little role at Laughing Ogre. But that wasn't true in many other places.

To understand the dueling priorities of comic shops, it helps to think of readers and collectors as circles on a Venn diagram. Some people buy comics to read them, and then carefully file them away with the idea that they might increase in value. That $2.95 copy of *Paper Girls* #1 may be worth $100 someday, especially if it's in mint condition.

At the same time, there are comic readers who are not really collectors. They may store old issues, but only for rereading. They don't fuss over mint condition, and even prefer to buy old comics in poor condition because the prices are lower. And there is a smaller group of collectors who are not really readers. They buy and sell comics with the idea that there is money to be made.

"My hard line is, 'Do not care about the value of something. Only care if you love it,'" said Dave DeMarco, co-owner of Legend Comics & Coffee in Omaha, Nebraska. "These are things that should be experienced, not bought and put away just to recoup some amount of money ten or twenty years later."

Customers often ask him to point out the new comics that will one day be valuable. The answer is that he doesn't know and nobody knows. For example, one of the most sought-after comics of the last twenty years is *Batman Adventures* #12, published in June 1993. It was a series aimed at younger readers, with art done in the style of the *Batman* television show of the time. The issue is valuable because it is the first comics appearance

Mile High Comics' flagship location in Denver has millions of back issues under one roof, including rare comics with prices north of $10,000.

of the villain Harley Quinn. Copies in near-mint condition are now selling for more than $600. It is only in hindsight that it made sense to stock up on that comic. Most collectors at the time were much more focused on other new releases, such as *Darker Image* #1, an Image horror title with superstar creators that was a massive hit, and now can be found in back-issue bins for less than the original cover price of $2.50.

Until you understand the dynamics of readers and collectors, many things about the comics industry look downright weird. Exhibit A is the collector's bible, the *Overstreet Comic Book Price Guide*. Released in a new edition each year, it lists market prices for comics as determined by a special panel of contributing editors. It also has articles about the history of comics and the current state of the market.[1]

Overstreet's ad pages are some of the most precious real estate in the industry for an antiquarian comics dealer. Many of the same dealers advertise year after year. And most have variations on this message: "Sell me your comics." One ad shows a comics dealer sitting in a living room with an older couple, like a life-insurance salesman or a funeral director. The ads are asking fans to sell their comic collections, knowing that there are many elderly collectors who no longer have the space or the inclination to maintain a lifelong hobby. Another ad shows a dealer pointing to a stack of cash. The message is that the dealers will pay you top dollar for your collection.[2]

The guide shows photographs of its dozens of contributing editors. The group is overwhelmingly white and male. In this crowd, there is sometimes grumbling about the way the back-issue market has been transformed by the Internet. Now anyone can set up an eBay account and become a dealer, often undercutting the prices of more experienced players. The big risk with an Internet sale is that the buyer may discover that the comic book is in poorer condition than advertised, or has undergone some unreported restoration to repair damage. This wouldn't be as much of a problem in a shop or at a convention, where the buyer could inspect the book before the sale.

To help rein in concerns about Internet sales, parts of the comics industry have embraced the practice of "slabbing" books, which, to a noncollector, looks like a ridiculous waste of money. Here's how it works: The owner of a comic book can mail it to a third-party certification company, the largest of which is Comics Guaranty Company. The company has experts examine the book and rate its condition on a scale from 0 to 10. Then the company seals the book in a rigid frame or "slab," with the condition score listed on the label. The cost of the service starts at about $20 per comic.[3] When the owner offers the comic for sale online, he or she can say it has a CGC score of, say, 9.2. Since the book is now sealed inside the slab, the buyer can be assured that there will be no damage during delivery.

The practical effect of CGC certification is that books with the highest scores are commanding prices much higher than the *Overstreet* values.[4] A book in 10.0 condition is prized, even though the casual observer is likely to see no difference between a 10.0 and a 9.6.

CGC keeps a census of how many copies of certain comics have been graded at certain levels. For the oldest comics, this shows how few copies exist in excellent condition, and helps push up values. A key issue from the 1930s or 1940s in top condition is coveted, with a few selling for more than $1 million.

Some buyers of the old issues love comics and have sentimental reasons for wanting to own them. But others in the market view comics as a commodity to be bought low and sold high, regardless of the content. And, as long as there are buyers out there who will pay steep prices, the market can continue to reinforce the idea that demand, particularly for the oldest or scarcest comics, will do nothing but rise.

I can't help but wonder, however, if large parts of the back-issue market are a bubble waiting to burst. Many comic shops that opened in the last ten years give little space to collectible back issues. New shop owners came of age in an era when old comics could easily be found in book form or digitally. Many of them do not have the collector's mindset. Meanwhile, back-issue specialists are having somber conversations with elderly collectors, followed by the exchange of cash.

"There are serious concerns about the values of Golden Age comics declining in the next ten years," said Michelle Nolan, the comics historian and collector. "This is what happened to the dime novels of the late nineteenth and early twentieth century. They are worth much less than they were in 1940 or so."

During the 2015 downturn, back-issue sales decreased for many of the shop owners I interviewed. The customers who wanted back issues tended to be older men, a slice of the core audience that was seeing attrition. And back-issue sales had largely moved to online retailers and conventions and away from local shops.

But it would be simplistic to say that the industry doesn't need the back-issue market. Several shop owners, even a few that don't focus on back issues, say that the idea of collectibility is an essential part of why people buy new comics.

"It's integral," said Dan Merritt, co-owner of Green Brain Comics in Dearborn, Michigan. "People need to feel like they are getting something for their investment past entertainment. It's not integral for everybody, but I think it's integral for the market. There has to be some awareness or some perception of value to make plunking down $4 per book reasonable to the general person. If you remove the idea of an aftermarket, then I think comics fall off a cliff. That's the macroeconomics of it. If you take away the aftermarket, you don't have conventions. You turn off the older generation that has been collecting, and you shut off eBay revenue. The industry collapses."

Putting aside the question of whether the back-issue market is an essential part of the comics market, there is another set of concerns about the ways publishers seem to cater to the desires of collectors and invite booms and busts. Over and over, the collectors have embraced certain types of comics, such as black-and-white titles in the 1980s or bagged special editions in the 1990s. The collector-fueled booms have been followed by busts.

In 2015, the best example may have been the proliferation of comics with variant covers. New comics come with a standard cover that appears on most copies, and in addition, publishers print alternative covers with the same contents inside. The variant covers often come in limited quantities as an incentive for retailers who reach certain benchmarks for ordering.

There were at least six variant covers that retailers could preorder for what turned out to be the top-selling title of November 2015, *Dark Knight III: The Master Race* #1, from DC. At the low end, stores could order one with a cover by artist Klaus Janson for every ten they ordered of the standard cover. At the high end, if a store wanted a copy of a variant by Jim Lee, it had to order five hundred of the standard cover.[5]

To provide some perspective, The Laughing Ogre, a large shop, sold 243 copies of *Dark Knight III* #1. For most stores, ordering five hundred of the issue would mean far exceeding the demand from local consumers and would leave many copies unsold. The only way this makes sense for the retailer is if the ultra-rare variant can be sold at a huge markup, and that's what ends up happening. On eBay, the Jim Lee cover, showing a bloodied

Batman with one fist raised and his other hand on the shoulder of his side-kick Robin, was selling for prices that started in the $300 range as of the summer of 2016.

Today, many if not most new comics from major publishers have at least one variant cover for each issue. New series often have a long list of variants by different artists. There are "sketch" variants, with pencil art before inks and colors; Lego variants, with key characters displayed in Lego form; and so on.

DeMarco from Legend Comics is one of many retailers who say variant covers have gotten out of hand. He likes some variants, such as when a certain artist does a series of alternate covers in a month, and the covers are widely available. He doesn't like it when a cover is intentionally made in small quantities to command a premium price.

"That doesn't grow the medium. It just plays a weird market game," he said.

Enough customers want to buy the covers, and enough retailers want to sell them, that this part of the market is going strong. So far, this is a boom without a bust. Chuck Rozanski of Mile High Comics speaks for many shops when he tells critics of variants to stop complaining.

"Here's a very simple thing: if you don't like variants, don't buy them," he said. "If you don't like them, just shut up. It's not your business. I make money off of them, so shut the fuck up. It's just that simple. If you don't like them, don't sell them. This is America, Goddamn it. There's allowed to be things that you don't believe in that occur that other people do believe in. And you're sitting there and saying it shouldn't exist because you don't like it? That takes a lot of fucking gall, asshole. Pretty simple."

In my hours of interviews with Rozanski, that was only time that this mild-mannered hippie was clearly pissed off. This gap between collectors and readers is the greatest disconnect I see in the industry. And if you would like to talk about it some more, I'm sure Chuck was just getting started.

10

Raina's World

IN THE young readers' section at The Laughing Ogre, filed under "T," is an author who has upended a number of notions about the comics market of the 2010s. The store keeps a stockpile of copies of titles such as *Smile, Sisters,* and *Ghosts.* Readers often refer to the author by just her first name, as if she's a friend: Raina.

"It's really relatable, especially to younger, female readers," said Lauren McCallister about Raina's comics. "Not that kids don't like crazy fantasy stories too. But it's a story about a girl that doesn't get along with her sister, or has to get braces. And there's something about the way it's drawn. It's easy to read and inviting to look at."

Raina Telgemeier grew up in the Bay Area and studied illustration at the School of Visual Arts in New York. Her early career looks like that of a lot of cartoonists, drawing and photocopying minicomics and selling them. Her big break was getting picked up by the Graphix imprint of Scholastic Corp. in the mid-2000s. Her first books were comics adaptations of *The Baby-Sitters Club* books by Ann M. Martin. Then, in 2010, came *Smile,* an autobiographical story about losing her front teeth when she was in sixth grade and going through years of treatments at an already awkward age.[1] Scholastic, with access to bookstores and school book fairs, helped put Telgemeier's work into the right hands. She became the top-selling comics creator in the

Raina Telgemeier drew big crowds and long lines at Cartoon Crossroads Columbus in October 2016. Here, fans read the author's books as they wait to meet her. *Photo by Fred Squillante* © The Columbus Dispatch.

country. In mid-2015, she had the top four spots in the *New York Times* best-seller list for paperback graphic books.[2]

She is big in comic shops, and also bigger than comic shops. Her success underscores two major changes in the market. First, she is someone whose work does not appear in periodical form before it gets published as a book. This is different from many other top-selling creators, such as Neil Gaiman and Brian K. Vaughan, whose comics often make their first appearances as periodicals. Second, her core audience is middle-grade readers, contributing to the diversification of comic shop customers.

The element that's missing in this description is the sheer scale of Telgemeier's following. To explain that, I'm going to flash forward to a few months after the period covered in this book. On a Saturday in October 2016, I was a volunteer at Cartoon Crossroads Columbus, a celebration of comics culture organized by group that includes Jeff Smith. Most of the events that day were at the Columbus main library branch, where comics creators were selling their work and appearing on panels.

I was working on the show's main floor when another volunteer came up to me with a worried look. She needed help with crowd control in the Telgemeier line. At that moment, on a separate floor, a line had formed to see a special presentation by Telgemeier. I came down to see hundreds of girls and boys and their parents, many of them clutching books and reading books. Some of them had planned to buy books at the show to be signed, only to learn that the books had sold out. Others had just learned that they needed to have tickets to have books signed. The crowd was simultaneously elated, chaotic, and grumpy.

For an hour or so, I helped keep the line organized so it would not double back on itself. During the lulls, I asked some of the fans which book was their favorite. The most common answer: *Sisters.*

Soon the doors opened and the line began to file inside. I remained in the lobby to help with the line for the book signing that would take place right after the talk. I barely saw Telgemeier that day, but I saw everything around her. She was adored in a way I had never witnessed with a comics creator.

Telgemeier has gained a huge following by selling work in a format that was almost completely absent from early comic shops. Whether you call it a graphic novel or a graphic book or anything else, the format's growing popularity is one of the key forces that has changed the direct market.

In the early days of the market, comic shops often stocked prose paperbacks along with periodical comics. The few comics in book form tended to be mass-market paperbacks that reprinted comic books or comic strips. And a few stores stocked imported comics that were in book form.

At Comics & Comix, the Northern California chain, the first graphic books that could be described as hits were the Marvel Fireside series from Simon and Schuster, according to former employees. The series began in 1974 with *Origins of Marvel Comics,* a collection of reprints of origin stories of Marvel characters.

Comics & Comix also had success with books from Starblaze Graphics, an imprint from the Donning Co. that began in 1978. It published fantasy and science fiction material, including collections of *Elfquest.*

"We were selling a zillion of [Donning's] books, enough that I was able to get a really big discount," said Dick Swan, a manager and later a co-owner of the chain. "And that was kind of the beginning of books selling a lot of copies. . . . Somewhere in the middle there, Marvel and DC started looking over and said, 'Hey, they're starting to sell a lot of these *Elfquest* books.'"

Those were the sales successes. There also were books that turned out to be influential but were not big sellers at the time, such as Will Eisner's *A Contract with God* in 1978.

Marvel launched its graphic novel line in 1982 with *The Death of Captain Marvel,* by writer and artist Jim Starlin. This was different from the Fireside series because Marvel was producing new work that was designed to be read as a complete story in one volume. DC began its graphic novel line a year later.

Along with original stories, Marvel and DC published paperback collections of stories that had been serialized in periodical form. One of the successful reprint volumes was Marvel's *The Dark Phoenix Saga,* which had initially appeared in *X-Men.*

Then came the three titles that helped define the format, *Batman: The Dark Knight Returns* and *Watchmen,* both from DC Comics, and *Maus* from Pantheon Book. The paperback editions, published in 1986 and 1987, were collections of material that had been serialized. The books inspired media coverage about the new graphic novel format and how comics were no longer just for children. And they sold like mad. Each title remains a strong seller thirty years later.

The format became a fixture in bookstores and libraries, along with comic shops. To feed demand, publishers began to collect more material in paperback and hardcover. This included reprints of many stories that used to be available only through buying back issues.

Dick Swan could see where this was heading, and he didn't like it. He knew that if old issues were widely available in book form, and the books were less expensive than the original comics, then the back-issue market would become less relevant. This was no small matter for a man who had gotten his start buying and selling back issues and whose stores were overflowing with them. His fears turned out to be justified. Bit by bit, the back-issue market has faded.

By the mid-1990s, a new kind of comic shop was emerging in which books were out front and displayed much like in a bookstore. One of trendsetters was Rory Root, co-owner of Comic Relief in Berkeley. Root and business partner Michael Patchen opened their store in 1987 on Telegraph Avenue. For the first few years, it looked like much like a typical comic shop. The walls had racks for new comics, and much of the floor space was

Comic Relief in 1993, early in its transition to being a bookstore more than a comic book store. *Credit: David Miller.*

taken up by tables with boxes of back issues. Over the years, the store made changes to better emphasize books.

Comic Relief became one of the most influential stores of its era, and Root was a leader among retailers. He was recognizable for his girth, his beard, and his fedora. And he is missed dearly. He died in 2008 at age fifty following surgery for a hernia.

While many retailers give Root credit for having one of the first book-centric shops, there were several others who had similar ideas. Among them was Joel Pollack, co-owner of Big Planet Comics in the Washington, D.C., area. Root, Pollack, and others were part of a group of like-minded retailers who had gotten to know each other through trade organizations and at conventions. Most of them came of age in the 1970s and became store owners in the 1980s.

"Rory did a lot of good things for the business of comics, perhaps the most profound of which was goading publishers and retailers to adopt his bookstore model with the comic book twist," said Joe Field, owner of Flying Colors Comics in the Oakland suburbs, eulogizing his friend in 2008.

"There's a hole in the comic book world . . . . and with the sadness of Rory's passing, there's also a real sense of gratitude for his key contributions to the ongoing health of the comics industry."[3]

The trend line has continued, with book sales rising each year and taking up a larger share of comic shop sales, based on interviews with retailers. Shop owners say that most people new to comics are looking at them in book form, not as periodicals. However, there are no data available about the share of book sales for comic shops as a whole.

"The role of a comic shop is to be a curator, is to be a gatekeeper, to help new readers find what they want," said Mark Waid, a prolific comics writer with recent runs on *All-New Avengers* and *Archie,* and co-owner of Aw Yeah Comics in Muncie, Indiana, from 2013 to 2016. "It is a great time in that more and more people are coming in and looking for things that are not Marvel and DC comics, that are looking for creator-owned stuff, that are looking for material based on creators rather than on franchises, and that's pretty cool. And frankly, it's healthier for the market because it brings new people in. Very few people walk in the door at age twenty-five and say, 'I want to start reading *Avengers*.'"

The changes are forcing creators, publishers, and retailers to adapt in ways that can be uncomfortable. "The paradigm shift seems to be away from monthly comics and toward trade paperbacks and stuff like that, which is great," Waid said. "It's better money for everyone in the long run and a better format. But it's the changeover that is dangerous. That's the part that could kill us because all comic book stores still depend on that Wednesday cycle. All comic stores are still budgeted for those people who come every Wednesday for their comics. We can't change overnight to deal more with a bookstore customer, people who only come in infrequently to pick up bigger amounts of stuff."

One hazard for comic shops is that the book business is much larger and more competitive than that of periodical comics. To illustrate this, let's go back to Laughing Ogre, where Telgemeier's *Ghosts* sells for the cover price, $10.99. A customer can get the same book from Amazon for $6.55, a 40 percent discount. And the Columbus library system has 531 copies in circulation.

Despite this, Laughing Ogre sells many copies of the book. But the store's larger opportunity is to serve customers who have become comics fans because of Telgemeier. If even one-tenth of her fans become steady comics readers, that is a large number.

McCallister has some standbys ready when a Telgemeier fan is looking for something else. There is *Roller Girl* by Victoria Jamieson. "That one is about a girl who decides to do roller derby," she said. "It's super cute. I like that one a lot because it's about how you can be a girl and not need to be into traditionally girly stuff."

And her recent favorite recommendation has been *Goldie Vance* by Hope Larson and Brittney Williams. "It's an easy pitch. It's basically *Nancy Drew* meets *Eloise*."

The best may be yet to come. McCallister looks ahead to when readers raised on Telgemeier will be old enough to read autobiographical comics for adults. Those are the kinds of comics McCallister writes and draws when she is not at the store, and she can see a day when there is a huge audience that has been steeped in the medium.

11

Re-Rebirth

THE LAUGHING Ogre headed into January 2016 with trepidation. The Christmas sales season had been decent, helping ease some of the anxiety about the market downturn. Now the store and the industry faced what are traditionally the slowest months of the year. In January and February, comic shops depend on their regulars. The regulars are some of the most dedicated Marvel and DC readers. And Marvel and DC seemed to be doing all they could to make those customers go away.

Eric Owens was one of dozens of Laughing Ogre customers who had cut back his purchases. He is a photographer and graphic designer, and has read comics since early childhood.

"Really I haven't lost interest. It just comes down to money," he said. "At $5 an issue, following a number of series is just far too expensive." Because of the cost, he gets most of his comics in digital form from a service that gives a big discount compared to the cover price. Even that is expensive for him. "If digital comics were 99 cents an issue, I would probably be subscribed to thirty or forty series a month."

Another problem for him was that Marvel and DC seemed to perpetually reboot their characters and series. This was done to attract new readers, but longtime leaders could get lost in the transition. "There are so many versions of Superman right now, I really don't understand what is going on," Owens said.

Of the two major publishers, DC seemed to have the most acute problem. In December 2015, only six of the company's periodical comics sold more than seventy-five thousand copies. Each of them featured Batman or a Batman-related character, and two were limited series, such as *Dark Knight III: The Master Race.* Meanwhile, the middle of the sales chart was a disaster zone. For example, *Action Comics* sold fewer than thirty thousand copies. The figures, from Comichron.com and ICv2.com, are estimates of the number of copies purchased by comic shops; the actual sales, by comic shops to customers, are not known.[1]

"With DC it's pretty clear," said Mark Waid, the comics writer who also is a former DC editor. He was speaking in early 2016. "They're just not doing well, creatively, on a sales perspective, on every level. It breaks my heart to say that because I love DC Comics."

Some of the sales slide could be attributed to changes in buying habits. For example, *Batgirl* sold only about twenty-eight thousand copies as a comic book, but sold relatively well when the single issues were collected in book form. This was in line with the comments of retailers, who said comics popular with women and younger readers were more likely to sell as books or in digital form.

Even with this caveat, it was clear that the post-*Convergence* sales slump had continued. Some titles got brief spikes because of special covers or other promotions, but the larger trend was an erosion of DC's sales. The company had lost its way. It needed to find a way to grab attention and get lapsed readers to come back. And it needed to act quickly.

In January 2016, DC copublisher Dan DiDio posted an image on Twitter of the word "rebirth" projected against a blue curtain. Comics news websites went bonkers with speculation. Then, in February, DC released a video of Geoff Johns, the chief creative officer, explaining what was afoot. "The whole point of Rebirth for all of us is to get back to the essence of the characters," he said.[2]

The company's entire superhero line would relaunch, and most titles would get new #1 issues. The publisher would try to get back some of what core fans had said was missing. In many cases, this would mean a return to concepts or designs from years ago or even decades ago. DC again would emphasize the legacy of its shared universe. To underscore this, the two longest-running titles would be the only ones to use numbering that reflected every issue that had been published. So, amid the wave of #1 issues, *Action Comics* would be #957 and *Detective Comics* would be #934.

Some of the most telling details had nothing to do with issue numbering or creative choices. DC announced that it would switch to shipping many of its titles twice per month, a doubling of the previous monthly schedule. In addition, nearly all of the Rebirth comics would have cover prices of $2.99, down from the prior price of $3.99. The new prices were addressing one of the biggest concerns of comic shop owners. For years, retailers had seen cover prices increase faster than inflation, which meant that many readers, especially young ones, couldn't afford to read as many titles as before. Readers were being conditioned to wait for comics to be collected in book form, in which multiple issues could be read in one sitting, often at a cost that was less than if purchased as single issues.

Another change was returnability. The first few issues of the new comics could be returned to the distributor for credit if stores found that they had too many leftover copies. DC and Marvel had both used returnability in recent years as a promotional tool to encourage large orders.[3]

For longtime fans, DC Rebirth had the whiff of the familiar, not just because it was a return to tried-and-true concepts, but because line-wide relaunches had happened before, and were happening with increased frequency. The biggest one was in 2011, when DC began "The New 52," canceling all of its superhero titles and then releasing fifty-two series that were a mix of renumbered old titles, such as a new *Batman* #1, and many titles based on new ideas or twists on old ideas.

The New 52 was a sales juggernaut, putting DC ahead of Marvel in market share for a short while.[4] Marvel came next with its own relaunches, starting with the renumbering of old series under the banner of "Marvel NOW!" in 2012. This was followed in 2014 by "All-New Marvel NOW!" and in 2015 by "All New, All Different Marvel." Then, in 2016, with adjectives seemingly in short supply, the company called its relaunch "Marvel Now," the same as the one in 2012, although with a different slate of new titles.

The first few relaunches sold well in part because of their novelty. It was a big deal that DC and Marvel would do line-wide events. But some retailers worried that the regular succession of reboots was diminishing the significance of each one, leading to a temporary boost in sales that would quickly recede. Sometimes the results confirmed those fears.

So what about DC Rebirth? The event began in May 2016 with the release of *DC Rebirth* #1, written by Johns and drawn by a succession of top artists. The company encouraged comic shops to open at midnight on the release date, May 31, the kind of fanfare that used to accompany a new Harry Potter book.

Laughing Ogre had limped through the first few months of the year. But Gib Bickel could see excitement growing with some of his regulars. He went into spring knowing that Rebirth was likely to be at least a short-term success.

"I thought we were near the bottom and almost anything would be better," he said.

On May 31, Laughing Ogre was one of many stores that held special midnight openings to mark the release of *DC Rebirth* #1. Bickel rang up about a dozen customers. Stores in larger metro areas reported much larger turnouts, which helped amplify the long-building hype. Within weeks, the event had been declared a smashing success by DC and by industry media.

In June, with a full month of Rebirth releases and Marvel's *Civil War II* #1, comics orders hit their highest level in more than twenty years, at least in dollar terms, according to Comichron.com. Among the caveats: June had five weeks' worth of new comic releases, compared to the usual four. And the perpetual caveat: the figures are estimates of orders by comic shops, not sales to customers.

In July, DC continued its momentum. The publisher led the industry in market share, with 35 percent of sales, narrowly beating Marvel's 34 percent. DC had not led Marvel for three years.[5] "With Marvel and DC it's often a tug of war, and right now DC is winning that tug of war," said Joe Field of Flying Colors Comics. The turnabout from just a few months earlier was breathtaking.

The question for retailers was whether DC's sales could be sustained. Brian Hibbs of Comix Experience had little doubt that the answer was "no." His two stores had huge increases in DC sales with Rebirth, and he wanted it to last, but his decades of retailing told him otherwise.

A wall of DC Rebirth #1 issues at The Laughing Ogre. *Artwork is* © *DC Comics.*

"It's really a matter of do they keep the quality of the comics up," he said. "If the comics are good, people will buy them. If they're not, they won't." He only needed to look back at the New 52 to see how a sales sensation can quickly lose momentum. With Rebirth, he suspected that sales would trail off when the creators were no longer able to keep up with the twice-monthly schedule, leading to last-minute fill-ins and a drop in quality.

The larger issue here is the publishers' reliance on relaunches and other stunts to inflate sales. Rebirth was the second time DC had done a major re-numbering in five years. Marvel had done this even more often, relaunching its main titles every year or two.

Take, for example, Captain America, one of Marvel's top characters. He made his debut in *Captain America Comics* #1 in 1941, with a cover of him punching Hitler. The book ran until 1949, with a brief return in 1954 in which Cap battled communists. Then, in 1964, the character was brought back as part of the new Marvel universe. He appeared as a feature in *Tales of Suspense* from issue #58 to issue #99. Then that title was renamed *Captain America* and ran from #100, released in 1968, to #454, in 1996.

Since then, *Captain America* has been relaunched or renumbered about ten times, not including spin-off series. Just since 2011, there have been five relaunches. Usually, this means Marvel has a new *Captain America* #1 to mark a change in the creative team or in the storyline. Now the milestone of a new Captain America comic, which used to be an event, happens about every two years.[6]

"All of the publishers overuse the #1 as a marketing tool, and so it loses value as a marketing tool over the long range," Hibbs said. "It gives them a short-term benefit and they get addicted to that short-term benefit, but it hurts them in the mid and long range." One problem with constant relaunches is that it hurts the back-issue market. *Captain America Comics* #1, or even *Captain America* #100, meant something because they were milestones in a much larger tradition. Hibbs and other retailers have a difficult time seeing why anyone would place the same value on what they see as artificial milestones.

But what really gets Hibbs upset is indexing these comics. It is easy to sort back issues when a series lasts five hundred issues. It gets more complicated when the numbers get repeated every few years.

"There was a sense of history and a sense that these things matter," he said. "It's not a smart move that the publishers are making to get away from their history and legacy, and make it confusing and difficult for people to collect their comics."

His criticism of Marvel and DC underscores a wider sentiment among retailers. They distrust the top two publishers, even though they depend on them. Many shop owners told me that they get most of their enjoyment from introducing readers to material from smaller publishers. These are many of the same shops in which *Saga* outsells just about any single title from Marvel and DC.

"Our base of consumers is stronger now than we've ever had it," Field said. "While things may not always resonate with a huge audience, there is enough of a breadth of material, with trade paperbacks and things going back thirty to fifty years, to the smaller publishers, meaning outside of Marvel and DC, that are continuing to put things out that are finding new audiences." So he is pleased that Rebirth is doing well in his store, but its success was not a matter of life or death for his business.

It should be noted, however, that there have been many times when the dominance of Marvel and DC seemed to be on the wane in comic shops.

Each time, the big publishers' difficulties were viewed with glee by some fans and retailers who were eager to see the "big two" replaced by a more nuanced market. In 1981, Pacific Comics looked like it had the talent to challenge the big guys. The same could be said of other independent publishers in the 1980s, such as Comico, Dark Horse, Eclipse, and First. It definitely could be said of Image in 1992, which showed that an independent company could hit the top of the sales charts.

Despite the many challenges, Marvel and DC still have about 70 percent of the market. Some of this is because of the companies' sheer number of titles, which shop owners say is flooding the market and crowding out other publishers—an argument, by the way, that has been made for decades.

One relatively new dynamic is that both Marvel and DC are owned by much larger media companies, and the owners are making their presence felt in a more visible way than before. DC has long been owned by Warner Bros., which is part of Time Warner; the recent difference is that DC relocated from New York to California, in part to be closer to other entertainment divisions of its corporate parent. Marvel was purchased by the Walt Disney Company in 2009, and has gradually been integrating into the structure of its parent.

"Comics are still a very small business when you take a look at media in general," Field said. "Even though comics drive the other media and drive a lot of the successful ventures in movies and TV and whatnot, comics themselves are still a small piece of that. So could the corporate overlords just say, 'Comics just aren't worth it?'"

The fear for comic shop owners is that Time Warner and Disney are so large that they will have no patience for comics publishing. After all, the companies would continue to own the characters and concepts from comics, even if Marvel is not publishing *Spider-Man* or DC is not publishing *Superman*.

There are two related, and somewhat contradictory, ideas at play here. One is that many shop owners have little affection for Marvel and DC and are trying to promote alternatives to reduce exposure to the foibles of the big guys. The other is that shop owners can envision a day when Marvel and DC no longer care enough about the market to flood it with comics and to relaunch its core concepts every few years.

In other words, DC Rebirth could be one in a long succession of reboots, to be viewed in hindsight along with the ones that will follow. Or maybe it's the last one, or close to the last one.

Whichever is true, the immediate popularity of Rebirth marked a return to form for The Laughing Ogre. The year of anxiety was over. The new employees who had started the previous summer were all still there, and had shown themselves to be good at their jobs. Bickel, even though he had shown few outward signs of worry during the tough times, could relax a little.

12

Deathmate (1988–94)

IN THE late 1980s, a number of baseball card shop owners discovered comics. This turned out to be a pivotal, and some would say unfortunate, turn of events. Card shops were going through a sales boom. Old-line producers such as Topps were getting competition from high-end newcomers such as Score and Upper Deck. Hot new rookie cards had skyrocketing values, with players, such as the New York Mets' Gregg Jefferies, becoming stars in the eyes of collectors before ever accomplishing much on the field.

The card frenzy gained momentum from media coverage about how these pieces of cardboard were turning out to be better investments than stocks. The collectors' outlook had many parallels with what had long existed in parts of comics fandom: a fixation with "mint" condition, a desire to possess scarce resources, and a zeal for obtaining complete sets.[1]

Card shops opened by the thousands, and many of them also had racks of new comics. The growth in the number of outlets selling comics, and a renewed focus on collectibility, meant that high-profile new releases were going to find audiences much larger than had been seen since the 1950s. It was a classic bubble, and would be followed by the most destructive bust of the comic shop era, much worse than the black-and-white bust.

"There's a phrase from Wall Street I learned after that: never confuse brains with a bull market," said Jim Hanley. "Ultimately, that's what we did. We thought we had the world by the balls."

His business had been growing almost nonstop. Then, in 1989, the *Batman* movie starring Michael Keaton was a surprising boon to comic shops. Demand soared for Batman T-shirts and other noncomics merchandise. At the same time, comics sales had a noticeable uptick, for Batman titles and many others. New comic shops opened, in addition to the card shops that also sold comics.

Batman mania was a warm-up for what was to follow. The market had a whole new generation of retailers with almost no experience, plus new buyers who were card collectors and mostly interested in getting what they thought would someday be valuable.

Into this volatile mix came *Spider-Man* #1, released by Marvel in June 1990. It was the adjectiveless Spider-Man comic, joining mainstays such as *Amazing Spider-Man* and *Spectacular Spider-Man*. The writer-artist was Todd McFarlane, who had made his name a few years earlier with dynamic portrayals of Spider-Man in acrobatic contortions.

The fact that the comic was the first issue of a new series, and had a star creator, meant it was going to be a sales success almost no matter what. But then Marvel took steps to appeal directly to collectors. The issue would be sold with two different covers, one with regular colors and one using silver ink. In addition, each of the covers would be available in a special collector's edition that came sealed in a clear plastic bag. A completist would need to buy multiple copies.

Spider-Man #1 sold about two million copies, almost all of them through comic shops, a figure that includes subsequent printings with additional covers. It was a record for the direct market, and the most of any comic since the post–World War II days, when comics were a mass medium.[2]

The record would not stand for long. In 1991, Marvel released *X-Force* #1, by another superstar artist, Rob Liefeld. The gimmick here was that the book came bagged with one of five trading cards inside the bag and visible. A completist needed to buy five copies. Total sales were five million, obliterating the numbers from *Spider-Man*.

Again, the record would not last. A few months later, Marvel released *X-Men* #1, a companion to its long-running *Uncanny X-Men*. The artist was Jim Lee, another of Marvel's biggest stars. The comic came in one of four covers that could be put together to make one long image of the team. A fifth cover, with a premium price, had all four covers in a gatefold. Sales were eight million, which remains the most ever for a single issue.[3]

Retailers recall how customers wanted to buy cases of the new comics, intending to store them rather than read them. The buyers did not seem to grasp that a comic book would not be valuable if the number of copies far exceeded the number of people who wanted to read it.

The number of retailers ballooned during this period, going from about one thousand stores in 1990 to an all-time high of about ten thousand in 1995, according to estimates from industry consultant Melchior Thompson.[4] This number is misleading, though. Many of the new "comic shops" were card shops that opened wholesale accounts with comics distributors but did not look anything like comic shops. Some didn't even have a storefront. Much like the sales figures for *X-Men* #1, the number of supposed comic shops had grown to the point that the numbers had little meaning in terms of understanding how many people were reading comics.

The hype about these comics was amplified by *Wizard,* a magazine about comics and pop culture that had started in 1991. Each issue had features about the "hottest" comics and creators on the market, and a price guide that showed how back-issue values were rising rapidly.

For consumers who wanted an easy way to buy multiple copies of a single issue, Steve Milo placed monthly ads in comics offering a discount on bulk orders through his company, Entertainment This Month. The ads touted comics as "red hot" or "can't miss," and often used the word "violent" as a selling point. For example, the Entertainment This Month ad copy used to sell *Nomad* #1 from Marvel in 1992 ran, "Nomad returns in the violent new series with stunning art! *Nomad* #1 includes a fold-out map cover! A can't miss!"

The cover price was $2, but customers could get it for $1.50 each if they bought three or more copies. The book was about a former sidekick of Captain America who was now in his own series that explored the gritty and violent side of the Marvel universe. *Nomad* lasted for about two years before it was canceled because of low sales. Today, just about any issue of the series, including #1, is available online for less than $2.

Milo was vilified by many of the retailers and mail-order dealers who competed with him. The prime example was Mile High Comics, which suffered because Milo's companies were helping drive up the cost of ad space in comics, making it so that Mile High ads no longer appeared.

"Steve Milo cost me ten years of my life," said Chuck Rozanski, Mile High's owner. He regards his former competitor with contempt, saying that Entertainment This Month and its affiliated businesses had an unsustainable model that threatened to put many others out of commission.

Milo says his sales peaked in 1992. Six years later, he would sell his business to an online startup. He thinks the comics industry, including his company, was mainly hurt by competition from other forms of entertainment.

"From my standpoint, we were more or less going against the tide," he said. "We just didn't realize it. We didn't realize that the paper industry would just get reduced every single year. The comic book newsstand would go out of business, which was our feeder system. It's almost impossible to find comic books outside of comic book stores now."

After leaving comics, Milo turned his attention to e-commerce companies. His current venture is a company that manages more than sixteen hundred vacation rental properties in Florida (I spoke with him by phone as he drove across the Florida panhandle). He no longer reads comics or follows the comics business in any way.

Meanwhile, at Marvel, Carol Kalish had been promoted within the sales department. She was looking at ways to develop new products, inside and outside of comic shops. This included greeting cards that were miniature comic books and would be sold in the greeting card aisle at stores. She had turned thirty-six in 1991, and had no signs of health problems.

On September 5 of that year, Richard Howell got a phone call at their New Jersey home from Kalish's assistant, who wondered where she was. Soon after, he got a call from a hospital. She had collapsed and died while walking from Penn Station to Marvel's offices in Manhattan. Doctors told him that she had a blood clot in her leg that came loose and moved through her system to block her heart.

"She collapsed on the street, and since it was Manhattan, nobody did anything," Howell said. "Finally somebody called an ambulance, and the ambulance couldn't get through the traffic in Manhattan. It's kind of almost encouraging that nobody stole her purse when she was there, so they knew enough to call me, but it was too late to do anything."

The news of her death began to travel through the network of comic shops she had nurtured. Shop owners remember getting calls from colleagues who were sobbing. "She was the patron of the art of comic retailing," Hanley said.

She was gone, right as the comics industry was about to do its best to destroy itself.

About a year after *X-Men* #1, Marvel's top artists announced they were leaving to start their own company, Image Comics. The creators—including McFarlane, Liefeld, Lee, and others—made the move because of frustration with the lack of creative control at Marvel, and because they were getting an unfairly small share of the financial benefits from their successes.[5]

Around the same time, DC launched a series of story lines designed to attract the collectors who had led to record-breaking sales for Marvel. The biggest of these was in 1992, the most audacious idea of all: the death of Superman.

"There was a whole peculiar circumstance with the death of Superman where news of it broke in the mainstream media long before DC wanted it to break," Hanley said. "That created a demand for books that were not in the store yet."

The character was going to die in *Superman* #75, which would go on sale Wednesday, November 18. Customers could buy a regular-format comic, or pay extra for a collector's edition that came in a black plastic bag. Hanley initially ordered three thousand of the collector's edition and two thousand of the regular edition. Then, right before the deadline to change orders, he increased it to ten thousand of the collector's edition, while keeping with two thousand of the regular one. This was more than he had ordered of *Spider-Man, X-Force,* or *X-Men.* He knew that if he was wrong and the comic was not a huge seller, it would be the biggest blunder of his career.

"The day before it shipped, I had a hard time sleeping," he said.

In the morning, his first store to open was the one on 32nd Street in Manhattan. He expected a line to form, considering all the publicity. He did not expect a line extending down the block and around the corner, which is what he got. He was astounded in the face of the largest crush of customers he had ever seen.

A few years before Superman "died," Jim Hanley's Universe held a fiftieth birthday party for the character, and had this window display. Superman © DC Comics. *Courtesy of Jim Hanley.*

He had no time to feel relief that the comic was selling. His focus turned to his other stores, some of which didn't have the staffing to handle the crowds. He jumped on an express bus and went to his store near Wall Street. There he spent hours working the door, letting customers in ten at a time. He waved people inside while he kept in touch with the other stores with a cordless phone pressed to his ear.

"By noon nobody else in town had a copy of the book," he said. "The news media was calling us trying to get copies. CNN came down to the store to get copies."

Some customers were not content to buy one or two copies. They wanted fifty, one hundred, or more. The sales that day were enough for a great week. And the boom would continue. The month was the best in the history of Hanley's business. The following month, December, was better than November. He gave out $30,000 worth of Christmas bonuses to staff, the most ever.

The market boom had been going for three years or more, depending on how you measure. It was long enough that predictions of an oncoming bust had already been proven wrong a few times. But the bust was near.

Superman remained dead for five months. The story that was supposed to change everything was undone quickly enough to cash in on a hot new story: the return of Superman. The rebirth began with *Adventures of*

Superman #500, released in April 1993. Retailers who underordered on the death made sure not to make the same mistake on the rebirth.

That comic book, in which Superman fights his way out of the afterlife, is what many store owners say was the beginning of the bust. Sales would have been great if not for inflated expectations, this idea that each new hit would be bigger than the previous one. Retailers were left with hundreds of unsold copies. Distributors had it even worse, with stockpiles ready for reorders that would fall far short of expectations.

And yet, *Adventures of Superman* #500 was a mere flesh wound compared to what was coming. The creators at Image Comics were finding that they were good at drawing comics and selling comics, but not good at getting them to come out on time. Retailers had made orders during the boom on books that were delayed and would not arrive until the market was in free fall.

The late books tended to arrive in waves, so stores had little to sell from Image for months and then were inundated. The result was that consumers pared down their spending because they couldn't afford the dozens of books coming out at the same time.

Around the same time, Image released a crossover story with another independent publisher, Valiant Comics. The result was a miniseries called *Death-mate*. It started out well, with a prologue in June 1993 drawn by star artists from each company, Jim Lee for Image and Barry Windsor-Smith for Valiant.

The plan was for each company to release two issues of the story, followed by a copublished finale. Valiant released its issues on time. Image did not. By the time the Image-published issues arrived in 1994, the bust had arrived in full force.[6]

Hanley cut back on orders as much as he could, only to find that his cuts were not enough to keep pace with the drop in sales. He had tens of thousands of unsold comics. For a while, he kept going with credit and the hope that the market would rebound. By 1996, with no good options, he and his business partner filed for bankruptcy protection.

Jim Hanley's Universe was able to stay open, but nearly every financial decision had to be approved by a court-appointed trustee. The bankruptcy lasted for seven years. Hanley and his partner regained control after they had repaid about two-thirds of the money they owed.

"It knocked the wind out of our sails," he said. "And, to some extent, it never came back."

He would remain in business until retirement in 2013, when he closed the stores and sold some of the assets to two of his employees. Looking back, he thinks of his comics career as two phases, before the bankruptcy and after. He has happy memories of the beginning and the early growth, when he was living his dream. And he wouldn't mind forgetting everything else.

Birth of *Bone*

The same year as *X-Force #1* and *X-Men #1,* an unknown cartoonist from Columbus released the first issue of *Bone.* Jeff Smith had grown up reading Disney comics and classic newspaper strips. He worked in animation, but wanted to focus on comics. *Bone* had a premise far removed from the popular comics of the time. It was an epic fantasy and a comedy, starring Fone Bone, a baldheaded white cartoon character in a world of swords and dragons. Smith began his promotion of the comic by traveling to the annual retailer conference held by Capital City Distribution.

"I was really small," he said. "I literally had an easel with a drawing of Fore Bone paper-clipped to it, and a few pieces of original art. What was interesting for me is that I was the only cartoonist there. Everyone else was just salespeople from those companies." His company, Cartoon Books, consisted of Smith and his wife, Vijaya Iyer. She handled most of the business affairs, in addition to her full-time job.

His first evening at the conference, he hung out in the hotel bar, where retailers were congregating. He chatted with store owners, and, if they asked, he showed them samples of his work. He found some immediate fans. "They connected to the idea of what I was doing, which was the idea of funny-animal comics like *Donald Duck* or *Pogo* or something like that," he said. "The retailers would go and get their retailer friends and bring them back over."

He didn't know it at the time, but he had stumbled into a marketing coup. His new friends were some of the most influential retailers in the business, such as Jim Hanley in New York, Rory Root of Comic Relief in Berkeley, and Joe Field of Flying Colors Comics in Concord, California.[7] They would go home and sell *Bone* with abandon.

Field remembers Smith as a kind of double prodigy, a skilled cartoonist and a talented marketer. "He was not waiting for people to come to his table," Field said, recalling a later appearance by Smith at a convention in San Francisco. "He was grabbing people and putting the book in their hands and saying, '*Looney Tunes* meets *Lord of the Rings*.'"

Sales started small. After about a year, Smith began to see a notable increase in orders. The momentum grew as the comic got glowing reviews and as Smith won industry awards. *Bone* had come out of nowhere to become enough of a success that Smith and Iyer no longer needed day jobs.

"Really, there were about twenty retailers that I knew were selling as many copies of *Bone* as they were *Batman*," Smith said. "Retailers would tell us they were giving copies of *Bone* to their customers and saying, 'Take this home. You don't have to pay for it [unless] you like it.'"

These stores were the outliers. The twenty top stores were part of a group of about one hundred stores that emphasized independent comics alongside mainstream publishers. "At that time, there were a lot of stores that only sold Marvel and DC books," said Iyer. "There was a huge swath of stores that didn't carry independent comics at all." But Smith and Iyer only needed the help of a few stores to break out into the larger culture. *Bone*'s collected editions would soon appear in libraries and bookstores. In 2005, Scholastic Corp. launched its new Graphix imprint with a color version of the first *Bone* collection. From there, the material went from a hit in the comics world to a mainstream hit.

None of that would have happened if not for the network of comic shops and their nonreturnable business model, Smith said. The lack of returns meant that a small company such as Cartoon Books could sell its products without the risk of needing to issue refunds for unsold copies. The risks were all on the retailers. By the time *Bone* got to bookstores, most of which require returns, the company was large enough to be able to handle it. "Early on, Vijaya and I realized that the real customer was not the person taking the book home and reading it. It was the retailers," he said. "It was actually just a stroke of luck that I started hanging out with retailers, but it was the best stroke of luck that I could imagine."

An outside observer could look at *Bone*'s success as oddly timed considering the prevailing trends of collectible covers and other marketing gimmicks. However, Smith thinks the industry's climate contributed to his success. Retailers who sold *Bone* were also selling *X-Men* #1 and the like, and making enough money that they could take risks by stocking more independent material.

Today, the early issues of *Bone* continue to sell in book form and are being discovered by a new generation. Meanwhile, the hot #1 issues of the early 1990s have largely faded, found in back-issue bins and the occasional collected edition.

Jeff Smith got an armful of Will Eisner Comic Industry awards in 1994, presented at the San Diego Comic-Con. Here he gets the back of one of the trophies signed by the awards' namesake. *Credit: Jackie Estrada.*

Smith poses with a statue of one of his characters, the Great Red Dragon, at the Alternative Press Expo in San Jose, California, in 1998. *Credit: Jackie Estrada.*

13

The Mailman (1994–2016)

IT WOULD not be difficult to frame the history of comics' direct market as the improbable rise of one person. This man was a fan and collector when Phil Seuling created the business model. Soon after, this man opened a comic shop in a basement. He later bought the assets of a regional comics distributor, entering a crowded market. His company survived and grew to become the largest distributor in the country. It remained the industry leader during the boom and bust of the early 1990s. And then this man and his company pulled off the greatest trick of all.

This man is Steve Geppi, owner of Diamond Comic Distributors. He grew up in Baltimore's Little Italy. As a child, he read every comic book he could find, starting with Disney's duck stories and then DC's superheroes. His love for comics did not fade when he was an adult. He worked as a letter carrier and used his spare money to buy old comics. He found he had a knack for selling comics, and began to rent tables at conventions.

"It's a classic case of turning a love, a hobby, into a business," Geppi said. "And I have to say for most of us it was not even a business attempt. It was more of a love that dragged us into a business."

I interviewed him at the suburban offices of Diamond International Galleries, a business that sells pop culture collectibles, one of eleven companies he owns in the Baltimore area. He trotted out to meet me, dressed in a black

T-shirt, shorts, and loafers. He gave me an off-kilter smile, like the kid who misbehaves in class. I had not seen a recent picture of him, and was surprised he looked almost the same as in photos from decades ago. He is stocky and medium height, with some gray at the roots of his slicked-back hair.

He took a leap of faith in 1974 when he quit his job at the Postal Service to open a comic shop. His sales at conventions had grown to rival the paycheck at his day job, so he thought he could make a go of it. He rented a space on Edmondson Avenue for $100 per month, down the steps from a television repair shop and a watch-repair shop.

Geppi's Comic World opened on July 1, 1974. It was maybe four hundred square feet, including a small back room. It had no cash register and no new comics, just one man's collection of old comics.

"It felt like going into someone's basement," he said. "Sometimes you would get there and see a sign that said, 'Back soon. Out playing basketball.'"

He placed print advertisements. That, along with the customers he knew from conventions, gave him steady traffic. The store exceeded his expectations. Soon he was selling new comics along with old ones. He opened additional stores around town.

This was the Steve Geppi people knew when he bought some assets of the bankrupt Irjax/New Media in 1982. He was a shop owner who seemed to think he had the chops to operate a much larger business, one of many people at the time who could be described that way. He called his company Diamond, a reference to the diamond symbol that appeared on the lower left corner of comics distributed to the direct market, and he built a base along the East Coast. One by one, he bought other distributors, expanding his regional footprint each time.

He knew that when he did a deal, it was an audition of sorts for the next deal. He made sure his reputation with competitors was impeccable. He was someone who could keep a secret if asked, and would honor his agreements. This was one of the reasons Bud Plant chose to sell his distribution business to Geppi in 1988. It was why Ron Forman and Walter Wang sold Comics Unlimited, another distributor, to Geppi in 1994.

The Comics Unlimited deal had the distinction of happening right as the market was heading into a nosedive. Shortly before the sale closed, Wang criticized some of Marvel's practices, and Marvel responded by cutting off all orders. It was a major change to Comics Unlimited's business fundamentals, and Geppi could have used it to wriggle out of the deal, which looked worse by the day, considering the deteriorating market. But he didn't. He made ten years of monthly payments for the sale.

"Steve Geppi was as gentlemanly and reasonable as anyone we ever dealt with," Forman said. "We got our 120 checks, each on time. We always remained friends."

His kind view of Geppi, however, is at odds with the public image of the man that was about to develop. From 1994 to 1996, the comics industry nearly destroyed itself. Depending on who you ask, Geppi helped save it or was one of the leading instigators of its near-demise.

In the summer of 1994, the comics business had retreated from the heights of the boom. Thousands of stores had closed, or soon would close.[1] Many that remained were choked with debt. But longtime players had seen previous booms and busts, and thought better days were ahead.

Diamond was the largest distributor, with Capital City a close second. Each company had nationwide networks of warehouses and stocked close to a full line of mainstream and independent material. After that were regional players with small slices of the market, including Heroes World Distribution in New Jersey and Friendly Frank's in Indiana.[2]

The business had settled into a near-duopoly in which most retailers across the country chose to buy from Diamond or Capital City. The distributors vied for customers by trying to have the best discount structure, the most reliable deliveries, and the most flexible credit terms. If one distributor did a poor job, a retailer could fall back on the other.

Marvel, the largest publisher in the industry, was in crisis. Its most bankable creators had left two years earlier to form Image. Marvel had flooded the market with new titles and found that many were not selling and that top titles were not doing nearly as well as before. Retailers told Marvel that the problem was low-quality products, but the publisher found its own scapegoat: the distribution system. The argument was that distributors were not working hard enough to sell Marvel's great titles.[3]

Since 1989, Marvel had been owned by a company tied to Revlon executive Ron Perelman. The new leadership had arrived just in time for the boom years, not knowing that those sales levels were not a sure thing.[4]

Marvel held an initial public offering of its stock in 1991. This imposed a new pressure on the company to increase its profit and sales, even in the face of strong headwinds.

Rumors began to fly that Marvel was going to buy out a distributor and sell directly to comic shops, cutting out the other distributors. The question then was who would sell? Steve Geppi was at his desk at Diamond in December. He overheard as his administrative assistant took a call from someone who desperately wanted to speak with Mr. Geppi. The caller was a woman who claimed to have information that would be of high interest. He motioned for his assistant to put the call through.

The woman said she was the mistress of an attorney who worked for Marvel, and she was upset because he had decided to go back to his wife. To get back at him, she was going to reveal Marvel's big secret: the publisher had agreed to a deal to buy Heroes World.

Geppi called everyone he could to try to verify the story. Marvel wouldn't talk to him. He recalls that he didn't get an answer until he reached Ivan Snyder, Heroes World's co-owner, who had known Geppi since the mid-1970s. Snyder has a different recollection, saying that he didn't speak with Geppi until after the sale had been publicly announced. What is clear is that Geppi knew about the sale before it was announced.

This was a doomsday scenario. Marvel would not buy Heroes World unless it intended to exclusively distribute through the company, Geppi thought. Despite its foibles, Marvel remained 40 percent of the market. Without it, Diamond and all the other distributors would face a financial upheaval.

The public announcement of the Heroes World deal was on December 28, 1994. Soon after, Marvel confirmed that Heroes World would have an exclusive contract. Any comic shop that wanted to sell Marvel comics would need to get an account with Heroes World.

Heroes World had a history with Marvel. Snyder had grown up in Brooklyn and was a certified public accountant by training. He joined the publishing division of Marvel's parent company in the 1970s and was part of the team that negotiated the original contract with Phil Seuling to distribute the company's comics. When he left Marvel, he made a deal to buy Marvel's mail-order business he had started within the company that sold toys and collectibles. He used those items to start a mail-order toy business selling Marvel products and also opened a retail store in New Jersey.

"I was amazed that people were driving two hours to come to a dumpy little store that was maybe 100 square feet," said Snyder, who now is retired in Florida. He was talking about his first store, a space that was mostly warehouse and only had a small retail area open to the public.

His company became known as Heroes World and grew to include eight stores and a distributor of comics and related merchandise. The mail-order division had a colorful catalog that showed the toys as illustrated by comics artist Joe Kubert, and the catalog turned out to be so popular that the company sold it on newsstands and in comics shops.

In the 1980s, Heroes World distributed comics to shops in the Mid-Atlantic and New England. One of its largest customers was Jim Hanley's Universe in New York. Its co-owner, Hanley, found that Heroes World had the best discounts, several percentage points better than competitors, which made a big difference. He praised Snyder for being one of the "smartest men in comics." With the Marvel deal, however, Heroes World was being thrust into a role for which it was not ready, Hanley said.

Behind the scenes, Marvel had been negotiating with Snyder for months to buy his company. He felt torn, knowing that the sale was a great opportunity for his company, and also knowing that it would do tremendous harm to his friends at competing distributors because they would no longer sell Marvel products.

"It was basically guilt," Snyder said. "Six or seven of the [other distributors] were probably going to be out of business, and I was not happy about that. But as it was pointed out to me, if I didn't sell to [Marvel], they would buy one of the others and I would be out of business."

He introduced himself to new customers with a message in the first Marvel-exclusive product catalog: "We realize that even though we might be your only source for Marvel Comics products, we still have to earn your business. Over the course of the next few months we will demonstrate that we mean what we say."[5]

The Heroes World deal led to a free-for-all among the other publishers and distributors. Small publishers and distributors could see a world coming in which the big players each had an exclusive partner and everyone else was cut off from the market. The big question was, what would DC do?

On April 28, Capital City co-owner Milton Griepp had a phone call scheduled with DC executive Paul Levitz. It was right before Capital City's retailer conference in Chicago, when retailers and vendors from across the country would gather.

"When Paul started off with something like 'It's good that you scheduled a call for today,' I knew immediately the next few days were going to have a heightened importance," Griepp said in the June 1995 issue of his company's trade magazine, *Internal Correspondence.*[6]

Levitz told Griepp that DC was signing an exclusive deal with Diamond. Griepp was not surprised. The rumors of a DC-Diamond pairing had been around for months. Capital City did not push as hard for its own exclusive contracts because Griepp and his partner John Davis disagreed with the idea in principle. Soon, when it became clear that exclusive contracts were the new way of doing business, Capital City signed up a few small publishers.

Retailers were furious at the actions of Marvel and DC, which they saw as a threat to the industry. From a shop owner's perspective, the new system meant they could no longer get all of their comics from one distributor. They would need to have a Heroes World account for Marvel, a Diamond account for DC, and a Capital City account for

Milton Griepp, photographed in the 1990s. *Courtesy of Milton Griepp.*

several independent companies. The practical implications were daunting. Three order forms. Three deliveries. Three billing systems. And it wrought havoc on the discount structure. Many retailers saw their discounts decrease because orders were being split three ways and were falling short of levels needed to qualify for additional savings.

DC's agreement with Diamond became public the day before Capital City hosted its retailer conference in Chicago. An event that was supposed to be festive instead took on the atmosphere of a wake.

"I was literally in tears out there, it was so awful," said Greg Ketter of DreamHaven Books in Minneapolis. "I saw the future, and it happened. You took out all the competition and innovation."

Griepp gave a speech about Capital City's plan to move forward, saying he would not let the recent changes destroy the industry. He was an analytical guy giving a speech to an audience that was sad and angry.

"Being at the Capital show was like taking a bath in emotion," said *Cerebus* creator Dave Sim, interviewed in that same issue of *Internal Correspondence*.

"They were waiting for Milton to declare war," he said. "All he had to do was start slow, explaining to them what they already knew. . . . They had been slapped in the face, first by Marvel and now by DC. He could have gone in and said it's time for everyone to stand up and be counted—'The only way to stop this madness, this cancer, is to isolate it. Every retailer who believes in a free marketplace must draw a line in the sand here and now. We have to tell the Paul Levitzes of the world that we are not pawns on his chessboard; we are not his minions; we are not his serfs.'"[7]

That was the kind of speech Sim might give, but not Griepp.

Meanwhile, Diamond and DC felt like they had no choice but to band together. "The whole system had come apart," Levitz said in our interview. "I did what needed to be done." He then cut off any further discussion of the topic, saying the specific business decisions of that time were "not anything we're going to go into."

Geppi summarizes the whole period: "It was a total clusterfuck. Nobody was happy."

Adding to the tension, it was revealed that DC's contract with Diamond included an option to buy the distributor. For DC, the option provided some insurance to stop Marvel from buying Diamond. In an industry already reeling from what was happening with Heroes World, a potential DC purchase of Diamond was horrifying for many retailers. The purchase option was supposed to be confidential, but it got reported by the *Comics Journal*.

"They put all kinds of onerous, onerous things on me," Geppi said about the conditions DC insisted upon. He signed the deal anyway because he saw it as the difference between life and death for his business.

He still resents the way he got treated by Marvel at that time. He recalls a visit to see Marvel officials in New York to discuss the ramifications of the switch to Heroes World. He and one of his associates walked into a conference room and were met by at least a dozen Marvel lawyers, which he saw as an attempt to intimidate. They worked out details of how Diamond accounts would make the transition to Heroes World. Through it all, Geppi remained businesslike.

At the end, he told the lawyers he wanted to keep the lines of communication open. He said that if Marvel ever wanted to come back to Diamond, he was open to the idea. One of the Marvel lawyers responded by making a face and giving an exaggerated "Nawwww."

Capital City vowed to persevere. It closed many of its warehouses and laid off workers to reflect the dramatic shrinkage of its product lines. By the beginning of 1996, Griepp and Davis needed to come to terms with a bleak future for the business they had built. "We could see that the larger consumer market was soft," Griepp said. "There wasn't going to be organic growth to pull out of a sort of survival mode."

They began to look for a way out of the business. And in comics distribution, there was always one guy who was buying. In July 1996, Geppi and Diamond bought Capital City.

Heroes World turned out to be a disaster for Marvel. Many orders were late and incorrect. The home office in New Jersey did not have mechanisms in place to deal with the high volume of complaints. Callers were often met by busy signals, or by operators who had little idea of how to fix complex logistical problems.

Snyder says many of the initial problems were because of a new software system that was not properly installed by Marvel, and that Marvel did not fix in a timely way, leading to mistakes with billing and managing inventory. He regrets the problems faced by retailers in those first few months, but also thinks that some of this was a normal part of what happens when a big distribution network makes major changes.

"It was a huge undertaking," he said. "Far more so than I probably first anticipated."

The Heroes World transition was just one event that preceded the financial collapse of Marvel. The publisher filed for bankruptcy protection in 1996. New managers came in to try to salvage something from the mess. One of the many changes, which took effect in 1997, was that Heroes World closed. Snyder retired to Florida and is not involved in the comics industry today.

Capping it all, Marvel signed an agreement to exclusively distribute its comics with Diamond, the last company standing.[8] The lawyer who had scoffed at such a possibility was no longer around.

The direct market that had begun with Phil Seuling and had grown to dozens of competing distributors was now down to one option for retailers. And many retailers were not happy about it. The Diamond exclusive era had begun, and continues to this day.

"People are saying 'Steve Geppi's a monopoly,' and I'm just trying to hang on here," Geppi said. He sold parts of his personal collection of vintage comics to make payroll and keep up with bills during the mid-1990s turmoil. Underscoring how much the industry had shrunk, Diamond's annual sales were much lower following the DC agreement than they were during the boom, he said. It would take years for Diamond to get back onto solid financial footing.

As an apparent monopoly, Diamond had reason to worry federal regulators would step in and force a breakup of the company. Indeed, the Justice Department did investigate Diamond in the late 1990s. Chuck Rozanski of Mile High Comics was one of the retailers who says he spoke extensively with federal officials. The government never brought charges, and Rozanski says a Justice Department official told him that there was no evidence that Diamond was using its status in a way that was harmful to the market.[9]

Rozanski met Geppi for the first time in the late 1970s when he visited one of Geppi's Comic World stores. Rozanski was unimpressed with the tiny and cluttered store, but was impressed with the owner. "He was unbelievably smart and aggressive, and a hustler of amazing talents," he said.

The key to Geppi's success was that he understood what the real game was, according to Hanley. Other distributors thought they would succeed or fail based on how well they served their customers, the comic shops. The best example of this was Capital City, whose approach made it a favorite of many of the best shops in the country. In contrast, Geppi saw that relationships with the publishers were just as important, if not more important.

"Supply was more important than customers," Hanley said. "And he built his business that way. So when Marvel decided to act crazy, he didn't go to customers, he went to the other publishers to get a corner on supply."

As Hanley sees it, Geppi's approach was rooted in his background as a dealer of Golden Age comics. In this realm, the person in control is the one who controls the supply. A dealer can have the grungiest store and the worst disposition, and will still be successful if he or she has comics that are not available anywhere else.

This is not how Geppi sees himself or his business. He agrees that there was an element of luck to his emergence as the last distributor. "Somebody had to be there at that time," he said. "I just happened to be that guy." But he thinks Diamond set the stage for its success by treating people well, including customers and publishers. In a fiercely competitive business, it helped to be liked.

The rest of the 1990s were an extended hangover for the comics business. The North American market was $300 million to $320 million in 1997, and then shrank in each of the following three years, according to estimates from Comichron.com and ICv2. Once growth returned, it was slow. (Figures are based on orders by comic shops, not sales to customers.)[10]

Then, starting in the early 2000s, more robust growth took hold and continued for more than a decade.

There are many theories about what set off the resurgence. Some point to the popularity of movies based on comic books. Others say that comic shops have successfully diversified their audiences, reaching women and younger readers in numbers not seen in decades.

The Diamond monopoly era now accounts for more than half of the time since Phil Seuling started his company in 1973. It has been a stable period, by the rough-and-tumble standards of comics retail, but has also seen several major flare-ups in conflict between retailers, publishers, and Diamond. Retailers' common complaint is that Diamond does the bidding of Marvel, DC, and other major publishers and does not act in the best interests of the people actually selling the comics.

One of the most consequential of these fights began in 2002 when retailer Brian Hibbs observed Marvel's tendency to be late with comics and to change the creative teams without notice. This was hurting comic shops because they would order based on when they expected a comic to arrive and whether the creative team was likely to boost sales, and then be stuck with the inventory if the actual product was not what Marvel had advertised.

Hibbs looked at Marvel's terms of service and found that the publisher was repeatedly violating its own rules. So, he pointed this out to the company. Even though he owned just one small store, he was well known in the retailer community for his monthly column, "Tilting at Windmills."

"I was trying to resolve this in an adult way, and Marvel wasn't having any of it," Hibbs said. "Not in so many words, they basically told me, 'Fuck off, little man.'"

So, he organized a class-action lawsuit against Marvel. It was a huge risk for him, taking on the corporation that was his largest supplier.

"I honestly believed that I was right," he said. "Marvel Comics taught me the difference between right and wrong in the first place. With power comes responsibility. With great power comes great responsibility. That's why I knew I was going to win on this."

Marvel's law firm flew Hibbs to New York for a deposition. The bearded San Francisco shop owner showed up to a room full of men in suits, while he was

Brian Hibbs

dressed in his usual flannel shirt and cargo pants. He remembers that they sat at a giant conference table that was a piece of a redwood tree that had been sliced.

The questions started aggressively. "It appeared to me that their law firm thought I was trying to scam Marvel," he said. "And so they were asking me the most basic questions about how comics retail works. Toward the end the tenor of the questions was changing and it seemed to me that they began to grasp that something was wrong on their end."

He went back to San Francisco with the sense that Marvel was now taking the case seriously. Then, in the information-sharing process to prepare for trial, Marvel disclosed that the number of late or changed comics was much larger than the retailers had realized. Hibbs had thought there were about twenty affected comics, and was mostly thinking of changing the company's practices going forward, having little awareness of how widespread the problem really was.

Near the end of 2003, Marvel and Hibbs settled the case, with Marvel agreeing to provide credits to retailers to make up for past errors and pay for the case's legal fees. It was an unambiguous victory for retailers.

Although Diamond was not a party in the lawsuit, the case got to the heart of the way major publishers were operating in the Diamond-exclusive era, Hibbs said.

While the case was still active, the major publishers began a new system called "final order cutoff," which let retailers change their orders up until just a few weeks before new comics were delivered. Shops still filed their initial orders three months in advance, but could revise the numbers for select publishers to respond to changes in shipping dates, creative teams, or for any other reason.

Officially, Hibbs's case was not the cause of final order cutoff, but he and other store owners say the timing shows a likely connection.

Despite the conflicts between retailers and publishers, comic shops had a steady period of rising sales, ending only in 2017. Considering the volatile nature of the business, this was a remarkable winning streak.

Tom Spurgeon, who runs ComicsReporter.com and is a former editor of the *Comics Journal,* says the overlap of generations of retailers makes this a dynamic period. "This is the last ten years of that first generation, and then you have this enthusiastic up-and-coming generation," he said. "It's a good time."

Some longtime retailers have come close to mastering the business model, almost making it look easy despite the risks, he said. At the same time, the most experienced retailers know that the next bust could be right around the corner. They have seen how good times turn to bad times.

"There are waves in this business," said Joe Field of Flying Colors Comics. He left a career in radio marketing and had the good fortune to open a comic shop in 1988, right before the 1989 *Batman* movie led to a resurgence in interest in the character and in comics. He rose to become a leader among retailers, serving on the boards of trade groups and coming up with the idea that has become the industry's top promotional event, Free Comic Book Day. Despite his enviable track record, he looks ahead with caution. "The retailers that have been able to persevere through all of that have learned to ride those waves. Sometimes there's an occasional wipeout and you get sucked under the tide, and there are times when you're riding high and you're on top of the world. For me, in all of that, the key has been how do you manage things, not just on the way up, but how do you manage things when things aren't going well. And that's, to me, the difference between the stores that last and the ones that don't."

But don't call him a pessimist. "We are the cockroaches of pop culture," he said. "We will survive a nuclear fallout. But the big companies that are losing lots of money and have unreal stock prices, they can last a long time, but we're more nimble."

Asked about Diamond, he said, "Unfortunately, I think Diamond is in a no-win position. They do an incredibly difficult job in an incredibly crowded market, and, for the most part, they carry it off very well. Are there glitches in the system? Yeah, you bet there are." The most common problems are orders that show up with damage or in incorrect numbers.

The fact that there is no other option for ordering new comics means that retailers and the distributor have no choice but to make this relationship work.

"It's like an old married couple," Spurgeon said. "They kind of function well together at this point."

Steve Geppi says he is semiretired. The joke around the office is that now he only works sixty hours per week. He remains the sole owner of Diamond Comics Distributors, but leaves the day-to-day management to others. He has a succession plan for when he passes away, which includes his children. "The kids all work in the business and they love it," he said.

Geppi's rivals from his early days are long gone. They moved on to other parts of the comics business or left comics altogether.

Despite being the last person standing, he had had more than his share of adversity. He invested heavily in real estate prior to the 2008 housing bust. That, plus some other business investments unrelated to comics, drained his personal fortune.

"I hit the trifecta," he said. "I had my wife leave me, financial problems, and my brother died. And when my brother died, I realized the other two weren't important. They could be fixed, and they were."

His financial problems led to the foreclosure of his palatial house in the Baltimore suburbs and to other court actions for an inability to pay debts. The Baltimore media and the comics media covered his travails, showing how one of the wealthiest men in his city, and most powerful men in comics, had fallen on hard times.

He gradually got his finances in order. He maintains that Diamond was never affected or in any way at risk because of his personal problems. "Diamond has been better than ever, the last three years particularly," he said.

I interviewed him right as DC Rebirth was being released, and he was in awe of the sales figures. Diamond had budgeted for 2016 sales to be slightly lower than 2015, and now the estimate looked way off, largely because of DC. "They're silly numbers," he said. "They're literally silly."

DC no longer has an option to buy Diamond. It took twenty years for Geppi to get that provision removed from his contract. His deal with DC in 1995 lasted eight years, followed by a renewal of eight years. Next was a shorter contract, in which DC again insisted on maintaining an option to buy Diamond. "I had to renew it for four years, which broke my heart, but we had some trouble at the time, and needed some covenants, and that was their ransom," he said.

In 2015, when negotiating the current contract, Geppi was able to get the provision removed. "They never wanted to buy us," he said. "It was all

Steve Geppi in the official photo used by his companies.
Courtesy of Diamond Comics Distributors.

about getting an advantage." The problem for him was the perception from other publishers that DC had favored status, something that Marvel would bring up from time to time. He is relieved those days are over.

14

The Moral of the Story

ON A Saturday in August 2016, The Laughing Ogre had just about all hands on deck. The store was hosting a signing for creators involved with the Cartoon Crossroads Columbus festival, which was having its second annual installment a few months later. The artists at the signing were an accomplished bunch, but one name jumped out: Jeff Smith.

I arrived at the store right before Smith was to begin, and had to drive around back to find an open parking space. At the door, employee Elissa Leach handed out plastic bags so that the staff could differentiate between books from the store and books that people had brought to be signed. Leach, herself a cartoonist, was a kind of reserve employee, only called upon for the busiest days.

Lauren McCallister was at the register. Later in the day, she was scheduled to sign some of her own comics. Also there were Sarah Edington and Trish Smith, both Valkyries. Smith was one of the employees who had left the previous summer because she was moving out of town. Since then, she had come back, and was close to full-time hours at the store. The only male employee that day, other than Gib Bickel, was Michael Cavender, one of the people who had started the previous fall. He had recently been promoted to assistant manager, joining McCallister in that role.

Smith made his way through the store, shaking a few hands. About a dozen people were in line with books, ahead of his arrival, and others milled around. He took a seat at a table in front of the back-issue area and greeted the first person. He had a black brace on his right hand and forearm, his drawing hand, because of nagging problems with repetitive stress injuries. Stacks of books were ready for customers to buy, including the one that had come out that summer, *Bone: Coda*.

The line was mostly parents and their children. Many of the parents read Smith's work when it was a self-published comic book in comic shops, and many of the children read it when it was color paperbacks in school libraries. He had sold millions of books and become a celebrity in the cartooning world. But this was his home store, a place where he had done signings before he became a big deal, and the whole event had a low-key feel.

Abby Richman, six, had drawn her own *Bone* comic, and she showed it to Smith. The characters were rendered in blue marker. He smiled and looked at each of the pages with her while her parents looked on. Her father, Dave, had been shopping at Laughing Ogre since he moved to Columbus for college in 1996.

"As I got to know Gib and the other people who work here, it created that sense of community, that this was my shop," he said. He remained a customer through the ownership changes because the place still felt like home to him. "The general vibe stayed the same."

Jeff Smith reads a *Bone* comic made by a young fan during a signing at The Laughing Ogre.

On the day of Smith's signing, one of the store's cofounders, Rod Phillips (*right*), stopped by with his daughter, Ava. He remains close friends with Gib Bickel (*left*), more than twenty years after they and Daryn Guarino started the business.

Near the front of the store, a customer asked Bickel for a recommendation to read to a young child. He pointed to a hardcover collection of *Owly* by Andy Runton. "It's strictly with pictures," Bickel said. "A lot of little kids love that because they can read without reading." Sold.

Along the foothills of the Sierra Nevada Mountains, Bud Plant continues to report for duty at his two-story warehouse. His second-floor office is filled with stacks of comics history, as are the hallways. Even the break room has boxes of books, bought for a song when some publisher went out of business. It is difficult to distinguish between the company's inventory and his personal collection. Case in point: the Betty Boop ashtray near the front entrance is not for sale.

"It's a fun business, as you can imagine," he said. "Every day, we get in groovy new stuff."

He turned sixty-four in 2016. He is in a long-term relationship with Anne Hutchison, a writer and book dealer. He has children and grandchildren and friends all over the country. And he has been in business long enough

Bud Plant in his element, standing among the warehouse shelves of his business.

that he knows the next market bust could be right around the corner. But he loves the work.

Of all the people still active in comics, Plant has the most direct connection to Phil Seuling and the dawn of the direct market. He knew all the key players, and was a confidant to many of them. In an industry that financially and emotionally ruined many people, Plant has remained well regarded by just about everyone with whom he has done business.

After my drive to visit him in Grass Valley, I could see that the place might be the secret to his longevity. It is a small town, dense with trees, and with mountains to the east. Downtown there is an independent bookstore where Plant works one shift per week, just because he likes the people and the books.

"We're all getting older, so at some point we may all decide to sort of retire," he said about himself and his small group of employees. Not today, though, and maybe not for a while.

In Denver, Chuck Rozanski doesn't discuss retirement. He has owned a comic shop since 1974, making him one of the last, if not the last, of the early shop owners to still be actively managing a store. He says Mile High's best days are ahead.

"We're the last ones that sort comics and actually care about comics," he said, seated in the second-floor office that overlooks the floor of his flagship location. "If you want an issue of *Cosmo the Merry Martian*, I'm it."

He doesn't specialize in key issues, such as #1s or first appearances of characters. He doesn't specialize in a particular era or genre. He buys and sells everything, and aims to be the place collectors will go to find the thing that's not available anywhere else.

Sometimes at night, before he locks up, he goes down to his warehouse shelves and runs his fingers against the spines of the books. "These are trades and hardbacks, and this is the largest repository of trades and hardbacks in the world," he said.

He is financially secure following a sale in 2016 of his previous warehouse. The building's value had skyrocketed because of Colorado's legalization of marijuana. Growers are only allowed to grow indoors in certain types of buildings, which led to bidding wars for the few existing properties that fit the bill. So he no longer needs to make money from comics. Why does he stay?

"I cannot explain my motivation," he said. "All I can tell you is that I cannot wait to get in here. I resent the time that I can't be here. I would rather be here working on this than just about anything in the world. I don't take vacations per se. I just really love this environment and the people that are in this environment. But mostly I just love the comics."

Jim Hanley is retired and living in Washington, D.C., with his brother. I met him for lunch at a restaurant there. He is dealing with health problems related to diabetes and was using a wheelchair because of a back fracture. Despite his ailments, he looks almost the same as photos from his glory years at his stores, except his hair is now white instead of red. "As Mickey Mantle said, 'If I knew I was going to live this long, I would have taken better care of myself.'"

Jonni Levas lives with her sister on the New Jersey side of the Philadelphia area. She turned sixty in 2016. She and Seuling shared a birthday, January 20, so she thinks of him that day more than any other. Her greatest pride is her daughter, who has completed a doctorate. She has come to terms with her life in comics to the point that she can talk about it, but some wounds are deep. "I think a lot of me is still back in 1985," she said.

My final interview with Bickel was the evening before the Jeff Smith signing. We sat behind the counter and I went through a list of follow-up questions.

Every few minutes, the other employees would all be busy, so he would get up to help a customer or to answer the phone. I asked him if there was a moral to the story.

"When I was a kid, I always said I was going to retire with a used book-store because there's nothing to me more enjoyable than sharing a really good book," he said. "At the time there weren't any comic book stores." He wanted to do this at retirement because he couldn't imagine anyone earning a living from recommending books. Through ups and downs, he found a way to do just that.

"There's nothing better than when someone says, 'I'm looking for some-thing new to read,'" he said.

Part 2

Notable Comic Shops of the United States and Canada

When I am visiting a new city, I often look for the nearest comic shop. Sometimes I find a business that appears on "best of" lists and has an owner reputed for his or her thoughts on all things comics. Other times the shop is a mess of back-issue boxes with a cranky guy behind the counter and a whiff of cat pee. Either way, I'm in my glory.

What follows in chapters 15 through 20 are brief biographies of forty-three notable stores in the United States and Canada. In my interviews for this book, I asked each person to name a few favorite shops. Then I added some shops I already knew and admired. (You can find a complete alphabetical list of the forty-three stores on page 241, and all of them also appear in the index.) My aim is to show the people behind the businesses, especially the ones who informed my research on the first part of this book but may not be prominently featured there. Inevitably, however, there are some great stores that I missed.

I did most of the reporting by traveling to visit the stores and interviewing the owners and managers. In some cases, when it was unavoidable, I did reporting by phone and e-mail, sometimes supplemented with work by colleagues who went to the stores.

One recurring theme is the way the best stores support comics creators. To help show this, I asked writers and artists (and one retailer) to comment about certain stores. Their responses appear throughout this section.

In my travels, I walked a lot, sweated a lot, and got lost on public transit more than once. Some of my favorite shops were ones that were new to me, such as Green Brain Comics in Dearborn, Michigan, and Aw Yeah Comics in Muncie, Indiana. I was happy to see how well my local shop, The Laughing Ogre, stacked up against its peers. And I could not help but buy something at just about every stop, including a stack of DC Comics reprint digests, the latest issue of *King-Cat Comics,* and, amazingly, a pack of trading cards featuring the sci-fi artwork of the French artist Moebius. The last, from Floating World Comics in Portland, Oregon, was so great and weird that I couldn't believe what I was seeing.

15

"All of the Above" Stores

SOME COMIC shops aim for the traditional audience of superhero fans, who tend to be male and skew toward middle age. Others put an emphasis on independent publishers and art books. Their audience tends to be younger, with more of a gender mix. And then there are stores that seek to appeal to everyone, the types of places you can bring your mother, your daughter, and the crustiest comic fan you know. The degree of difficulty is high, but when the stores succeed, the results are sublime.

Aw Yeah Comics

107 N. High Street
Muncie, Indiana

If anyone wants to know how to run a successful comic shop in a small city, go to Muncie and pay close attention to Christina Blanch. Her store has built an audience by turning people into fans and by meeting the needs of existing fans. The staff has a knack for identifying good comics and selling the heck out of them.

"This is the comic shop that I want to shop in," Blanch said. "We have something for everybody. There's no negativity."

Aw Yeah Comics in Muncie, Indiana.

She opened the store in 2015 with business partner Mark Waid, an acclaimed comics writer who was her boyfriend at the time. They have since broken up, and Blanch became the sole owner. Waid was not a full-time presence at Aw Yeah, so his departure doesn't seem to have changed much about how the store runs.

Blanch gave me a tour of the two-story, century-old space. The area near the front entrance is books and other items that may appeal to the general public, such as movie and television adaptations and *Star Wars* merchandise. The middle area is designed for the regulars, with racks of comics and books. In the back is the kids' section, with a big sofa and chairs, and comics, books, and toys intended for all ages.

"Every time that a kid comes in here, they leave with a comic book," she said. She means this literally. There is a stack of comics for children, including extras from Free Comic Book Day and overstock. Every kid gets one.

Upstairs is the store's event space, which was being renovated when I was there. The second floor is mostly open, but also has boxes of back issues and shelves of discount books. I spotted a stack of DC digest-size paperbacks and had to stop the tour to go through all of them. Among my finds: a digest with reprints featuring the Justice Society of America, the 1940s superhero team that inspired the Justice League and many others.

The store has a loose affiliation with two other Aw Yeah Comics stores, one in Skokie, Illinois, and one just north of New York City. The name comes from an all-ages comic whose creators, Art Baltazar and Franco Aureliani, are among the co-owners of the Illinois and New York stores. The Muncie store has an indoor mural painted by Baltazar, showing the cartoon animals that populate the comic.

Blanch came to Muncie in 2000 to attend Ball State University and never left. She grew up in the Indianapolis area, which is about an hour's drive southwest. Outside of her work at the store, she is finishing her dissertation in education, raising a teenage daughter, and occasionally writing comics. She is a regular on comic convention panels, talking about the intersection of comics and pop culture. She and Waid became comics retailers in 2013 when they bought into an existing store in town, Alter Ego Comics, that had run into financial problems. In 2015, they closed that store and then opened Aw Yeah in a different location.

Muncie, with about seventy thousand people, has some familiar markings of an industrial city that long ago lost its industry: vacant or underused factories and empty storefronts. And yet, when you stand outside Aw Yeah, downtown looks vital. The shop's immediate neighbors include Savage's, a bar and restaurant, and Dan's Downtown Records. This cluster of businesses is part of an attempt to revitalize a central business district that has struggled for decades.

Because of the location, Aw Yeah gets foot traffic from people who aren't comics fans. Blanch and her staff have managed to turn casual visitors into comics readers, and they have helped build audiences for small-press comics that would go virtually unnoticed in most shops.

One such title is *Squarriors,* a postapocalyptic story about warring clans of small animals such as squirrels, published by Devil's Due Entertainment. The store's assistant manager, Kyle Roberts, liked the comic and promoted it relentlessly.

"We have this tiny little book and it's a huge seller in our store," Blanch said. "It's kind of just amazing."

Big Planet Comics

4849 Cordell Avenue
Bethesda, Maryland
(one of several locations)

Most of the people who walk in the door of this suburban shop probably do not know that the man behind the counter has been a part of comics retail almost since its dawn. While many of his contemporaries have retired or moved behind the scenes, Joel Pollack is still the guy at the register. His prominence is partly because of his love of the business and partly due to necessity. Rents in this part of the Washington, D.C., metro area have risen so high that he and his longtime business partner have cut costs by working nearly all of the hours themselves.

Pollack is the founder of the Big Planet chain, which has grown to become a group of four stores throughout the region. The other three are now owned by other people, all of whom got their start with Pollack in one way or another. The stores share a logo and a website, but each location has its own personality. The Bethesda store is about eleven hundred square feet. It is located in the community's old downtown, a walkable area with restaurants, coffee shops, and apartments.

"Sales are pretty strong right now, but the big problem is there's such a massive number of titles being published," Pollack said. "There are few really big titles and lots of niche titles."

He was born in 1949 and grew up in the Washington area reading comics. An aunt who lived in Manhattan knew one of the staff members at DC Comics, and because of this, Pollack got to visit the DC offices as a child and met some of the creators. If he wasn't hooked already, he was hooked then. His favorite artist was Carmine Infantino, known for *The Flash* and *Batman*, and later the company's president.

Pollack wanted to draw comics himself. He had illustrations published in fanzines and other places. But he realized he didn't have the chops to make a living with his art. He tells a story about being in line at a convention with his portfolio and comparing his art samples to those of the next guy in line. Pollack saw that his work wasn't good enough. That other guy was Howard Chaykin, who would become one of the top artists in the business.

Joel Pollack.

Pollack attended Phil Seuling's first New York comic convention in 1968 and later became a dealer at local conventions, buying and selling comics and original comic art. He did this while working a day job at his father's drapery business.

By the mid-1980s, the nation's comics business had grown to the point that Pollack decided the time was right to open his own store. Big Planet Comics started in 1986, not far from the current location. Pollack got involved in national retailer organizations and became part of a core of store owners who traded ideas.

In the 1990s, he was one of the first comics retailers to focus more on comics in book form and deemphasize back issues. Books had more appeal to women and other audiences that were less likely to be hardcore fans. One of the best sellers for him and many others was *Sandman*, written by Neil Gaiman, whose collected editions helped solidify the book side of comics as a viable format.

Today, Big Planet's Bethesda store is more of a book shop than a comic shop. This has its pluses and minuses. Pollack has been frustrated that comics publishers are collecting nearly everything in book form, a switch from a time when only the best work, or work likely to be popular, got released in book form. So, while he would like to stock most new books, and used to be able to do so, he has to be much more selective in his ordering.

On the day I was there, Pollack did a brisk business. A student from nearby American University came in and signed up for a pull list, which means the store will order and hold specific periodical titles for that customer. Also, a man came in with his young daughter and was excited to see a new Bone book from Jeff Smith, *Bone: Coda*. He bought the book and talked with Pollack about their shared fondness for Smith's work.

It was just another Tuesday for Pollack, a man who has been behind the counter for thirty years, and has been part of the world of comics for as long as he can remember.

Challengers Comics and Conversation

1845 N. Western Avenue
Chicago, Illinois

The tables and overstuffed chairs at Challengers Comics and Conversation are supposed to tell you something about the store. At least that is the intent at this place, where the owners sweat just about every detail.

"We want people to have a chance to browse and look at the books they like, rather than being rushed out of the store in a this-is-not-a-library sort of way," said W. Dal Bush, a co-owner. "You really need to create a space that people feel like they can enjoy, basically. Just enjoy being in the shop."

Bush and his business partner, Patrick Brower, opened in 2008. They had met as coworkers at Graham Crackers Comics, a chain in the Chicago area, and both had become store managers at the time they left to start their own business. They obtained a bank loan right before the economic downturn led to a seizing up of the financial system. So they had financing but were opening at a time when consumer spending was way down.

They found a space in a new building on Western Avenue at the edge of the increasingly affluent Wicker Park neighborhood. There they built a store that emphasizes simple design, with a red-and-white color scheme, wide aisles, and bright lighting. One of the co-owners is there almost every hour the store

Challengers Comics and Conversation, Chicago.

is open, and they are recognizable for their uniform of dark suits, dark shirts, and ties. The rest of the staff are part-timers, and mostly suit-free.

The store has given Bush and Brower the chance to put into effect the ideas they had talked about for years but felt they could not do at Graham Crackers. For example, Challengers puts almost no emphasis on collectible back issues. The few back issues in the place sell for $1 each. The store's focus is on new comics, collected editions, and art prints. Displays put an emphasis on books that are accessible to a broad audience, rather than catering just to superhero fans.

"If someone comes in and says, 'I haven't read anything. What's good?,' something on this table is bound to be for them," Bush said, referring to the table near the entrance.

Among the books on display there: DC's *Prez,* a satire about a teenage president of the United States; and Image's *Paper Girls,* a science fiction story that follows teenage newspaper carriers in the 1980s. The owners also place an emphasis on local creators. Among the people featured when I was there was Lucy Knisley, who writes and draws autobiographical comics.

Challengers has earned a loyal following in the competitive Chicago market and has a shelf full of local and national awards. And yet the business is still finding its way financially. Sales growth has been constrained by the neighborhood-centric nature of the Chicago comics scene, in which many customers shop at the nearest store rather than traveling across the city, Bush said.

His hope is that the store will continue to build an audience to the point that the owners can take a breath and make plans for the long term. For many successful comic shops, that means the owners can step back from day-to-day operations. When asked if that's his goal, Bush said, "We don't want to be those guys who are working in a store until they die."

Lucy Knisley on Challengers:

Challengers is the coolest place, and best comic shop. They cultivate a relationship with readers and creators that I've never seen in another shop. I've spent many hours as both a customer and an author at Challengers, signing and browsing and chatting with Patrick and Dal. I bring every comics colleague from out of town to the store for a visit, to sign their amazing art wall and meet Patrick and Dal and the awesome staff. When I was a week overdue to deliver my son in the middle of last summer, I waddled the mile and a half from my house to the store, where they gave me comic recommendations to survive the end of pregnancy, and water to survive the walk back. I'm so glad to live so close to this store, and to know the staff so well.

Lucy Knisley is a cartoonist whose books include Relish: My Life in the Kitchen *and* Something New.

Comicopia
464 Commonwealth Avenue #13
Boston, Massachusetts

With four employees and less than a thousand square feet, Comicopia is a wonder, an uncluttered shop with a huge selection in a tight space. But you have to work to find it. The business has an inconspicuous storefront on the ground level of a grand old residential building.

The manga section at Comicopia in Boston.

The location, on Commonwealth Avenue in Boston's Back Bay neighborhood, is in a high-rent district right next to an astronomical-rent district. Owner Matt Lehman likely would be priced out, except that he bought the store's real estate back when prices were within reach. Later he bought an efficiency apartment in the building, which also functions as overflow storage for the store.

"People joke about having a Bat-Pole," he said, a reference to the fireman's pole that connected Wayne Manor to the Batcave on the 1960s *Batman* television show. "That would be logistically infeasible and probably illegal."

He came to the Boston area in the early 1980s to attend MIT, where he studied math. He had grown up on Long Island reading DC Comics and remained a devoted fan. After college, in 1986, he got a job at New England Comics, a chain of shops in the Boston area.

He became a manager and met a fellow employee who would become his business partner. The partners opened their own store in 1989 in Brookline, an inner-ring suburb. They moved to the current location, a snug nine hundred square feet, in 1991.

Almost immediately, Comicopia got a reputation for being one of the best, which Lehman sees as a bit of happenstance. The *Comics Journal* had a report in July 1992 about the top ten shops in North America, based on a reader survey.[1] To Lehman's surprise, his store was on the list, even though his business was relatively new. He suspects that voting was light, especially for the stores near the bottom of the top ten, but he's not complaining. Or maybe he's just being modest.

Comicopia has a broad selection of mainstream and small-press titles. If the store has a specialty, it is Japanese comics, or manga, which take up several large bookcases. Lehman nurtured his audience for manga by learning the material well enough to attract existing fans and help develop new ones.

He has help these days from Morgana Hartman, whose title is "manga maven." Yes, it says that on her business cards. She consults with Lehman on ordering, and sets up displays such as the shelf labeled "Manga for people who hate manga."

She thinks many comic shops have untapped audiences for Japanese comics that have been translated into English. "They don't stock the product and they don't know the product," she said.

Comicopia has tapped the audience to a notable extent. Manga is about 20 percent of the store's sales. From just one small location, the store has become the second-largest comic shop account in the country for Viz Media, a leading manga publisher, according to Lehman. The largest is Midtown Comics in New York and online, which is the country's largest seller of new comics.

Lehman, now the sole owner after buying out his partner, says he continues to enjoy the work of running the store. His greatest disappointment is that many mainstream comics and their publishers seem to have lost much of what made him a fan. He is tired of publishing stunts, such as the way Marvel seems to kill a major character every few months simply to goose sales, with little doubt that the character will return after a brief hiatus.

"I'm pretty jaded about a lot of stuff, especially a lot of superhero stuff," he said. "More and more these days it's became transparent that it's just a bunch of cogs to [Marvel and DC]. It's just intellectual property for them to generate the real revenue, which is TV and movies and licensing."

That said, he continues to be excited about the comics coming out from many other publishers. This includes hits, such as Image's *Saga*, and many smaller titles that he is happy to put into the hands of readers.

Comix Experience
305 Divisadero Street
San Francisco, California

First, Brian Hibbs is a comic shop owner with two stores in one of the most competitive markets in the country. Second, he is a columnist who writes about the industry with a refreshing lack of regard for pissing off the powerful. The column is a side gig, but it has made him a celebrity among retailers, most of whom have never walked up the hills of San Francisco to his main store on Divisadero Street.

"The only reason people know about my store is I have a column and I'm a loudmouth," he said, interviewed in the cluttered back room that serves as his office. He has long hair and a scruffy beard.

His storefront is small enough to be easy to miss if you're not looking for it. Out front are display windows with neon signs of the logos for Superman, Batman, and Green Lantern, all DC Comics characters. Already, a visitor can tell that Hibbs is an old-school DC guy, which helps explain the intensity of his disappointment over the company's many misfires.

Comix Experience in San Francisco.

The store is small, with about sixteen hundred square feet open to the public. It is brightly lit and has wide-open sight lines to the displays of books and comics. This is a neighborhood store. The staff knows its regulars well enough to hand-sell a new series that deserves support. That is what happened with *Sandman,* a DC series that started a few months before Comix Experience opened in 1989. It was written by a then-unknown Neil Gaiman, and it became a hit, thanks to its own quality and the efforts of stores such as Comix Experience.

Hibbs did the same thing with *Saga,* which is his current top seller. "We looked at *Saga* and said, 'Holy shit, this comic is fucking great,' and we hand-sold it," he said.

In 2013, Comix Experience became a two-store operation with the purchase of Comic Outpost, a shop on the southwest side of San Francisco near the border with San Mateo County. Hibbs changed the name to Comix Experience Outpost, but left the store's character mostly intact. Unlike the flagship store, which has almost no back issues, old comics are a focal point at the Outpost.

Hibbs was born in Columbia, Missouri, a college town, and grew up in Brooklyn and then in San Francisco. Starting in his late teens, he worked at Best of Two Worlds, a shop owned by longtime Bay Area retailer Robert Beerbohm. Hibbs was just twenty-one when he opened Comix Experience.

"I couldn't have fallen backwards into a better time to open up," he said.

Any youthful inexperience was mitigated by good luck with market timing. He opened in April 1989, a few months before the *Batman* movie led to a boom in interest in the character and other comics. His business grew, and he got a side gig in 1992 writing a monthly column for *Comics Retailer,* a trade magazine aimed at his peers.

The column, titled Tilting at Windmills, followed an essay he wrote for the magazine in September 1991 about ethics among comics retailers. It began with this:

> From numerous conversations in the aisles of San Diego, messages on computer networks across the country, and letters and articles in the pages of many of the industry magazine forums, it is obvious to me that both the industry and medium of comics are presently at an ethical crossroads. Most of the concern comes from ethical questions (not necessarily stated) about the nature of comic book speculation and pricing. From my particular vantage as a retailer,

I can see several ways that the retail community can take positive steps to expand the consciousness of the medium as a whole.[2]

His voice here is demure compared to what would follow in later years, but the subject matter would come up frequently: the way the comics industry can prey upon buyers' desire to spend money on something they think will appreciate in value, even if there is little evidence that the item in question will become rare enough to be sold for a premium. His main example in the first column was *Spider-Man* #1, published in 1990. The comic was sometimes called the "adjective-less" *Spider-Man* because it was joining three other ongoing titles featuring the character, *Amazing Spider-Man, Spectacular Spider-Man,* and *Web of Spider-Man.* It sold more than two million copies, which was huge for the time. The large number of copies would imply plenty of supply to meet demand, and therefore little chance of the comic rising in value. But that's not what happened. Soon after the release date, some shops were selling the comic for $5 to $10 per copy, and many customers were willing to pay it. The whole thing made Hibbs feel sick.

"Capitalism does not have to be rapacious," he wrote in the 1991 essay. "I freely admit that I want as much of my customers' money as I possibly can get, but I want to know that they received value in exchange. This is why they continue to give me their business."

His column ran in *Comics Retailer,* followed by its successor publication, *Comics & Games Retailer,* and then several websites. It now appears at ComicsBeat.com. In his writing, he reserves his most withering scorn for the publishers. This is on display in a column from March 2016 where he discusses DC's just-announced "Rebirth" initiative. He proceeds to list seven reasons that the plan was unlikely to succeed, while also giving the company credit for at least trying. He reserves his most scathing comments for DC's main competitor, Marvel.

"But Marvel doesn't, as far as I can possibly tell, give a crap about their customers, or their needs," he writes. "And this really discourages me. All I can figure is that they think that if they've got nearly 50 percent market share, then they're doing everything correctly, and can't do any better. . . . Even if you think that you're doing everything right, there's an enormous amount of hubris in thinking you can't do better—in not wanting to learn from the people who are on the front lines who are the ones dealing with, day-to-day, your customers."[3]

Heroes Aren't Hard to Find

417 Pecan Avenue
Charlotte, North Carolina

Near the end of 2017, Shelton Drum could relax at last. He had made it through a transformative year for his shop, Heroes Aren't Hard to Find, moving from his longtime rented location to a nearby building he had bought, and surviving a turbulent stretch in the comics market.

The ups and downs in the market were nothing new for him, but the relocation was a risk. Yet he pulled it off with aplomb, making the new space look and feel enough like the old one that his longtime customers still felt at home.

"It's so comfortable," he said. "We're enjoying it so much. By buying the building, we have so much more security and less stress."

The new location is a little smaller than the old one, about 2,000 square feet instead of 2,400. It helps that the basic setup is almost the same, and some familiar decorations from the old store—such as the life-size Spider-Man and Doctor Octopus hanging from the ceiling—have been installed in the new one.

This is a happy chapter in what has been an eventful life in the comics business. Drum began selling comics in 1974, buying space at a twice-monthly flea market. The rent was $40 per month. If you liberally assume another $10 in expenses, he was looking at an outlay of $50.

He started by selling from his own collection, and later new comics he bought from a distributor. He developed a network of regular customers who depended on him. Then he got more involved in comics in 1977 by helping organize a small convention. All of that was a prelude to his first retail storefront, which he rented in 1980, a space the size of a closet that he got for $75 per month.

"The door was literally not wide enough to walk through with a comic box," Drum said.

He was far from an instant success. Sometime in those early years (he thinks it was 1982 or 1983), he was behind his counter when a man came in waving a knife and demanded cash. Drum reached down to the cardboard box that held the cash and handed over the full amount: $62. The man was soon caught by police and the money was returned. The part that makes Drum laugh is the dollar figure, which was a decent day's business at the time, and seems like nothing today.

The relatively new storefront of Heroes Aren't Hard to Find. *Credit: Shelton Drum.*

"There were any number of times that any intelligent person would have given it up, but I was stubborn and didn't have anything else I was passionate about doing," he said.

He also had his parents to serve as a financial safety net. "They bailed me out so many times," he said.

He was raised in Newton, North Carolina, a small town about forty miles northwest of Charlotte, and grew up around the auto-salvage yard his father owned.

"I got a feel for how to treat people from him," Drum said. "He was pretty well-loved and respected in the community."

Heroes Aren't Hard to Find provided the name and much of the organizational muscle to start Heroes Convention, which began in 1982 and has grown to become one of the top stops on the country's comic convention circuit.

The store occupies a rarefied place within the industry. Drum's peers from other shops say they look up to him. Joe Field, a longtime leader among retailers, is one. "I'd love to do what Shelton Drum does," he said. "He has one of the best setups of all in that he does a ton with back issues, and that's great because he loves that part of the business, but he also does a lot with cutting-edge indie stuff. It's a very vibrant arts community, and he's very connected."

The store also has the distinction of having employees go on to become comics professionals. Among them is Matt Fraction, who worked there in the late 1990s and has been a top-selling writer for Marvel and now Image.

By the time Fraction got a job at Heroes Aren't Hard to Find, it had already been through booms and busts. Drum had a peak of six locations in the region before the mid-1990s crash. By 1997, he had sold all but one store to other people.

Asked how he has been able to stay in business this long, Drum said, "Stubbornness. Refusing to give up."

Now he has a dedicated enough customer base that he can survive the occasional dips in the broader comics market, such as the one that hit right about the time he was moving the store in 2017.

Lately, he spends much of his time buying and selling old comics, which is the part of the business he has long enjoyed the most. He has an experienced staff that can handle most of the day-to-day issues at the store. He is so confident in his staff that he took a two-week vacation to Britain in the summer of 2018, something that would have been unheard of for him a decade or two ago.

He doesn't plan to retire, but can see himself making a transition to taking more time off.

"If I retire, what am I going to do? Go sell comic books?"

This is an enviable dilemma. He has spent his professional life doing the thing he would do for fun if it wasn't his job.

"I count my lucky stars every day," he said. "I've been in the business so long that I've had the opportunity to and ability to do the business that I want to do. I'm an old school comic book fan."

Matt Fraction on Heroes Aren't Hard to Find:

I think Shelton's success comes from a few things. Who he is, as a person, first of all. He loves this stuff. He loved it as a kid and he loves it now. You can still see it in his eyes. He's gregarious without being, like, obsequious. He was a pop culture curator before we knew we needed curators, and the kind of retailer that knew every customer, knew what they liked (even if *he* didn't, particularly, and that's crucial), and Shelton knew how to grow the reading world of his customers without making his store feel like a used-car lot. He not only loves comics but he loves getting people *into* comics, you know? He's not a gatekeeper. You don't have to pass a test, you don't have to win a trivia contest, you don't have to have any bona fides to be welcomed at Heroes Aren't Hard to Find. He's the opposite of Comic Book Guy on *The Simpsons,* from stem to stern. And he's been at it now so long his customers have kids and even some of those kids have kids and he's making sure that comics pass generation to generation like a genetic trait.

Also he's indefatigable. And he always has been.

This is also the same stuff that makes Heroes Aren't Hard to Find a good store. Shelton is what makes HAHTF a good store. And he brings people in that, like him, share love and zeal for the art form and medium and can help spread the gospel.

Matt Fraction is a prolific writer of comics. His credits include cocreations such as Casanova *and* Sex Criminals, *published by Image Comics, and mainstream titles such as* Invincible Iron Man *and* Hawkeye, *published by Marvel.*

Packrat Comics

3872 Lattimer Street
Hilliard, Ohio
(second location in Marysville, Ohio)

Every time I go to Packrat Comics, it seems to get bigger. This shop in the Columbus suburbs has an ever-expanding mix of comics and games, and a well-stocked children's section. The store is now about 6,000 square feet, which would feel vast, except that it is spread out among several rooms, including a gaming room filled with tables.

Co-owners Jamie and Teresa Colegrove have been at this since 1993, which was the same year they got married. They raised their children at the store, and one of their sons now manages a second location up the road in Marysville. All along, their top priority has been to have a shop that that appeals to the entire family. It is colorful and well-lit, with just about every detail selected to be as welcoming as possible to customers who may be new to comics.

I am far from alone in thinking Packrat is uniquely good at what it does. The store won the 2015 Will Eisner Spirit of Retailing Award, arguably the most sought-after prize in the business.

The Colegroves opened the first incarnation of Packrat in 1993 in London, Ohio, a county seat on the western fringe of the Columbus metro area.

Packrat Comics in Hilliard, Ohio.

"Our first building got condemned, so we had to move overnight," Jamie said.

They took a break from the business from about 2000 to 2003 and then reopened in Hilliard, the suburb where they had long lived. They have been together, in business and in life, for so long that they can't imagine it any other way.

"I would be weird not working with her," Jamie said.

Teresa quickly added, "It's weird when he's not here. I miss him a lot when we're not working together."

Vault of Midnight

219 S. Main St.
Ann Arbor, Michigan
(two other locations)

If only every college town—or every town for that matter—had a comic shop like Vault of Midnight, located in downtown Ann Arbor. With an inviting layout and a loyal following, the store's three co-owners have hit upon a way to do comics retail that clearly works.

The business started in 1996 with the comics collections of its founders, Steve Fodale and Curtis Sullivan. They started small at a time when comics retail was

Vault of Midnight in Ann Arbor, Michigan.

struggling, but they had the advantage of fresh energy at a time when many competitors were under duress. The business grew and moved around within Ann Arbor. Along the way, one of the employees, Nick Yribar, became a partner in the business, and those same three co-owners remain in charge today.

Vault of Midnight now has three stores: Ann Arbor, Detroit, and Grand Rapids. I'm going to focus here on the flagship in Ann Arbor, which has been at the current storefront since 2006.

Ann Arbor is an affluent college city, with much of its economy tied to the University of Michigan. It's a great market for comics. Vault of Midnight has enough of a core audience of comics fans that the store might not need to try that hard to appeal to the general public. What makes this store special is how effectively its owners have set up their space to be an enticing entry point for people who are not already fans.

"We want folks who don't read comics to read comics," Yribar said, interviewed alongside Sullivan at the store. "Nothing is more important than that."

First, the location: The Ann Arbor store is in the heart of downtown, a short walk from the city's famed Literati Bookstore and surrounded by restaurants, bars, and boutique retail. The location has much higher rent than if it were in a strip mall at the edge of town, but the benefit is the constant foot traffic, which provides a steady supply of people who don't ordinarily read comics or are lapsed comics fans.

When you walk in the front door, there is a display of geek-centric T-shirts and tables with an array of comics in book form, selected to appeal to the general public. This often leans heavily on indie publishers and material aimed at younger readers, along with a few mainstream titles.

The store has one of the largest book-of-the-month programs I've seen. When I was there, the book was *The Prince and the Dressmaker* by Jen Wang, the story of a prince who has a secret life as a dress-wearing fashion icon, and his friendship with the dressmaker who knows his secret. This book gives a good idea of the owners' approach to selecting the book of the month. They want something that is a good read, appeals to a broad audience, and might not be noticed by many customers if not for this special promotion.

And the promotion is substantial. The store sells the book at a discount, has prominent displays at each location, and holds at least one event to support the book. It is not unusual for Vault of Midnight to sell several hundred copies during the month, which is a remarkably high number.

While the owners spend much of their time and energy trying to attract new fans, the core of the store's success is the way it holds onto its most devoted customers. The Ann Arbor store has about 1,000 customers who have a pull list, meaning they have a list of comics that the store sets aside so that the customers don't miss a single issue. The pull list customers do much more than pick up the comics they ordered. This audience includes the most prolific buyers of comics in book form, and of comics that are not on their pull lists. Every new periodical comic is bagged and boarded, so a customer can't take it down from the shelf and look through the pages. I've seen this in other stores, but usually only in ones that cater to hardcore collectors, which is not the vibe at this store.

Sullivan tells me this is because he and the other co-owners want to make sure that the comics stay in good condition.

"The comic books get really, really dogeared when they sit on the shelves," he said. "They're resealable and we encourage people to open the books. They are in no way intended to keep people out of the books."

Also, he notes that the store gives away the bag and board with each comic. Many other stores charge for this. I suspect that this practice is popular with customers who are existing fans, who would be buying bags and boards anyway.

Vault of Midnight also is a board game store. This is a growing part of the business, which is now about 30 percent of sales. There is an existing crossover between comics and board game customers, which makes games a natural fit. There is cross-pollination, with some customers coming in to look at games and stopping to check out comics.

The owners know what they're up against, competing with Amazon and persevering in a climate that is challenging for stores with physical locations. This is one of the best stores I've seen for having a coherent vision for the future and an ability to execute the vision. The key is attracting new customers and making the store a destination.

"The shop has to be clean and bright and welcoming," Sullivan said. "No dead bugs in the window."

ALSO IN THIS CATEGORY:

Alternate Reality

4110 S. Maryland Parkway
Las Vegas, Nevada

Three miles east of the Las Vegas strip, in an unassuming shopping center, sits a great comic shop. Alternate Reality has been in the city since 1995, and its owner, Ralph Mathieu, has been in comics much longer than that. He sells mainstream comics along with a deep selection of manga, minicomics, and European titles.

Ryan Claytor on Alternate Reality:

> Alternate Reality's store image is immaculately kept. It's one of the (very few) stores my wife will request we visit. Patrons are greeted with organized areas, constantly curated shelves, and a clean, welcoming aesthetic. Last but not least, Ralph Mathieu is one of the nicest guys I've had the pleasure of meeting.
>
> He also supports local artists by designating a section of his store as an art gallery and signing space. Beyond the gallery, which regularly rotates artist exhibitions, the remaining walls of Alternate

Reality serve as a more permanent display for Ralph's extensive personal original art collection, including work by heavy hitters such as Dan Clowes, Tony Harris, and J. H. Williams III, to name but a few.

Ryan Claytor is the cartoonist and publisher behind Elephant Eater Comics. He teaches comics and visual narrative courses at Michigan State University.

Casablanca Comics

151 Middle St.
Portland, Maine
(one other location)

Years ago, I came upon Casablanca Comics by accident during a trip to Portland, Maine. It was the stuff of fantasy for a comic book reader, walking around in an unfamiliar city and finding a great shop right in the middle of a random downtown block. Casablanca Comics has now been open for more than thirty years, with more than twenty years in the same downtown Portland building. It is a linchpin of the Portland-area comics scene, including owner Rick Lowell's work as an organizer of the annual Maine Comics Arts Festival.

"We have worked hard to have a carefully curated store that is accessible to new readers as well as longtime fans," Lowell said. "We are purely comics with very little other merchandise. We don't carry games, toys, cards."

In 2018, the store relocated within its building, moving to a larger basement space that was open because a Videoport, a beloved video store, had closed. The location is in Portland's Old Port shopping district, which has become a hub for high-end retail. A second Casablanca location is in Windham, just outside Portland.

Lowell often gets asked about the origins of the store's name. His answer is succinct: "It's Rick's place," a reference to Rick's Cafe in the movie Casablanca.

Cosmic Monkey Comics

5335 N.E. Sandy Boulevard
Portland, Oregon

In a city rich with comic shops, this is the favorite of many residents. Cosmic Monkey epitomizes the idea of an "all of the above" store, with big selections of new comics, books, minicomics, and back issues. A well-stocked children's section is right inside the front door. Old hardwood floors in the front of the store help make the place feel like it has been around a while, but Cosmic Monkey opened in 2003 and has been in its current space in the Hollywood neighborhood since 2006. Although it is not a comics–coffee combo shop, it may feel that way, with the popular Case Study Coffee just a few steps away in the same retail complex.

Happy Harbor Comics

10729 104 Ave N.W.
Edmonton, Alberta

It is not unusual to see an artist drawing comic book pages during store hours at Happy Harbor Comics. The store has an artist-in-residence program that selects creators and then pays them for thirty-two-week stints of drawing comics and engaging with the public. The program is one of many things Happy Harbor does to nourish the local comics scene. The store, in its current location since 2011, is on the large side, with more than seven hundred slots for new periodical comics and a deep selection of graphic novels. "The goal is to be bright, clean, and accessible," said owner Jay Bardyla.

The Laughing Ogre

4258 N. High Street
Columbus, Ohio

Jeff Smith on The Laughing Ogre manager Gib Bickel:

He's just friendly. You just want to be his friend. I think a lot of people feel that way when they go to the store. . . . He's a real proponent of comics as an art form, of comics creators as authors. But he also loves the Hulk and Spider-Man, just like he's a big kid.

Jeff Smith is a Columbus-based cartoonist best known for Bone. *He is president and artistic director of Cartoon Crossroads Columbus, or CXC, an annual celebration of cartoon arts.*

Star Clipper

1319 Washington Avenue
St. Louis, Missouri

Star Clipper is a store that died and came back. The business was a St. Louis mainstay, opening in 1988 and then closing in 2015. The co-owners of another area business, Fantasy Books, stepped in to buy some of the assets and offer jobs to the employees. The result is the new Star Clipper in a different location. The store retains much of the welcoming vibe of the predecessor. "We actively try to dispel the stereotypes so often associated with comic shops," said Keya Matanagh, the store manager. "There is no boys' club atmosphere here." But the new store is more than just a copy of the original. For example, it has added board games and role-playing games, which are a small but growing part of the sales mix.

Strange Adventures

5110 Prince Street
Halifax, Nova Scotia
(one of three locations)

Calum Johnston has worked for more than two decades to build his stores into a destination for locals and visitors to this part of Atlantic Canada. The flagship location in downtown Halifax is on the ground floor of a stone building built in 1820. "Our aim is to share the comic book love," Johnston said. "The more folks reading and enjoying comics, the better it is for the industry as a whole from retailers to suppliers to creators and customers." In interviews with Canadian comic creators, this store, along with the Beguiling in Toronto, were the two that elicited the most unsolicited praise. People adore this place, for its deep selection and helpful employees, and for its location, just a short walk from the Atlantic Ocean.

16

Comics Galleries

I WANT to roll my eyes when a comic shop uses the word "curated" to describe its selection. After all, any decent retailer is going to put thought into what to sell and how to sell it. And yet, "curated" is an accurate way to describe the layouts at the following stores. Each of them feels a bit like an art gallery, emphasizing small-press material and art prints. A hand-stapled minicomic is as likely to get shelf space as prominent as *Batman*. Mainstream titles are on the shelves and are a key part of the businesses, but they often are not where the owners' hearts are.

I'm calling this subset of stores "comics galleries," because their look and feel are often more like a gallery or a museum store than a typical comic shop. They are passion projects by owner-operators, and places where the enthusiasm can be infectious.

Books with Pictures

1100 S.E. Division St. #103
Portland, Oregon

The newest store to be featured in these pages, Books with Pictures is tapping into and contributing to the growing popularity of comics for audiences

Books with Pictures in Portland, Oregon.

outside the traditional core of white men. It is doing so in a city already rich with great comic shops.

Katie Proctor opened the store in May 2016. She was a comics fan who had worked as a tech consultant and dreamed up the idea of opening the kind of shop that she thought was missing from the market.

"We needed a store that was not just welcoming to everyone but was explicitly open to everyone," she said.

The store got off to a rollicking start with an opening-day signing by married comics writers Kelly Sue DeConnick and Matt Fraction. The place's identity was close to fully formed from the start, with comfortable seating and an inviting children's section.

Books with Pictures is located on the east side of the Willamette River, near the border between Ladd's Addition, a residential area, and a riverside industrial district. The building, a former auto service garage, has high ceilings and about 1,000 square feet open to the public.

The store is set up to appeal to everyone and gets a lot of customers who are new to comics or have never been in a comic shop.

"I have a lot of customers who are women in their fifties and their sixties and I don't think a lot of shops can say that," Proctor said. "They're really fun to sell Bitch Planet to."

Bitch Planet is the critically lauded series from Image Comics, created by DeConnick and artist Valentine De Landro. It's a science fiction story about women who are sent to an off-planet prison because authorities have deemed them "noncompliant."

"Your grandma would love Bitch Planet," Proctor said.

Alissa Sallah on Books with Pictures:

Books with Pictures is a prime example of the evolution of comic stores. It casts a wide net in genre, format, and style of comic throughout the store. Most importantly, its focus is on opening the door for new readers. For a medium to grow, it needs new voices and new audiences to stay fresh. Books with Pictures offers many options for new readers of any age or experience level, and I've seen first-hand the creation of these new fans. The employees are helpful and knowledgeable about a range of comics they sell, but never talk down to anyone. This is the key to which shops do the best in my experience, the ones that make comics as a whole seem like a fun new adventure for anyone.

Alissa Sallah is a comics artist and a recent former employee at Books with Pictures. She previously worked at The Laughing Ogre in Columbus.

Desert Island

540 Metropolitan Avenue
Brooklyn, New York

The largest sign on this storefront still has the name of the business that used to be there: "Sparacino's Bakery: Italian French Sicilian Bread." When Gabe Fowler rented the space, he added "and Comic Booklets" to the sign.

Desert Island in Brooklyn.

The sign, which has gone through several permutations since then—the "comic booklets" part is no longer there—is one indication of the playful vibe at Desert Island. Another is the ever-changing display in the front window. When I was there, a red papier-mâché dragon was menacing a diorama of a medieval town.

I visited the store on a hot and muggy July afternoon. Fowler is behind the counter most days, but wasn't there on the day I was in town, so we traded questions and answers later via e-mail.

"We aim to knock you out with unexpected discoveries and associations between very different varieties of comics, art books, zines, and printed ephemera," he said.

When he opened Desert Island in 2008, he sought to combine the qualities of two stores: Printed Matter in Manhattan, a nonprofit bookstore that specializes in publications made by artists, and Quimby's Bookstore in Chicago, a shop that specializes in small-press comics and art books. (Since my visit, the founding owner of Quimby's opened a Quimby's location next door to Desert Island, a move made with Fowler's blessing.)

Desert Island has a snug 380 square feet open to the public, but it doesn't feel cramped. A half-dozen customers were there with me, spread out among a rack of new comics, tables and shelves with books, and a spinner rack with minicomics. Fowler stocks a wide array of zines, minicomics, prints, and other self-published items, usually on a consignment basis to start. Any artist can submit work.

Desert Island also is a publisher. It has a free quarterly comic anthology called *Smoke Signal,* which Fowler describes as a "sampler of cutting-edge comics and art." And that's just one part of Fowler's work beyond running the shop. He has been an organizer of comics festivals, such as Brooklyn Comics and Graphics Festival and then Comic Arts Brooklyn. As of 2016, the latter is one of the major stops on the festival circuit for independent comics, drawing top artists from around the world.

Floating World Comics

400 N.W. Couch Street
Portland, Oregon

In a region dotted with comic book shops, Jason Leivian couldn't find one that matched what he wanted. He took this as the sign he needed to open a business. More than a decade later, he has built Floating World Comics into a destination for independent publishers and art books, which he sells alongside new releases from major publishers.

It wasn't easy. He was in his midtwenties when he began the business in a studio at an artists' co-op space. Start-up costs were about $12,000. He took his promotional tips from artists and musicians, and he built a customer base from those communities. He moved to a storefront and then to the larger current storefront.

"For all of my twenties, I was, like, working jobs I didn't like," he said, interviewed at the store. "But once I figured out what I wanted to do, I just did it."

The shop is located just north of downtown Portland in a neighborhood called Old Chinatown, or Old Town. It shares a space with Landfill Rescue Unit, a record shop, and the combined retail space is about two thousand square feet. When you enter, the records are to the left and the children's comic section is to the right.

Floating World Comics, Portland, Oregon.

"We wanted it to be obvious and accessible," Leivian said. "Kids just make a beeline to this section."

The children's titles include many old standbys, such as *Tintin, Asterix,* and *Pippi Longstocking.* Moving into the main part of the store, the focus is on comics in book form, as opposed to periodical comics. Mainstream periodical comics—your *Batman* and *Spider-Man* floppies—are here, but you need to look for them along a side wall, and a small selection of back issues is in a back room.

One of the focal points is a table near the front, stocked with a variety of material Leivian has put there to appeal to walk-in customers. This covers some familiar titles such as *Saga* and *The Walking Dead,* and some more obscure ones, such as *Lose* by Michael Deforge and *Janus* by Lala Albert.

"If someone comes in and doesn't know anything about comics, I want them to go to this table and everything's cool," Leivian said.

Farel Dalrymple on Floating World:

Floating World is one of my favorite stores in the world and has been pretty much my main local comics shop for the past nine

years, since I moved to Portland. Jason has the best selection of stuff
I like: independent books, a lot of foreign stuff, and great art books.

He has a distinct vision and made a cool and comfortable area to
buy books. The location is convenient, right downtown, and close
to a bunch of galleries and comic book artist studios. I usually run
into a bunch of cartoonists and friends whenever I go in there.

Farel Dalrymple is a cartoonist whose books include
Pop Gun War *and* The Wrenchies.

Secret Headquarters
3817 Sunset Boulevard
Los Angeles, California

The cozy space doesn't look much like a comic shop, and that's the point.
Co-owners Dave Pifer and David Ritchie want a vibe more like a cigar store
or an old social club. They do this through attention to details such as soft
lighting, dark wood fixtures, and leather armchairs.

"You could definitely make a store look really good and be smart and be
extremely custom if you just gave a shit and put real money into the layout
and the construction. Hell, yeah," Pifer said. "I mean, think about it, bike
shops, coffee shops, clothing stores, record stores. You name nearly any other
retail industry and there's just got to be a range of styles and looks. But for
some reason, comics is almost the exact same thing no matter where."

He describes a typical comic shop this way: "No thought to lighting, wire
racks everywhere, crappy tables, white boxes everywhere, posters covering
the windows."

The co-owners met in high school in the late-1980s in the Miami suburbs
and have remained friends ever since. Ritchie was the first to move to Los
Angeles, where he worked for a small chain of skateboard shops. Pifer was
next and worked in film production. They talked about opening a business
together.

One of their friends from Florida, Tate Ottati, had started Tate's, a successful comic shop in the Fort Lauderdale area. They asked him for advice.

"I was like, 'Are you fucking nuts?'" Ottati said. He advised them that
Los Angeles had a number of established stores and competition would

Secret Headquarters in Los Angeles. *Courtesy of Secret Headquarters.*

be brutal. Later, upon seeing his friends' vision in action, he learned that there was room in the market for a small store that provided something the others didn't.

In 2005, with about $30,000 worth of financing from credit cards, Pifer and Ritchie opened Secret Headquarters in the gentrifying Silver Lake neighborhood. For about the first three years, the shop struggled to gain an audience, and Pifer worked long hours by himself. In hindsight, he can see that $30,000 was not enough and that the place needed a larger initial investment so that it had the range of products that would better attract customers. Instead, the growth was gradual, with small increases in sales that allowed the co-owners to stock more items and make improvements to the layout.

An essential ingredient for success was the neighborhood, Pifer said. The surrounding residential areas started to attract more families, and more people who were likely to want to buy comics. That said, he doesn't want to leave the impression that his customers are some kind of "hipster class," as he puts it, even though the neighborhood has a reputation as a hipster enclave. The residents are diverse in just about every way, he said.

The shelves and tables are filled with periodical comics and books, with a broader selection of zines and art books than a typical comic shop would have. At the same time, mainstream comics are an essential part of the mix.

Secret Headquarters now has six full-time employees, including the owners, plus four part-time employees. It is a destination for fans of comic shops when they are in the Los Angeles area, including several of the owners of other shops profiled in these pages. Some of those people walk away amazed by the look of the place, but question how a store with such small square footage and seemingly expensive design can make money. Pifer says the costs of having an attractive store are not prohibitive, and he wonders why more of his peers don't do it.

ALSO IN THIS CATEGORY:

Isotope Comics Lounge

326 Fell Street
San Francisco, California

James Sime has terrible timing. He opened his comic shop in San Francisco in 2001, right as the dot-com bust socked the local economy. He went into it with panache, dressed in an array of suits and athletic shoes and maintaining a handlebar mustache and super-spiky hair. And he has survived, largely because customers responded to what was a different kind of shop. He turned out to be on the leading edge of boutique-style comic retailers, which take design cues from shoe stores and art galleries. Isotope is a short walk from the center of the city, a small storefront that you might miss if you aren't looking for it.

Jamaica Dyer on Isotope:

James Sime wants you to have the best night of your life. He could be running an Italian restaurant where the waiters dance routines in between dishes, or a tiki bar with mai tais to die for, but we're lucky enough that he chose to bring his flair to comics. I've done many events at Isotope over the years, and I wish I could hire him to be my personal publicist, publisher, and ringleader. At signings, James will set you up in the center of the store, and make sure every person who wanders in—whether they came to see you or not—gets to know you with gusto, and leaves with a smile and a freshly signed book. His enthusiasm is contagious.

Jamaica Dyer is a cartoonist living in Oakland whose books include Weird Fishes, Lake Imago, *and* Mixtape.

Southern Fried Comics
136 E. Front Street
Hattiesburg, Mississippi

This small shop looks like an art gallery, with white walls and wood floors. Co-owners Jamye Foster and Barry Herring opened the place in 2010 and treat comics as art, but without being stuffy about it. "Our goal is to be inclusive, so both lifelong readers and those who are reading their first comic book feel like they belong," Jamye Foster said. "I believe what makes the store truly special is Barry's commitment to helping people find comics they will love. We have kids who have grown up at the store, and they love talking with Barry about their favorite books and characters."

Southern Fried Comics in Hattiesburg, Mississippi. *Courtesy of Barry Herring.*

17

Old School

I WISH I could go back and walk the aisles of the great comic shops that are gone, such as Comics & Comix in Berkeley, Victory Thrift in Queens, and Jim Hanley's Universe on Staten Island. The next best thing is to visit stores that retain some of the DNA of the old days. Most of the following shops have roots in the 1970s. They are the survivors of decades of booms and busts, and they have some stories to tell.

Comic World

1204 4th Ave.
Huntington, West Virginia

Kathleen Miller was eighteen years old and so nervous her legs were shaking as she signed a lease for the business she would soon name Comic World. That was in 1980 and she is still going strong today, and behind the counter for nearly all of the store's hours.

Her customers called her "The Comic Lady" and she let it stick. The nickname was because there were few women in the business of selling comics anywhere. She was the only female owner of a comic shop she knew of, and was one of the first in the country.

Kathleen Miller at Comic World in Huntington, West Virginia.

Her immediate concern was staying in business long enough to cover the one-year lease. She learned on the job and found she could make a good enough living to get a second lease.

"I feel like I've been lucky. I never dreamed I'd do this for thirty-eight years," she said, interviewed in the spring of 2018.

She has spent her entire life in Huntington, a city on the Ohio River that is home to Marshall University. Growing up, her family didn't have a television and she wasn't allowed to read comics. She read her first comics in high school, and her early favorites were Classics Illustrated.

She dropped out of high school and got married, and her husband was a comics fan. They began to amass a collection and started to sell comics at a monthly flea market. This is what led to the shop.

As with many early comic shops, her greatest competition was a local newsstand. She began to order her comics from Phil Seuling and Jonni Levas's company, Sea Gate Distributors, which gave her the advantage of getting her shipments earlier and being able to guarantee that she would have all the titles her customers wanted.

She survived the market bust of the mid-1980s largely because she rarely ordered much more than she thought her customers would buy that month. This was unlike many other retailers who stockpiled comics in the hopes of selling them for big markups, part of the boom and bust in black-and-white comics.

"I kept strict inventory," she said. "I didn't lose my shirt buying *Adolescent Black Belt Hamsters* thinking it would be the next *Teenage Mutant Ninja Turtles.*"

The business grew, and she and her husband opened three more stores in other West Virginia cities. At their peak, they had a half-dozen employees. They got divorced in the late 1980s and he took over one of the stores, which soon went out of business. She eventually closed all but the original store, which today looks much like it did then.

The store still has superhero murals that have been there for decades. Miller has resisted the urge to paint over them because longtime customers don't want to see them go. New comics and books are racked along one wall, and most of the rest of the space is taken up with back-issue boxes.

I could have spent all day going through the store's back issues, and ended up buying an old issue of DC's *Doom Patrol.* Miller's personal tastes lean heavily on some of the best mainstream comics of the 1980s, such as Frank Miller's *Daredevil,* and a large share of the back issues are from that era.

She has been sustained by a core of loyal customers mixed in with an ever-changing array of college students and others. And she has no plans to stop anytime soon.

DreamHaven Books

2301 E. 38th Street
Minneapolis, Minnesota

DreamHaven Books is the only store I have seen that feels the way people describe the earliest comic shops. It has been a reverse evolution for the store and its owner, Greg Ketter. Today, he has one location on East 38th Street, packed with loosely organized odds and ends. His back-issue comics far outnumber new comics. He has a large and deep selection of science fiction books. Comics pioneer Robert Bell, and many others of his generation, would feel at home in a store like this.

As told earlier in these pages, Ketter opened his first comic shop in 1977. At his peak in the 1990s, he had three locations. When people ask me to

DreamHaven Books in Minneapolis. *Credit: Aaron Coker.*

name my favorite comic shop, I say it is DreamHaven, circa 1995. That store had a full selection of new comics, plus shelf after shelf of alternative comics. When I was a college student, it was the place I bought my first issue of *Palookaville, Eightball, Acme Novelty Gallery,* and other titles that were part of the creative renaissance in alternative comics. Before that, the most sophisticated title I had read was *Sandman,* which felt like checkers compared to the chess that was *Acme Novelty Gallery.*

Ketter, whom I never met at the time, had set up his shop in a way that appealed to many audiences and exposed people to comics they might not otherwise have considered buying. His tastes were, and remain, impeccable.

"I always wanted to do more than just comic books, and a lot of comic stores never did. They pretty much stuck to comics," he said.

He was an early advocate of the work of Neil Gaiman, writer of DC's *Sandman* and later a best-selling fantasy book writer. Gaiman, originally from England, moved to a house a short drive from Minneapolis, and Dream-Haven became the place he bought his books and comics. Ketter formed a partnership with Gaiman as the exclusive seller of certain editions of books.

In 1997, Gaiman wrote this about the store on his blog:

> I like Greg Ketter and the staff, I love getting my books there (they
> have things I never see anywhere else that I WANT). I'm sure that
> lots of bookshops sell the *annotated archy and mehitabel,* but if I
> walk into DreamHaven something like that is the first thing I see.
> Happiness. . . . Some people think I have a stake in the shop or
> something, and I don't, other than a desire to still have it around
> as somewhere to do my shopping or to do signings or to phone
> and ask weird book-related questions. I've seen too many good
> bookshops go down in the last decade.[1]

Ketter gradually downsized his business to one location, and then briefly
closed altogether, before reopening in his current spot. His stores were hurt
by changes in their neighborhoods and by an increase in competition. One
of the competitors was Big Brain Comics, which itself has now closed. It
was owned by a former employee of Ketter's, continuing a long tradition of
comic shops helping train the people who become their rivals.

He has had a good life in the business. He has reached a point where
he sells only what he wants to sell, works only when he wants to work,
and doesn't worry too much. He chooses not to stock most new periodical
comics because he has found that there are too many titles for a small store
to be able to offer a broad selection. He focuses on comics in book form,
new and used, and continues to sell back issues from a stockpile that goes
back decades.

You can find Ketter there on most days the store is open. "I'm having so
much fun with it these days," he said.

Excalibur Comics

2444 S.E. Hawthorne Boulevard
Portland, Oregon

At Excalibur Comics, regular customers get welcomed with "Hiya, hon."
The greeter is Debbie Fagnant, the co-owner, who is often stationed at the
register near the front door. If you shop here, she probably knows your
name and your tastes in comics.

Debbie Fagnant at Excalibur Comics in Portland, Oregon.

Excalibur is the ultimate old-school store, with a large back-issue selection that takes up the center of the floor. While there, I bought DC's *Adventure Comics* #425, published in 1972. I got it for the Mike Kaluta cover of an explorer hanging from a mountain pointing a pistol at an oncoming Pegasus. The insides were pretty cool too, with the Pegasus story drawn by Alex Toth, a comics legend whose work has been used to teach drawing to the generations that followed.

Excalibur is in a residential area just east of the Willamette River, a neighborhood that exudes a kind of hip affluence, with a succession of cafes and brewpubs. "We're going through kind of a hipster shift," Fagnant said. What does she think of the changes? It's complicated. The old middle-class neighborhood has faded, subsumed by new residents and the businesses that have sprung up to serve them. And yet this has been good for Excalibur. The business has thrived, helped by the influx of people who already are comics readers and have disposable income.

The store was started in 1974 by Fagnant's parents and has been in its current location since 1983. It began with a mix of paperbacks and comics. The local news distributor provided the comics, with the option to return anything that was unsold. As the store grew and evolved, comics took up a larger share of the space, and Fagnant's parents switched to getting material from a comics distributor. They are now co-owners with her, although she is the day-to-day manager.

"There are customers who remember my sisters and I when we were knee-high to a june bug," Fagnant said. "When I have kids, they'll grow up in these aisles too."

Kurt Busiek on Excalibur:

> This has the best back issue selection in town. . . . It's become a nice ritual. Wednesday after work, we come down here to get the new comics and say hi to Debbie, [who has] beaucoup charm.

> *Kurt Busiek, who lives just outside Portland in Washington State, is a comics writer known for his past work on* Marvels *and* Avengers, *and current series such as* Kurt Busiek's Astro City *and* Autumnlands.

Mile High Comics

4600 Jason Street
Denver, Colorado
(and two other locations in the Denver area)

Mile High Comics is uncategorizable. It is, by far, the largest single-location comic shop in the country, with sixty-five thousand square feet. Owner Chuck Rozanski, who is there almost every day, is one of the pioneers of comics retail. On my first and only visit, I thought of the film *Synecdoche, New York,* about a playwright who builds a production that grows to cover several city blocks and has a narrative with no ending.

"It's a temple," said Jim Shooter, the former editor in chief of Marvel Comics and a close friend of Rozanski's.

The building is a warehouse, located in a warehouse district. The floors are concrete and the ceiling is several stories high. Despite the vast dimensions, the main entrance for customers is a single metal door.

About thirty people work for Mile High, most of them at this main store. There also are two smaller locations in the Denver area. The employees have their own lingo. The "ocean" is the term for the back-issue area that is open

Chuck Rozanski in July 2016.

to the public, as in, "I was thinking of putting these comics in the ocean." But the ocean is not even close to the largest stockpile of back issues. That is in the rear of the store in rows of high metal racks, where the bulk of the store's ten million comics are located. This area is off-limits to the public, but if you ask, an employee will look up a specific comic and retrieve it.

There are shelves full of new action figures, and display cases with vintage action figures, even though Rozanski says he doesn't like selling toys. The same cases have commemorative plates, such as one with a platinum-edged image of Lieutenant Commander Data from *Star Trek: The Next Generation,* available for $200.

At a supersize store, it makes sense to have supersize decorations. Above the shelves is a life-size X-wing from *Star Wars,* seemingly made out of cardboard. Along a side wall is a two-story-tall Sentinel, the deadly robot villain from *X-Men*—only this Sentinel is done in the style of a Lego figure.

On the day I was there, the store hosted a poker tournament, with the proceeds going to Rainbow Alley, a local community center for lesbian, gay, bisexual, transgender, and queer teens. In recent years, Rozanski has became a dedicated fund-raiser for gay causes. His social life has come to revolve around one of the region's oldest LGBTQ organizations, the Imperial Court of the Rocky Mountain Empire.

While he is happily married to a woman, he feels a kinship with the group, and has become a devoted fan of drag shows. He even has a drag persona, Bettie Pages, who comes out for special occasions. "When I'm Bettie, I'm a very different person."

Bettie has an origin story. Rozanski got sick in 2003 and was later diagnosed with West Nile encephalitis, a potentially fatal inflammation of the brain. When he recovered, he had to work to relearn basic tasks of his life. In 2007, he got the illness again, which doctors told him was highly unusual. This time his recovery took even longer. It was then, while traveling for work, that he went to his first drag show, accompanied by a friend who was more familiar with the territory. Rozanski loved it.

"Somewhere along the line, wherever Bettie was hiding, Bettie came out as a result of my illness," he said. "I never had been in a gay establishment in my life, and now I live there."

He also lives at his store, spending time there seven days a week and working long hours most of those days. "Given my choice, twenty years from now I'd be sitting right here at this same desk," he said. "I'll just have twice as many comics. People ask me about owning ten million comics and what it feels like and I tell them, 'It's a good start.'"

ALSO IN THIS CATEGORY:

Escapist Comics

3090 Claremont Avenue
Berkeley, California

Escapist Comics has filled some of the void that was left by the closing of Comic Relief, a beloved and influential store that had operated for more than two decades in Berkeley. When Comic Relief closed in 2011, Jack Rems bought the store's inventory and hired some of the staff to start Escapist Comics in a different location. "If you like comics and like to talk about comics, this is a good place to be," said Paul Purcell, the store manager. The place has an old-school feel, with overflowing stacks of books and comics and an upstairs section with vintage back issues.

The Million Year Picnic

99 Mt. Auburn Street #2
Cambridge, Massachusetts

Generations of Boston-area comic fans have a fondness for this small basement shop, located in Harvard Square since 1974. The space is stuffed with comics and books, including an area for small-press comics. Hanging from the ceiling is a paper mobile made by cartoonist Gary Panter, a one-of-a-kind item that is not for sale. While I was there, I spent much of my time in the cozy back-issue area, which was rich with material from the 1960s and 1970s. The store's founder, Jerry Weist, died in 2011. In addition to comics, he loved science fiction; his store's name is the title of a Ray Bradbury short story.

18

Pop Culture Stores

BLAME IT on *Batman*. The 1989 movie showed that there was a market for noncomics merchandise featuring comics characters. Comic shops were some of the first businesses to benefit from this, and spent that year selling T-shirts, hats, and various tchotchkes with Batman logos. Around the same time, some comic shops began to sell vintage toys.

Since then, noncomics merchandise has continued to grow as a segment of comics shops' incomes. Some shops have embraced this more than others, to the point that when you walk in the door of these businesses, you feel like you're in a toy store. Almost always, the toys are in front for the casual buyer, and the comics are in the middle and back.

Of all the categories in this list, this is the one with the fuzziest borders. Every one of the shops below could be called "All of the Above" stores, and all have a solid selection for buyers who only want comics. The main difference is in the vibe. The following are big and colorful and prominently feature stuff that isn't comics.

Austin Books & Comics
5002 N. Lamar Boulevard
Austin, Texas

Bruce Banner was an ordinary scientist until the day he was bombarded with gamma rays that turned him into the rampaging green beast known as the Hulk. At some point in his adventures, he was frozen in place. Now he stands, his face in permanent rage, to greet customers at Austin Books & Comics.

Okay, not really. But the eight-foot Hulk statue at this landmark business is almost disturbingly lifelike. The store's owner, Brad Bankston, bought the statue and had an artist replace the painted eyes with glass eyes and sculpted eyelids. Ever since, employees have gotten used to the way parents barely notice the statue but their children are sometimes transfixed by it. And dogs. Customers sometimes bring their dogs inside, and a few of the canines let out a yelp at the sight of the green berserker.

Despite the giant Marvel superhero statues (there's a life-size Silver Surfer not too far from the Hulk), Austin Books & Comics has a selection that goes much deeper than Marvel and DC. The space is gigantic for a comic shop, with six thousand square feet. It is located about three miles north of the University of Texas at Austin campus.

"The main thing we try to get across is that this is an organized, clean, comfortable place for you to explore your fandom no matter who you are," said Brandon Zuern, the store manager. "We want to reach everybody. Everybody who walks in here we're going to talk to like they're the customer of the day."

He started working at the store twelve years ago as an entry-level clerk, a refugee from a call-center job. Now he is the day-to-day manager, which allows Bankston to focus on other aspects of what has grown into a collection of retail businesses. The other ventures, all in the same strip, are Outlaw Moon Games & Toys, a store that sells role-playing games, board games, and vintage toys; Guzu Gallery, an art space; and the Sidekick Store, a seller of clearance comics.

Austin Books & Comics was started in 1977 and is the self-described oldest continuously operated comic shop in Texas. Bankston, whose family had owned a comic shop elsewhere in Texas, bought Austin Books & Comics in 1994.

When you enter, to your left is a wall of new releases and to your right is the children's section. Deeper into the shop are shelves of toys and collectibles. At the very back is a section for back issues. The comics, whether new

Austin Books & Comics in Austin, Texas. *Courtesy of Brandon Zuern.*

or back issues, are held in custom-made wood displays, as opposed to the wire racks and white cardboard boxes that many stores use.

On most days, you can't get more than a few steps inside before someone greets you. The employees are trained to say hello to everyone and to be on the lookout for customers who may need extra help finding something.

The welcoming vibe has helped turn casual buyers into more dedicated fans. One notable example is Annie Bulloch. She was a recent college graduate when she came to the store in the late-1990s. She had heard good things about *Daredevil,* the Marvel comic, but had found other comic shops were unfriendly to women, and messy.

"Once I found Austin Books, there was really no reason for me to go anywhere else," she said.

She became a regular. In 2011, after a move to Houston, she and two partners opened 8th Dimension Comics & Games. She says Austin Books was part of her inspiration for how to lay out a store in a way that is welcoming to both diehard fans and neophytes.

This kind of story has become familiar to Zuern. His store has been around long enough that it is a local institution, and its best qualities are often imitated.

Midtown Comics

200 W. 40th Street
New York, New York
(has two other locations in Manhattan)

Midtown Comics is the largest comic specialty retailer in the country in terms of sales, a fact that is far from obvious if you're standing on the sidewalk at the entrance to the company's main store near Times Square. The shop is on the second and third floors, above Bazaar Perfumes ("We carry all kinds of name brands") and Maoz Falafel & Grill and next door to a two-story McDonald's. To get to the comics, you follow the signs and take a narrow staircase or an elevator.

The store is filled with a sensory overload of comics, books, toys, and games. Customers pack the aisles, a mix of regulars and tourists.

Midtown, started in 1997, has three locations, all in Manhattan, plus headquarters and a warehouse on Long Island. The stores do a brisk business, but they are not the only reason for the company's leading status. The

Though not the flagship store, this Midtown Comics location
near Grand Central Station is pretty big.

company has grown to became a national and international player through its website, MidtownComics.com, which now accounts for more than half of annual sales.

"We're always encouraging new readers," said Dimitrios Fragiskatos, a veteran Midtown employee who was manager of the location near Grand Central Station when I visited there in 2016. "The industry in general is going in a good direction."

By that, he means that comics readership is diversifying, with more women, more young readers, and people from diverse backgrounds. Midtown's managers try to lay out the stores in a way that will be welcoming to people who have never been in a comic shop, while also seeking to retain longtime fans. The specific details are often simple, such as wide aisles, bright lighting, and uncluttered shelves.

"Eighty percent of the comic stores I've been in just seem like dungeons," he said. "Part of me revels in it because that's where you'll find that underpriced, treasured book. But it's not appealing to the people we aren't used to that climate, mostly families and kids who want to get into comics."

Tate's Comics + Toys + More
4566 N. University Drive
Lauderhill, Florida
(second location in Boynton Beach)

Tate Ottati used to get annoyed when people said his business was not a real comic book shop. The comment often was a dig at his store's authenticity by fans who saw shelves of toys and Japanese animation products alongside the comics.

"Now we just say, 'Maybe we're not just a comic book store,'" he said, speaking from his flagship store near Fort Lauderdale.

He has long sideburns and makes prolific use of the word "fuck" and its variants. When he says "comic book," he strings it together to sound like "comibook," like a hyper kid rather than an entrepreneur who has been at it for more than twenty years.

Tate's Comics + Toys + More epitomizes the idea of a "pop culture store," a business in which comics are on close to equal footing with other products that appeal to geeky audiences. Other comics retailers point to

Tate Ottati behind the counter at his store,
Tate's in Lauderhill, Florida. *Courtesy of Tate's.*

Tate's for the way it has developed a slate of in-store events, helping create a sense of community with the store at the center.

The store has been successful enough that he has opened two other outlets, one in the same complex that specializes in board games and role-playing games, and one about a fifty-minute drive away that is a smaller version of the flagship.

The main store is 10,600 square feet, which makes it one of the largest comics retailers in the country. It is colorful and bright, with life-size statues of Iron Man, the Hulk, and Optimus Prime. About 40 percent of the space is for comics and books; another 40 percent is for toys; and the rest is for "other," a category including Japanese snack foods, among many other items.

Despite his experience, Ottati says he remains baffled by aspects of the comics industry. He doesn't understand how a title can be a best seller at one store and barely sell at another. His case in point is DC's *Sweet Tooth* by writer/artist Jeff Lemire, which never did well for him during its years of publication. "A good friend's store was selling twenty-eight copies of that book, and I was like, 'How the fuck are you selling twenty-eight copies of that book?' We were selling like one."

He also is frustrated that comics publishers don't do more to promote their products. He thinks the recent run of movies based on comic books is an opportunity publishers are largely letting go to waste.

"Whose fault is it that you're not even getting 1 percent of the people seeing the movie to buy a comic book?" he said. "I know that if you advertise your product, people will buy your product."

Ottati opened his first shop in 1993, at the age of seventeen, when he was still in high school. Shortly before that, he was in an economics class in which students played a stock-picking game without investing actual money. He was inspired to invest about $1,500 of his own savings in Marvel Comics, which had recently held an initial stock offering. He bought low and sold high, ending up with tens of thousands of dollars that were the seed money for his store.

His first space was about eight hundred square feet. He sold new comics along with his own collection of back issues and toys. His father, who had a day job as a teacher, worked the register every day. "It kind of evolved," Ottati said. "It was just comic books and then my Japanese animation collection, my Transformers, my Star Wars, my G.I. Joe, and I put it in the store. It was just my collection, and I said, 'Let me just see what sells.'"

He met the woman he would marry when she was a customer. They now have a son and daughter, whose bios are listed on the company's website along with the employees. Daughter RJ, who was six when I interviewed her father, said the best part of working at the store is "getting to take home anything I want and eating Pocky." Pocky, for the uninitiated, are chocolate-covered cookie sticks, a Japanese snack food that is a perpetual seller at Tate's.

ALSO IN THIS CATEGORY:

Atlantis Fantasyworld
1020 Cedar Street
Santa Cruz, California

Started in 1976, this is one of the oldest shops in the country still operated by one of its founders. Joe Ferrara, recognizable for his Santa-like white beard, is an elder statesman in comics and has made many friends of retailers, writers, and artists. His business has evolved to become a pop culture store, with racks full of toys and science fiction novelties to go along with new comics.

Dick Swan on Joe Ferrara:

Santa Cruz is over the hill from San Jose, so it's a little bit isolated. Everyone here knows Joe Ferrara. He's a singer and plays in clubs, so he's a local celebrity outside of his shop. His store won the Will Eisner Spirit of Comics Retailer Award in 1996, arguably the biggest award in the business. Soon after, he started facilitating the judging of the award, and, when Will Eisner died in 2005, Joe became the presenter. Among comics retailers, Joe is an integral guy.

Dick Swan, who lives in Santa Cruz, was a key player in the
Bay Area comics scene, starting as a teenager at Comic World in
San Jose. He went on to be a co-owner and senior purchaser at Comics &
Comix, and then was owner of Big Guy's Comics in Mountain View.
He now sells comics at shows and on eBay.

Comicazi

407 Highland Avenue
Somerville, Massachusetts

Among the thousands of action figures displayed at Comicazi, the one that caught my eye was Uncle Jesse, the white-bearded bootlegger from *The Dukes of Hazzard*. The price was $29.99 for the 1981 vintage toy, part of a near-complete set of Dukes. "We love every toy that's ever been made," said Robert Howard, one of three co-owners at the shop in Somerville's Davis Square, just outside Boston. Comicazi, pronounced "Kamikaze," is a place where you can get lost. It has vintage toys, new toys, role-playing games, board games, and science fiction paperbacks. Other shop owners and managers in the Boston area look at Comicazi with some envy because of the store's large footprint and its success in developing a regular schedule of free events. The calendar has game nights, book clubs, and author signings. All of this is in addition to its main business: selling new comics.

Dukes of Hazzard action figures at Comicazi.

Forbidden Planet

832 Broadway
New York, New York

Open late, with music often blaring and tourists in the aisles, this is the latest incarnation of a store with a rich history. Forbidden Planet started in the United Kingdom and opened in New York in the early 1980s. Now, after several moves and ownership changes, the current store has toys and pop culture gear up front, along with a big selection of comics and books. If you're in New York and visiting the landmark Strand Bookstore, Forbidden Planet is just a few doors away. In most cities, this would be the best comic shop in town. In New York, one of the capitals of comics retail, the store is one of many solid destinations.

19

Comics and . . .

FOR AS long as there have been comic shops, retailers have tried variations on double-barreled stores. One of the most common pairings has been comics and role-playing games. It makes sense because there has long been an overlap between people who read comics and people who play games such as Dungeons & Dragons and Magic: The Gathering.

Today, there are comics and games stores in just about every major and midsize market. Some have been around for decades. Many are role-playing-game stores that happen to stock a few comics. Others, including a few on this list, are comic shops that have a small display of games and game accessories. Less common are stores that have broad selections of comics and games under the same roof and are perceived as the real deal by fans of both.

While the comics-games pairing is well established, the comics-coffee combination is relatively new and growing. The coffee business provides a buffer against the ups and downs in the comics business. Regular coffee customers sometimes become comics fans through a kind of retail osmosis, according to the store owners.

And there are other pairings out there, such as comics and records. I can only wonder what combinations, good and not so good, may be next.

Amalgam Comics & Coffeehouse

2578 Frankford Avenue
Philadelphia, Pennsylvania

When Ariell Johnson was a student at Temple University, she looked forward to Fridays, when she would visit to the neighborhood comic shop and then go across the street to the nearby coffee shop to read and relax. And then the coffee shop closed. She was struck by how much this disrupted one of her favorite parts of the week.

Years later, in December 2015, she opened Amalgam Comics & Coffeehouse. The business inspired local and national media coverage, as it was one of the only comic shops in the country owned by a black woman. Johnson, who is in her midthirties, did so many interviews with newspapers, television stations, and online outlets that she got used to telling her story. She told about how she had become a comics fan as a child in the 1990s when she saw a promo for the *X-Men* cartoon with a glimpse of Storm, a black female superhero with the power to control the weather.

"Up until that point, I had never seen a superhero who looked like me," she said when I interviewed her. "She's brown and she's defiant and she's hurling lightning at people and I thought that was just incredible."

Ariell Johnson. *Credit: Steve Ling.*

Amalgam's comics selection is a mix of top sellers from major publishers and small-press comics from diverse creators. The store has titles such as *Brother Man,* about a black crime fighter, and *DayBlack,* about a former slave who was turned into a vampire.

"Our customer base is very diverse," Johnson said. "I do get a lot of support from the black community, people who make real treks to the store, from out of state. We also have the traditional, quote unquote, comic book fan."

She spent her twenties working as an assistant manager for a retail business and doing bookkeeping jobs for nonprofit groups. Once she decided she wanted to start her own company, she got a job at a coffee shop to learn that side of the business.

She obtained financing for Amalgam with help from family and through a crowd-funding campaign, among other sources. She found a space in the Kensington neighborhood, a gentrifying area about two miles east of Temple University. The store is about two thousand square feet, divided almost equally between comics and coffee. It has three full-time employees, including herself, plus six part-timers.

Johnson has dealt with some dizzying ups and downs in her first year owning a business. She was surprised by all the publicity when she opened, which likely helped attract customers. At the same time, the neighborhood and her block have been disrupted by construction, making it difficult for customers to find parking and navigate sidewalks. The good news about construction is that some of it is for new housing that should increase foot traffic.

She works exhausting hours, waking up before sunrise and getting to the store by 7 a.m., and then keeping at it most nights until about 11 p.m. She tries to avoid the store on Mondays, when it is closed, and for at least parts of Sunday. Her home is just a few doors away, which makes for a short commute but means she almost never feels like she is away from work.

The store was eight months old when we spoke, and she was looking forward to when she would have a year of results to review and have a basis for comparison of new results. Until then, every season and every obstacle is new, and she is trying to stay nimble.

"You're kind of figuring it out and tweaking it as you go," she said.

Source Comics & Games

2057 Snelling Ave N.
Roseville, Minnesota

As a concept, it makes sense to open a store that sells comics and role-playing games. The audiences overlap, at least somewhat, and the combination provides a safety net when either side sees an ebb in popularity. But it is difficult to pull off a store that will be regarded as authentic by both fan bases.

Bob Brynildson, co-owner of Source Comics & Games, has come close to cracking the code. His store has been in business in one form or another since the 1980s, and has earned credibility with comics enthusiasts without sacrificing its status as the region's top game store.

The key, he says, is that the two sides of the business function as one, with employees who are experts in comics and games. So there are no "game guys" who give a puzzled look when they get a question on comics.

Source Comics & Games in Roseville, Minnesota. *Credit: Aaron Coker*

"We fight that," he said. "We've been fighting that for our livelihoods, since the beginning of our days."

The Source is a roomy ten thousand square feet, and aims to have a full selection of comics, role-playing games, and board games. "We're completists," he said. There are sixteen employees, eight of whom are full-time. They dress in uniforms of a red shirt and a black vest.

Sales are split almost 50–50 between the two sides. Among games, his top sellers are board games such as Catan and Ticket to Ride. Next are tabletop role-playing games such as Dungeons & Dragons, followed closely by trading-card games such as Magic: The Gathering.

The comics selection is vast, with just about everything sold by the major publishers, plus a large selection of independent titles.

Brynildson opened Legacy Games in St. Paul in 1988. In 1991, he joined with an existing comic shop, the Source, which had a flagship location in Minneapolis. The combined business was also called the Source. In financial trouble almost immediately, it went bankrupt in 1992. Brynildson and partner Jerry Corrick bought the company out of bankruptcy and put all of their inventory in a new store in Falcon Heights, just north of St. Paul. A few years later, Dominic Postiglione also became a co-owner. In 2012, the store moved a few blocks north into a larger location in Roseville, another suburb.

The gregarious Postiglione, known to people in the store as "Nick Post," died in 2014. He was just fifty-two, and his passing was widely mourned in the comics community.

"On my one visit to the Source, after I got done being impressed with the sheer scope of the place, I was even more impressed by how much of a community space it was," wrote Charles Brownstein, executive director of the Comic Book Legal Defense Fund, an advocate for free expression in comics that has been supported by the Source, in an obituary. "The back of the store was occupied by giant gaming tables, which were going to be used for a tournament later in the day. The endcaps of each graphic novel bookshelf were stuffed with small press comics from the local area and all over the country."[1]

Brynildson and Corrick have continued without their partner, with the laid-back Brynildson serving as day-to-day manager of the store and Corrick doing most of his work from behind the scenes.

The Source's owners have one other store, Uncle Sven's Comic Shoppe, at 1838 St. Clair Avenue in St. Paul, which they bought in 2012 because

Uncle Sven's Comic Shoppe in St. Paul, Minnesota. *Credit: Aaron Coker.*

otherwise it was likely to close. More than any other store, this is one for which I have a sentimental attachment. I shopped there when I was a student at Macalester College in the 1990s, and one of my first stories for my college newspaper was a profile of the shop, which then-owner Ken Svendsen clipped and had hanging on the wall for years. Most of the staff were known by nicknames, such as "Evil Erik" and "Colonel Dave." The store had a hall of fame of notable customers, which consisted of hand-drawn "plaques" on the walls near the ceiling.

Uncle Sven's customers were a mix of college students, neighborhood kids, and longtime fans. I would walk there from campus on a Saturday and be gone for much longer than I planned because I got into a long talk on some geeky subject. The place packed an incredible amount of stuff into 290 square feet.

"We just picked it up because we didn't want it to die," Brynildson said.

He has kept almost everything the way he found it. And it turns out Colonel Dave still works Fridays.

ALSO IN THIS CATEGORY:

Criminal Records

1154-A Euclid Ave N.E.
Atlanta, Georgia

Since its start in 1991, Criminal Records has sold comics alongside recorded music. The store has attracted a loyal audience and survived some wild ups and down in both categories. "The two cultures mix nicely and we're able to expose our customers to new things," said Eric Levin, the owner. The tidily packed store is located in the Little Five Points neighborhood, a trendy area dotted with bars, restaurants, and small shops. Levin sells a mix of returnable and nonreturnable materials. His comics and new vinyl are mostly nonreturnable, meaning he is stuck with any unsold inventory. At the same time, his CDs and video discs are returnable to the vendors for credit. And it all seems to work, and has for a long time.

The Dragon

55 Wyndham St. North, Unit T-19B
Guelph, Ontario
(two other locations in region)

The Dragon is "a completely inclusive shop," said owner Jennifer Haines. "When I opened the store, I knew I wanted it to be a place that families and women especially would feel comfortable entering." The main location, part of a downtown mall, is brightly lit and has wide aisles. This is a comics and games combo store. Games sales have steadily risen in recent years to near parity with comics.

Sophie Campbell on The Dragon:

I love Jenn, and The Dragon is a super great place. It's really well-organized, it's bright and open, the staff is friendly and helpful and knowledgeable, and it's welcoming to all kinds of people. And they stock a lot of my books, so that helps too.

Sophie Campbell is a cartoonist whose work includes Wet Moon *from Oni Press; she also has been an artist on titles such as* Jem and the Holograms *for IDW Publishing.*

8th Dimension Comics & Games
15210 West Road
Houston, Texas

One of the better comics and games stores, 8th Dimension has distinguished itself with clever events and promotions. The store, whose name is a reference to the 1984 movie *The Adventures of Buckaroo Banzai across the 8th Dimension,* is located in a suburban-style strip mall near the Houston city limits. Its events include in-store ladies nights and social hours, plus remote promotions such as a pop-up shop at a local movie theater when a comic-themed movie is playing. Co-owner Annie Bulloch says the store aims to do things the right way, in how it treats customers and employees and how it tries to expand the audience for comics.

"It's what Superman would want us to do," she said.

20

Best of the Best

IF I intended to open a comic shop, I would go to the following five locations and take copious notes. I would follow the owners around and watch how they did everything. I would look for what can be imitated, and then imitate the hell out of it. I have been to many comic shops, and these are the ones that do almost everything right.

The Beguiling
319 College Street
Toronto, Ontario

The relocation of The Beguiling in early 2017 was an event greeted by fans with the trepidation associated with high-risk surgery. There was a real chance that one of the finest comic shops in the world was going to lose much of what made it special.

This was a potential tragedy brought on by Toronto real estate developers who had big plans to build condominiums along several blocks of beloved and quirky retail space and housing. One of the only good things to come out of the run-up to the move was a blowout sale of much of The Beguiling's inventory, an event that I wish I could have gotten to. The store's

The Beguiling in Toronto, exterior.

The Beguiling, interior.

deep selection was one of the things that made it special, and the sale of accumulated stuff must have been one for the ages.

The store had to move on, and did so in the middle of a Toronto winter. The new location was about a mile away. At first, owner Peter Birkemoe and his staff had the difficult task of fitting the store's diverse material into a smaller space. Instead of a rambling old house, this was a traditional storefront. It felt new in an unsettling way, as if the decades of history of The Beguiling had been replaced with something that could not live up to the store's tradition. This was still a great store, just not The Beguiling.

But this story has a twist. The shop's two neighboring storefronts became vacant, and Birkemoe rented them. He and his crew opened up entryways inside to turn the narrow shop into a sprawling space. They renovated the basement to create an area for back issues.

I visited the new address for the first time after this expansion had taken place and more than a year after the move from the prior location. The new shop had acquired a lived-in feel that reminded me of the old shop. And, with the newly rented areas, it had more space than the house ever did.

As a business, The Beguiling made it through the transition without losing its core customers.

"The loss was inconsequential," Birkemoe said.

This question would be crucial for most comic shops that depend on regulars for the large majority of sales. Yet The Beguiling is one of the few stores that has been able to develop a different model. The store gets a large share of its sales from a division that sells comics to schools and public libraries, and this business is not at all tied to physical retail concerns like foot traffic. Also, The Beguiling is a destination in a way that most shops aren't, so its customers include many people visiting from out of town who are eager to buy material they can't find at home.

The Beguiling is, and has long been, much more than a store. I learned of it from cameo appearances in autobiographical comics by Canadian artists. Then I found the store online, particularly its gallery of original art for sale. One of these days, I swear, I will buy a Jason Lutes page from *Berlin*. Then, on my first visit to Toronto, I walked down Markham Street and came to the previous location.

I went in with unreasonably high expectations. I walked away with a new understanding of what a comic shop can be.

The first floor was like a bookstore. I looked for books by Michel Rabagliati, a Quebec cartoonist, and found that nearly all of his published works were on the shelf, even the ones in French that had not yet been translated. That by itself was impressive. Then I asked the clerk about one volume, *Paul à Québec,* and whether an English version was forthcoming. He said Rabagliati was switching to a different English-language publisher, and it was not yet known when the book would be released in the language.

This turned out to be the first of several short conversations between me and the clerk that afternoon. Each time, it was clear this guy knew his inventory to a ridiculous extent, and that he wanted to sell me stuff. Unlike many employees in comic shops, he gave a shit.

I made my way through the store. Up the narrow staircase, on the second floor, were periodical comics and back issues. I dug through a back-issue bin and found old copies of *Batman and the Outsiders* for a dollar each. The title, drawn in the 1980s by a succession of great artists, is a must-buy whenever I find it so inexpensively.

By the time I left, I had spent more money than was prudent. The clerk encouraged me to come back during the Toronto Comic Arts Festival, held each May and cosponsored by the shop. The following year, I followed his advice, and now go to the festival whenever I can.

In the spring of 2016, five years after my first visit to The Beguiling, I interviewed Birkemoe and realized that he was the guy behind the counter on that initial visit. Co-owner at the time, he was now the sole owner. I had assumed, incorrectly, that a store as good as The Beguiling must be run by some beard-stroking sage behind the scenes, and certainly not by someone about my age.

"I'm not a natural-born salesman," he said. "I'm a natural-born evangelist for comics."

He is at the store six days per week. He started there as an employee in 1996, working a few shifts for store credit, and bought the place with a partner in 1998 when the original owners decided to move on to other things.

The founders, Steve Solomos and Sean Scoffield, started small in 1987 and moved around to several addresses before they came to the two-story house that would become the store's long-term location. The owners were artists themselves, and they attracted artists and supported the work of artists. But the name of the store hinted at a fondness for mainstream creators such as Barry Windsor-Smith, the artist of a gorgeously drawn short story called "The Beguiling" that appeared in a 1983 issue of Marvel Comics' *Epic Illustrated* magazine.

Almost from the beginning, the store had a reputation, good and bad, for fussing over high art and looking down on everything else. Solomos spoke about this when he appeared at a Toronto comics convention in 1990, assuring the audience that he and his partner were not "arty farty pigs."

"We're capitalists," he said in a transcript later published in the *Comics Journal*. "That's why we're in business. That's what we're here for. We like money. The only difference is we like to be able to sell the stuff that we like. It's very simple, and we hope we can reach a climate one day where we can go to a party or a wedding and not be too embarrassed to tell people that we either read comics, collect comics, or sell comics. Maybe that day will come."[1]

Birkemoe led the business to growth while keeping the main store recognizable to longtime fans.

And this doesn't include side ventures, such as the Toronto Comic Arts Festival, started in 2003 by Birkemoe and The Beguiling's longtime manager, Christopher Butcher. Butcher left his job at the store in mid-2017 to work for Viz Media, a comics and anime company. He will continue to oversee the festival, an event that gets bigger every year.

Birkemoe still devotes most of his time and attention to the store. My most recent interview with him was in the store's basement as employees prepared the nearby back-issue area for opening. The place was continuing to grow and change. I wouldn't go so far as to say I like the new location better than the old one, but I can see how the current spot is more sustainable than an old house. This is a business that can go on as long as Birkemoe wants to do it, and I hope that's a long time.

Chicago Comics

3244 N. Clark Street
Chicago, Illinois

Some comic shops are almost like cults of personality. The owner is a regular presence behind the counter and has a gift for gab that attracts customers and keeps them coming back. For many successful stores, it is difficult to imagine the business continuing if that key player is no longer there.

None of this can be said about Chicago Comics. The store is one of the best I have ever seen and routinely shows up on lists of top comics retailers in the country. And it does this with an owner, Eric Kirsammer, who stays a few steps away from the public.

"A lot of people don't even know I'm the owner, which I'm totally fine with," he said, interviewed on a weekday morning before the store opened.

He often starts an hour or two before opening. When the customers get there, he does paperwork or organizes shelves while his employees do most of the interaction with the public. The long, narrow space is about twenty-two hundred square feet. It is stuffed without being cluttered.

Eric Kirsammer, owner of Chicago Comics.

"Going into this from the first day, I didn't want to be the guy behind the counter, because I felt like that was the downfall of some stores that closed," he said. "The store itself should be the thing that draws people."

He came into the business by happenstance. In 1991, he was in his late twenties and worked as a designer of retail interiors. He was a comics fan and a regular customer at a shop called All-American Adventures. The owner of the store was having financial problems, and Kirsammer bought a stake in the business. Soon after, the owner left and Kirsammer became the sole owner, almost by default.

He used his background in retail to make some big changes. First he changed the name to Chicago Comics. Then, in 1993, he moved two blocks down the street in Chicago's Lakeview neighborhood, going from a rented space to a building he had purchased. He could afford it because the area was still years away from being prime real estate.

Now, decades after he got into the business, he has become a quiet leader in the local and national comics scene. He added a second store in 1997, buying Quimby's in the Wicker Park neighborhood, which specializes in small-press comics and art books. He also was a longtime board member of ComicsPro, the trade organization for comics retailers, stepping down in 2016.

His stores have helped many artists find their audiences. At Quimby's, just about anyone can put a self-published comic on the shelves and sell it on consignment. Chicago Comics also has an area for self-published and small-press work.

Keiler Roberts, a Chicago artist, began to share her comics with the public when she started selling at Quimby's in 2009. "That was a big moment for me," she said. "I've been a painter and been shown in galleries, but I felt more proud to see my minicomic on a bookshelf than see my painting on a gallery wall."

She went on to collect some of her comics in a book, *Miseryland,* published in 2015, about her funny and frustrating life as the mother of a toddler. The book has received glowing reviews and was picked up by a national distributor. Despite her strong ties to one of Kirsammer's stores, she's never met him and isn't sure she would recognize him. When she thinks of Quimby's, she thinks of the regular staff, which is exactly what Kirsammer wants.

"There is such a strong energy when you go into Quimby's," she said. "It's like the books hum, you know? They came straight from the hands of people who made them and put them on the shelf. There's something, I don't know, deeply inspiring."

Flying Colors Comics & Other Cool Stuff
2980 Treat Boulevard
Concord, California

More than once, someone has asked Joe Field if his shop is part of a chain. His response is "Yes, it's a chain of one."

Flying Colors is in a shopping center in Concord, east of Oakland, with a Trader Joe's, a Jimmy John's, and other chain stores. The shop is one of the cleanest and best organized I've ever seen. Employees, an unfailingly helpful lot, are dressed in matching shirts with the store's logo. When people think the place may be a chain, they probably mean that it doesn't seem as scruffy as most comic shops.

On a Saturday at the store, classic rock played on the sound system, and a mix of children and adults made their way through the aisles. A grade school–age boy asked a clerk if the store had any *Deadpool* comics. The clerk responded by turning to the kid's grandmother and advising that *Deadpool* is far from children's fare. The family had walked right by the store's well-stocked children's section, located to the immediate left of the front entrance.

Flying Colors devotes about half of its shelf space to books and most of the rest to comics. The selection is deep for any store, but especially for a store in the suburbs. At the same time, there is plenty for an old-school comics fan. I spent a good twenty minutes going through a bargain back-issue bin, and picked up an issue of DC's *World's Finest Comics* from the 1970s, featuring a short story drawn by one of my favorite artists of the era, Don Newton.

Field opened Flying Colors in 1988, leaving behind a career in radio promotions. He had been a comics fan since childhood, and knew the Bay Area scene because he was co-organizer of WonderCon, a major comics convention that began in Oakland in 1987.

"I sometimes, only half jokingly, say that my wife and three daughters were my marketing research team back them," he said. "When we were going to research getting into the comics business and opening a store, I took them with me on various trips to look at other comic shops and other businesses and would have them shop the stores and then go back out to the station wagon and get their notes."

Joe Field in the children's section of his store,
Flying Colors Comics in Concord, California.

His aim was to have a store that would appeal to entire families, not just a clubhouse for young men. To make it happen, he drained his retirement fund from the radio, along with his savings, and got a loan. His startup costs were about $50,000, which made his shop unusually well capitalized for the era.

Field picked close to the perfect time to open. The *Batman* movie had its premiere the following summer, leading to a heightened interest in comics. It was the start of a five-year boom in comics publishing. He learned how to manage inventory and employees, and was good enough at it that in 1994, when the industry went into a tailspin, he survived.

Almost from the start, he has been a leader among retailers. He has joined some trade groups and started others, and was one of the last people standing in groups that are now defunct. With this background, he is proud of ComicsPro, a group he helped found in 2004. The trade association for retailers has lasted longer than all of the others, and now has about 150 member retailers, which include many of the largest and most established shops and chains of shops. Its annual meeting has become an event. In 2016,

DC Comics chose to announce details of its Rebirth publishing initiative at the ComicsPro meeting in Portland, Oregon.

And yet, Field's claim to fame in the industry is not ComicsPro or anything to do with Flying Colors. It is Free Comic Book Day, an idea that he proposed in a 2001 column in *Comics & Games Retailer* magazine. He suggested that the comics industry should take a lesson from Baskin-Robbins's free scoop promotions.

The first Free Comic Book Day was in 2002. Publishers worked with Diamond Comics Distributors to offer a selection of comics for which retailers would pay a nominal fee, and which they would then give away to customers. More than fifteen hundred stores participated that first year, and the number has gone up every year since, Field said. At his store, there were seven hundred customers.

"People respond to the word 'free,'" he said. "That's the most powerful word in marketing." The event is by far the largest promotional event in the comics industry.

Because of Free Comic Book Day and ComicsPro, and maybe because he's been around for a while, other retailers often cite Field as a role model. "That guy is a comics retailing legend, an innovator," said Brandon Zuern, manager of Austin Books & Comics. "He's done more to expand comic retailing that just about anyone."

Shelton Drum, owner of Heroes Aren't Hard to Find in Charlotte, North Carolina, is more succinct when talking about Field: "He's like a retail god to me." Their admiration is mutual. And their stores are a lot alike, with material for many audiences and an eagerness to sell it.

Green Brain Comics

13936 Michigan Avenue
Dearborn, Michigan

In 1989, a young woman got a job at a comic shop, and she never left. She later started dating a machinist, and they bonded over a shared affection for comics. They got married. Soon after, they bought the store from the owner, who was retiring. The business has changed addresses and changed names and is now Green Brain Comics, with a giant retro roof sign that is hard to miss on the main drag of Dearborn, just outside of Detroit.

Katie and Dan Merritt at their store, Green Brain Comics in Dearborn, Michigan.

On a winter evening, co-owner Katie Merritt was behind the counter, dressed in black and with black-rimmed glasses. Framed behind her was a photograph of the store's original owners on the day of the original ribbon cutting.

"We gravitate toward where our strengths are," Katie said. "I do most of the bookkeeping and paperwork. Dan does the ordering and inventory tracking. What we share is the ideas. I could wake up at 2 o'clock in the morning and say, 'Here's a thing we should do at the store.'"

She was talking about her husband, Dan Merritt, who had a bushy beard and was dressed in red flannel.

In 1999, when the Merritts bought the store, the comics market was "in the dumper," Dan said. Comics publishers and retailers were still recovering from the industry downturn of the mid-1990s. The store cost about $30,000, which included a lease, some inventory, and a core of loyal customers.

"In a lot of ways it was perfect timing. We bought low and have been riding the wave ever since," Dan said.

Early on, they noticed a steady increase in sales of trade paperbacks, multi-issue stories collected from periodical comics. Today, books are about 35 percent of sales and periodical comics are 65 percent.

While the store sells plenty of Marvel and DC, the owners' hearts are with smaller publishers. "As soon as we see that faded interest in the big companies from a customer, we take that customer by the hand and take them to the other half of the store," Dan said.

That said, his top-selling comic book is *Ms. Marvel,* published by Marvel. The series features a Pakistani American girl who has the power to lengthen her arms, increase the size of her hands, and otherwise change the shape of her body. It has been a critical hit and a solid middle-tier seller for the publisher. For Green Brain, the title has resonated with a large local community of Muslim Americans and with young female readers.

The Merritts bought the building in 2014, relocating the store from a rented space down the street. The shop walls are painted aqua green. To understand its layout, you need to know that families tend to park in the back lot and use the rear entrance, and other customers tend to come on foot or find on-street parking and use the front entrance. So the children's section is in the back, and the indie comics section and books are close to the front.

Outside of the shop, the co-owners are among the organizers of ComiqueCon, a Dearborn convention that made its debut in 2015, notable for featuring female comics creators and for drawing creators from across the country. The Merritts also help put together Kids Read Comics, now called the Ann Arbor Comic Arts Festival, an annual event that features authors of all-ages comics.

This work, inside and outside the store, has made the business a favorite of many comics artists and writers. And yet, perhaps because of its location off the beaten path, Green Brain does not often show up on lists of the best in the country. This is a store richly deserving of a higher profile.

David Petersen on Green Brain Comics:

> It's the type of store that wouldn't put off the non-comic-buying community. I think there is an unflattering mental image of what the inside of a comic shop is supposed to look like, and Green Brain is one of those welcoming stores that doesn't feel seedy, like a boys' club, or unfriendly to outsiders. It's anything but.

David Petersen is the writer-artist of Mouse Guard
and lives in the Dearborn area.

Legend Comics & Coffee

Omaha, Nebraska

The first incarnation of Legend Comics was like just about any comic shop. Opened in 2007, its chief assets were its location, in a neighborhood that had no other shop nearby, and three gregarious co-owners. But something was missing.

While Legend had no competitors in the immediate vicinity, Omaha had several established shops that had followings from longtime readers. To succeed, Legend would need to convert people to the comics habit.

The solution turned out to be coffee. Less than two blocks from Legend's first location, a developer was renovating an old grocery store building. Legend's co-owners inquired about the space, and those conversations led to the current store, which began selling comics in 2010 and coffee in 2011.

"All of our customers, save for maybe a few percent, are brand-new people," said Dave DeMarco, a co-owner. "They are straight up like, 'What are

Dave DeMarco and Wendy Pivonka behind the counter at
Legend Comics & Coffee in Omaha, Nebraska.

these comic books and how can I get involved?' And I am pleased to be their landing pad."

The space covers 2,250 square feet on the main floor, more than twice the size of the first location. About one third of it is a full-service coffee shop, with a drive-through window. When I was there, most of customers on the coffee side were on laptops or their phones. If anyone wants to look at a comic, there is a long shelf of used trade paperbacks for browsing and purchase.

The coffee side has its own sign out front that says Legend Coffee, which makes it look like a separate business next to Legend Comics. Inside, the coffee shop is separated from the comics by a wall with a large half-wall opening.

DeMarco previously worked at another Omaha-area comic shop. His business partners are a married couple, Jason Dasenbrock and Wendy Pivonka, who founded the store before DeMarco joined, after having done many other things, including working in restaurants.

Legend is designed to serve as a neighborhood coffee shop and to get some of the coffee customers interested in comics. The comics side is more than holding its own. When the current location opened, it inherited the 170 or so "pull list" regulars from the first address, meaning customers who visit weekly or close to it. That number grew to nearly 500 within a year, and continues to grow.

"Even if the market plummets, we have very loyal customers," DeMarco said. "We have customers who come from Lincoln, who drive an hour, past five other stores, to come to us."

The co-owners are quick to note that they did not come up with the idea of combining a coffee shop with a comic shop. They saw it at Cup O' Kryptonite, a shop that opened in Des Moines, Iowa (about two hours from Omaha), in the early 2000s and has since closed.

"It was a wonderful store," DeMarco said. "They were super friendly and helpful and it was a cool layout."

One day at Legend, an unfamiliar person came in and talked about how impressed he was with the store's layout. He mentioned that he was one of the cofounders of Cup O'Kryptonite, and the employees at Legend began to do some gushing of their own.

"Wendy was like, 'You're the reason we did this. We're so thrilled you gave us this inspiration.' And he got a little misty," DeMarco said.

The original founders of Cup O'Kryptonite have moved on to other things, but some of the people behind it now own Capes Kafé in Des Moines, a coffee shop with a small selection of comics.

I should note that Cup O'Kryptonite was a store that was close to my heart for a number of reasons. I grew up in the Des Moines area and was a high school classmate of Matt Johnson, one of the shop's original co-owners. Whenever I was home to visit family, I went to the store, and I wished there had been a store that good in the city when I was a kid. Then, from 2004 to 2008, when I moved to Des Moines to cover politics for a news outlet there, I became a regular customer. The store was ahead of its time.

Legend is indicative of a boomlet of stores that combine coffee and comics. It is too early to say whether this trend has staying power, but the underlying idea seems to be a good one. DeMarco says the key ingredient is that the staff needs to be welcoming to people who are coming in because of the coffee shop and may not know anything about comics.

"Be good to people, because the Comic Book Guy stereotype from *The Simpsons* needs to stop," he said. "That's the thing that hurts the comics industry the most. [A comic shop employee] can still be a fat nerd with a goatee, like I am. That's fine. I accept my lot in life. But hopefully he's a nice nerd with a goatee."

Notable Comic Shops of the United States and Canada

THE FORTY-THREE notable comic shops featured in part 2 are listed below in alphabetical order. Page numbers in parentheses refer to the main discussion of each shop in chapters 15–20.

Comic World, Huntington, West Virginia (199)

Comix Experience, San Francisco, California (175)

Cosmic Monkey Comics, Portland, Oregon (186)

Criminal Records, Atlanta, Georgia (224)

Desert Island, Brooklyn, New York (191)

The Dragon, Guelph, Ontario (224)

DreamHaven Books, Minneapolis, Minnesota (201)

8th Dimension Comics & Games, Houston, Texas (225)

Escapist Comics, Berkeley, California (207)

Excalibur Comics, Portland, Oregon (203)

Floating World Comics, Portland, Oregon (193)

Flying Colors Comics & Other Cool Stuff, Concord, California (233)

Forbidden Planet, New York, New York (217)

Green Brain Comics, Dearborn, Michigan (235)

Happy Harbor Comics, Edmonton, Alberta (187)

Heroes Aren't Hard to Find, Charlotte, North Carolina (178)

Isotope Comics Lounge, San Francisco, California (197)

The Laughing Ogre, Columbus, Ohio (187)

Legend Comics & Coffee, Omaha, Nebraska (238)

Midtown Comics, New York, New York (212)

Mile High Comics, Denver, Colorado (205)

The Million Year Picnic, Cambridge, Massachusetts (208)

Packrat Comics, Hilliard, Ohio (181)

Secret Headquarters, Los Angeles, California (195)

Source Comics & Games, Roseville, Minnesota (221)

Southern Fried Comics, Hattiesburg, Mississippi (198)

Star Clipper, St. Louis, Missouri (188)

Strange Adventures, Halifax, Nova Scotia (188)

Tate's Comics + Toys + More, Lauderhill, Florida (213)

Vault of Midnight, Ann Arbor, Michigan (182)

Epilogue

A Golden Age of Art and Anxiety

I AM writing this in August 2018, two years after the period covered in the rest of these pages. It would be too simple to say that these two years have been an extension of the trends that were in place before. This is true in a big-picture sense, with sales continuing to decline for periodical comics, major publishers devoting much of their energy to hyping big events, and most of the sales growth happening for comics in book form. But the actual unfolding of events was far from a straight line for the retailers who lived through it.

There were scary moments, including a stretch in 2017 when Marvel seemed to be unable to do anything right from a sales perspective, producing loads of bad comics and displaying an inability to sell enough of its good ones. While sales were down in most shops, there was something incredible happening in the broader world of the medium, of which comic shops are only one part. The past two years were an amazing time for comics as art. It was also a time when there were more good comics than the market could possibly support, with earnest and capable small publishers barely getting by while they contributed to this embarrassment of riches for readers.

So here we go, from the lows of a despised comic called *Secret Empire* to the highs of artistic triumphs such as *My Favorite Thing Is Monsters*. Retailers saw it all and most of the good stores survived. Yet the ups and downs of the period serve to underscore long-term concerns about their economic footing, with a creeping sense that things are getting tougher just about every year for physical retailers and comic shops especially.

Ask retailers about *Secret Empire* and their expression is likely to be one of weary resignation. This 2017 miniseries was the culmination of several years of Marvel stories about what happens when Captain America turns out to be a sleeper agent for Hydra, the Nazi-descended terrorist group. The answer, at least from a sales perspective, was that many customers got upset and didn't buy the book.

The title suffered from a twin affliction of many recent superhero comics in its reliance on nostalgia and shock value. The series name is itself a reuse of the title of a landmark Captain America storyline from the 1970s in which Cap uncovers a massive conspiracy that goes all the way to the president of the United States. Considering that Captain America is the ultimate patriot, the realization that his country was corrupt led him to break down and adopt a new superhero identity for a while, calling himself Nomad.

The original story is a time capsule of Watergate-era attitudes as filtered through the mind of a dynamic writer, Steve Englehart, who was assisted in writing parts of the story by Mike Friedrich. It's a wild ride, with steady action and over-the-top pathos. Most importantly, it was something new, a fresh approach to a character who was already decades old.

Then, in 2017, Marvel decided to recycle the title *Secret Empire* in a story about the same character and with a whiff of similar themes as the world gets betrayed by the supposed good guys. The nostalgia is thick at the macro and micro levels, as scenes and dialogue are often packed with callbacks to stories from months, years, or even decades ago. But this is no romp. One of the early issues ends with Captain America ordering the execution by firing squad of Rick Jones, a beloved Marvel character whose previous roles include a brief time as Captain America's sidekick. There is no rescue here. Rick dies. A later issue shows the character Black Widow bloodily torturing a Hydra agent to get him to give up information.

It didn't help that these issues were coming out at a time when the country was going through anxiety about an apparent resurgence of Nazism. Marvel had turned Captain America, a character whose co-creators were Jewish and who was shown punching Hitler on his first cover, into an actual Nazi.

"Over the course of eighteen months, the story of Captain America's turn towards outright fascism has caused pain, anger and outrage and ultimately just wasn't worth the offense, the excuses or the effort," said a review from Kieran Shiach for Polygon.com.[1]

Sales started strong. The first issue, *Secret Empire* #0, sold 162,718 copies, making it the top-selling title of April. After that, it came out twice per month. By *Secret Empire* #5, sales were down to 87,675 and stayed at about that level until the final issue. To understand retailers' frustration, you need to look beyond the sales of the main title and look at the many companion miniseries and tie-ins, whose sales were often dreadful. One example is *Secret Empire: Brave New World,* which sold less than 15,000 of its final issue.[2]

"*Secret Empire* was the worst selling event. It was almost a non-event," said Dan Merritt, co-owner of Green Brain Comics in Dearborn, Michigan, talking about sales in his store.

He sees the series as a microcosm of Marvel's last few years. Would-be hits were disappointments, while many of the company's lower-profile titles were excellent and often failed to find an audience.

This touches on a much larger controversy at Marvel. Many of the titles that Merritt likes star female or minority characters, some of whom are using superhero names that once were used by white characters. One of the most successful examples is Ms. Marvel, a Muslim American whose series has been both well received by critics and a strong seller. Her precursor was a white woman who now goes by Captain Marvel and has her own series. Others were less successful, at least in terms of sales.

The new characters contributed to a backlash from some fans and retailers. "What we heard was that people didn't want any more diversity," said David Gabriel, Marvel's vice president of sales, in a March 2017 interview with ICv2. "They didn't want female characters out there. That's what we heard, whether we believe that or not. I don't know that that's really true, but that's what we saw in sales."

"We saw the sales of any character that was diverse, any character that was new, our female characters, anything that was not a core Marvel character, people were turning their nose up against," he said. "That was difficult for us because we had a lot of fresh, new, exciting ideas that we were trying to get out and nothing new really worked."[3]

His comments led to a backlash of their own. Gabriel quickly issued a statement backtracking a bit. He said that many of the new characters have been warmly received by fans and retailers, and that their positive reception needs to be balanced against the concerns of others who say Marvel is abandoning its core characters.

"We are proud and excited to keep introducing unique characters that reflect new voices and new experiences into the Marvel Universe and pair them with our iconic heroes," he said.[4]

Soon after, the public gave Marvel an unmistakable sign about its appetite for diverse characters. Marvel Studios' movie *Black Panther* was a huge hit in 2018 and featured a mostly black cast. One of the breakout characters was Shuri, a scientific genius and the sister of the title character. This was a loud rebuttal to the idea that a proliferation of minority female characters was harming Marvel, and showed that the company's film division was a few steps ahead of the comics division in terms of storytelling.

Marvel's publishing woes were a leading reason that the comics industry as a whole was down 6.5 percent in 2017, with $1.01 billion in sales, according to ICv2 and Comichron. Comic shops account for slightly more than half of these sales, with the rest coming in bookstores and other outlets. Looking just at comic shops, 2017 was much worse, with sales of $515 million, down 10 percent.[5]

The results were a shock to many retailers. Despite some short-term busts, sales had been growing each year for more than a decade, forming what was likely the longest period of steady growth in the industry's history. To understand this, it helps to realize that 2016, despite having a few months of sluggish sales that caused a brief panic by retailers, still ended with growth for the industry. To have sales go down year over year was a huge blow, considering that rents and other expenses were continuing to increase.

"Independent retail is a really tough business under the best of circumstances," said Griepp of ICv2. "We've just had weak sales in the core product line of comic stores in the last year or so and that exposes other problems."

While Marvel got much of the blame, there was softness almost across the market for periodical comics. DC was down from its the highs of when it started the *Rebirth* branding, although it still had healthy sales. Image continued to have a few solid hits such as *Saga* and *The Walking Dead,* but was having less luck with a large number of new titles that came and went.

Griepp sees the sliding sales for periodical comics as the biggest long-term concern for comic shops. Periodicals, as opposed to comics in book form, continue to be the core product at most shops, with many customers making weekly or near-weekly visits to pick up new comics that come in each Wednesday.

The decline in periodical sales has been gradual but steady, with books and other products picking up the slack at many shops. But what if publishers respond to the long-term trend by de-emphasizing periodicals? That would be catastrophic for many stores. Griepp describes this as "an existential threat to comic stores, not because they're economically unhealthy but because they're diminishing in importance in publishers' eyes."

For now, however, the big moments in mainstream comics continue to happen almost always first as single issues of periodical comics.

The sluggish market of 2017 led to some shops closing their doors for good. There are no figures available for the store count and the number that closed in this period, so it is difficult to tell if this is just the normal churn of openings and closings.

Meltdown Comics in Los Angeles closed in 2018, marking the end of a shop that was once a trendsetter in selling small-press comics and had grown to include a comedy club among other side businesses.

"As is the case with all good things, at some point they must come to an end," said co-owner Gaston Dominguez-Letelier in a blog post. "Meltdown Comics is no exception to this rule and so, after 25 years coveting every comic treasure we could lay our hands on, I'm sharing that on March 30th I'll be closing our doors for the final time."[6]

It was not clear how much of a role finances played in his decision. Meltdown appeared to be a successful business, and Dominguez-Letelier said his desire was to move on to other things.

A few months earlier, Zanadu Comics in Seattle closed after an unsuccessful attempt at crowdfunding to help stabilize its finances. The store had been open since 1975.

"The good guys don't always win," said an announcement on Zanadu's website. "Unfortunately, our world is harsher than that of comic books and

Meltdown Comics in Los Angeles, photographed in 2017. *Credit: Francisco Dominguez.*

after 42 years of battling in the trenches of comic book retail, Zanadu Comics closed its doors at the end of January 2018. Believe us when we say that this decision was not made lightly. There are hundreds of reasons we could list, but the truth is that the money coming in did not equal the money going out."[7]

Perry Plush, who described himself as Zanadu's "president and janitor," continues to sell comics through an online store.

"I've got too much comic book ink in my blood to stay away from comics too long," Plush said in an interview with ICv2. "I just feel like I'm morphing into something new."[8]

Many of the stores that stayed open needed to cut staff or go into debt to make it through this period of slow sales. In some places, natural disasters or other local factors made a bad situation worse. 8th Dimension Comics

& Games in Houston faced a massive disruption from Hurricane Harvey in August 2017. The saving grace was that the store didn't flood, while areas near it were under water.

8th Dimension's co-owner Annie Bulloch says the hurricane made a sluggish year for comics sales much worse. Her store was able to persevere in large part because its sales of role-playing games had grown earlier in the year, providing a small cushion ahead of the storm. While 2017 ended up being a down year for sales at the store, it was not catastrophic.

Compared to the misery of a natural disaster, the misfires of comics publishers are a minor concern. But the latter was still depressing for Bulloch as a fan and as a business owner.

"It's like [the major publishers] desperately don't want people to read them," she said. "There are tons of weird choices, and it's tiring for longtime readers."

Secret Empire was a leading example of this, greeted with offense or indifference, neither of which is good for business. In the store, people were more likely to talk about major stories from fifteen or twenty years ago than the one happening right then, she said.

"People just go, 'Maybe I'm done with this hobby,'" she said.

She responds to this type of sentiment by pointing out the many good and great titles out there. In 2018, one of the pleasant surprises has been *Domino* from Marvel, a fun and action-filled series featuring a second-tier character. The lesson for her is that the major publishers are doing many of the big things poorly but still manage to be brilliant with lower-profile characters and concepts. That's far from a vote of confidence, but it's about as good as a retailer can muster after a rough stretch.

One other change for Bulloch was the dissolution of the Valkyries, the international group for women who work in comic shops and libraries, for which she was a co-administrator. The group came under fire for not being inclusive enough for nonwhite members. Jazmine Joyner, owner of Visionary Comics in Riverside, California, wrote an essay for The MNT, a comics news and commentary website, about how she didn't feel welcome in the group.[9]

The Valkyries' co-administrators issued a statement in September 2018 saying it was time for the group to disband because of legitimate concerns being raised that it wasn't doing enough to support marginalized women.

One of the larger problems was that running the group had become too much work for the co-administrators to do effectively, and attempts to bring in others to lighten the load had not worked, the statement said.[10]

Bulloch told me that one other problem was that the membership had stagnated at about 600, and that included many people who were not active. The lack of growth in active members meant there wasn't much of a pool from which to find new leaders. Reaction to this reasoning leaned toward the negative, with some fans saying the Valkyries had responded to adversity by quitting.

The larger point for the group's leaders was that they all had demanding jobs and lives, and not enough time to make the group as good as it could be.

"We were all volunteers," Bulloch said.

Mainstream comics from Marvel, DC, Image, and others remain the core of most shops' sales. There have been some notable critical and sales successes for those companies in the last few years. For instance, DC's main Batman title has been on a stellar run from writer Tom King and an array of artists. And just about everything Jason Aaron writes for Marvel is good and sells well, including runs on Thor and Doctor Strange.

But if you're seeking the comics that are likely to go down in history as some of the finest of this era, or maybe any era, they aren't in the mainstream and almost all made their debut in book form. An example that stands out is *My Favorite Thing Is Monsters,* the mind-blowing debut from Emil Ferris, published by Fantagraphics.

A brief aside: There is no smooth way to make the transition from talking about an entertaining run on Doctor Strange to talking about a book that has transformed the way many readers view the comics medium. Yet this is the world in which comics retailers find themselves, selling both of those products, sometimes to the same customers, and depending on both to make a living.

If there was any prerelease buzz about *My Favorite Thing Is Monsters,* I didn't see it. But I have a vivid memory of the first time I became aware of the book. I was at my local shop, The Laughing Ogre, and assistant manager Lauren McCallister had a copy behind the counter that she was showing off like a newly found treasure.

MY FAVORITE THING IS
MONSTERS

EMIL FERRIS *"Absolutely astonishing."* —Chris Ware, *Building Stories*

"I loved the book immediately," she told me later. "In addition to being beautifully drawn and visually really interesting, it combines a murder mystery with a coming-of-age story and sort of uses one genre to enhance the other."

The story is told in the form of a drawn journal of a young girl living in 1960s Chicago. The art, which is ballpoint pen on lined notebook paper, shows how the protagonist uses her love of horror movies to process the confusing and tragic events around her. By using the conceit of a journal, Ferris dispenses with much of the language of comics, such as panels, in favor of a free-flowing design. Her drawing is incredibly detailed and packs an emotional punch.

Ferris was fifty-five when this, her debut book, was published. It was a passion project, done over many years while she recovered from health issues. She described some of what went into her design choices during an October 2017 panel in Chicago.

"The format is called, 'I did not know what the fuck I was doing,'" she said. "Honest to god, the format is called, 'Let me just do this thing the way I want to do it because I'm insolent.'"

She added, "It wasn't that I didn't love comics, because I do. It's that I couldn't stay within those little boxes if I tried."[11]

The book came out in February 2017, a paperback priced $39.99. Considering the complexity of the story, the high cover price, and the fact that Ferris was an unknown creator, this looked like a work that would be embraced by critics but not excite the sales charts. Yet it turned out to be a sales success right from the start. Within weeks, it was on *Publishers Weekly*'s graphic novel bestseller list, and Fantagraphics had ordered a second printing.[12]

I could go on at length about the great books of 2017 and 2018, but I'll limit myself to just one more: *Spinning,* the first graphic memoir from cartoonist Tillie Walden, published in 2017. The author was already a known quantity in comics, despite being barely old enough to vote. She was a student at Vermont's Center for Cartoon Studies and published her early work online. She found an audience with drawings of ornate buildings, simply rendered figures, and elegant lowercase lettering. Her 2015 short story "I Love This Part" is a heartbreaker about two teenage girls who fall in love.

Spinning tells the story of Walden's years as a competitive figure skater. It's incredible because it succeeds as a conventional narrative, as opposed to serving as just a showcase for Walden's ability to compose mind-blowing pages. This book makes me even more excited to see what she does next, and I hope she remains on her prolific course.

When I look at mainstream comics and the broader world of comics in general, I continually come back to some nagging questions of whether the comic shop business model is helping or hurting today's shops. I'm not talking just about issues of profits and viability. This is also about the art, and a question of whether comic shops are still the nexus for most of what is new and good in the art form. The answer is that some shops—many of which are profiled in these pages—remain vital to helping great work find an audience. But the comics ecosystem relies less on shops than before, and this reliance seems to be going down, not up.

There are many things filling the gap. Conventions, including a promising array of small press and "comic arts" festivals, have become some of the leading ways that up-and-coming creators get their work into the hands of readers. Many of the best bookstores now have well-stocked comics sections. Children's comics are a large and growing category, but most of those sales are through bookstores, libraries, and at school book fairs.

Add to this the continuing rise of Amazon as a competitor and the ongoing difficulties of being a physical retailer of anything, and it becomes clear that comic shops face some formidable challenges. The good news is that the best shops know what they're up against. When I asked them how they intend to survive and thrive, their answers were remarkably similar.

"There are things that we absolutely cannot do," said Brian Hibbs, at a panel discussion that I led at Flying Colors Comics in 2017. "We cannot compete on timely shipping. We cannot compete on a whole range of things. But I don't know that it matters a whole bunch because we're a fringe business, right?"

He was just getting started, and he soon shifted to talking about what comic shops do better than Amazon.

"Someone who doesn't know anything about comics could certainly go to Amazon and get some sort of recommendation from the algorithm," he said. "It's totally, totally different than if you walk into a well-appointed comic shop that's got quality staff. They're going to take you by the hand in a way that Amazon can't. . . . It's not an algorithmic thing, it's sort of a human emotional spark thing. I always say our job is to start fires. Our job is to be caught on fire by a piece of artwork, a writer's words, the synthesis of those two things, and then to fan that flame out to everyone else in the whole rest of the world. If we do that right, and we often do, then when we create that spark in you then you create that spark in other people, then it becomes a firestorm."

His comments were like a pastor trying to motivate the flock, and he got a spontaneous round of applause from an audience consisting largely of other comics retailers and longtime fans.

So, back to the question: Is the comic shop business model helping shops? First, a refresher of what the model is. Comic shops order nearly all their products on a nonreturnable basis, unlike most media retailers, which can return unsold items for a credit. At the dawn of the model, one of the key attributes was that shops received a higher wholesale discount than news-stands did for the same products. Today, the discount advantage is not nearly as much of an edge because the competition is giant companies such as Amazon, with incredible buying power, as opposed to a corner newsstand.

The business model was made for 1973, and the modifications that have taken place since then have not come close to addressing today's competitive landscape. At the same time, questioning the effectiveness of the model is largely beside the point. The model is not going to change unless publishers, Diamond, and the retailers themselves all want it to, and there is nothing close to consensus about this.

Most of the best shops are succeeding in spite of their business model, not because of it. They have mastered retail fundamentals to such an extent that they can coexist with an underlying system that is not much of an asset. And this is a good thing. The story of comic shops is one of survival, adaptation, and support for art in the face of a brutal market. The cockroaches persist, and that counts for something.

After making it through the challenges of 2017 and much of 2018, comic shops were looking forward to some potentially lucrative nuptials. One of the big publishing events of the summer was Batman marrying Catwoman, the culmination of a long-building story. Yes, this was a publishing gimmick, but Tom King's run on Batman had earned enough goodwill from fans and retailers that there was some genuine excitement.

The Batman-Catwoman romance was nothing new. The characters had been flirting since the 1940s, and an alternate version of them had gotten married and had a daughter who became a superhero in her own right, the Huntress.

DC was promoting the heck out of this event, knowing that comics weddings are great for sales, with examples such as the wedding issues of *Spider-Man* (in 1987) and *Superman* (1996). The publisher encouraged shops to buy vast quantities, with more than twenty variant covers. Some retailers responded by planning elaborate promotions, with wedding cakes and formalwear.

Then, days before the comic was released, the *New York Times* ran a story about it that included the revelation that the wedding issue would end without a wedding. The headline: "It Just Wasn't Meant to Be, Batman."[13] Indeed, Catwoman decided she couldn't go through with it. And, because this is a superhero story, it turns out that Bane, one of Batman's villains, helped orchestrate this change of heart.

"Unbelievable heel turn from DC this morning," said Brian Hibbs, posting on Facebook the day of the *Times* story. "I feel really really bad for the scores of retailers who bought 5,000 (!!!!) copies each to get exclusive variant covers that are now essentially unsalable."[14]

In writing about the chaotic world of comic shops, I often found Gib Bickel of The Laughing Ogre to be a voice of reason. That was certainly the case with the Batman wedding.

Yes, it was a bad thing that DC spoiled the story's ending by leaking it to the *Times*, he said. Yes, that probably hurt some stores that planned big events and ordered thousands of copies. I could tell a "but"was coming. But, he said, the story itself was well executed and satisfying for longtime readers.

"It was a good story. It was heartbreaking. It was solid," he said.

He sees this as a failure of DC's marketing and a creative success, which he thinks is much preferable to a marketing success that was a creative dud. He has seen enough comics events come and go that he doesn't get that excited when one incites outrage. Even *Secret Empire* didn't bother him much.

His main concern is that the store is doing well: 2018 is looking better than 2017. He's having fun.

"I'm doing what I'm supposed to do," he said.

Acknowledgments

This book grew from many conversations between Gib Bickel and me about our mutual interest in the history of the comics business. During my regular visits to The Laughing Ogre, we often would go off on tangents about the quirks of the comic shop model. One day, he said that a pioneering retailer had recently died and that somebody should interview those that remain. Well, here it is, Gib. Thank you, and your entire crew, including Michael Cavender, Sarah Edington, Juan Laura, Elissa Leach, Lauren McCallister, Alissa Sallah, Trish Smith, and the owner, Christopher Lloyd.

Several people helped me with reporting, whether by checking out stores on my behalf or by giving me a place to stay in my travels. They include Kasia and Ron Cristobal, Melissa Goldstein, Steve Olson, Alexandra Salerno, and Allison and Josh Jarmanning. Special thanks to Ryan Claytor, who has been to more comic shops than anyone I've known, and who gave me a long list of his favorites that turned out to be exceptionally reliable.

Thank you to the Cloud County Historical Society Museum in Concordia, Kansas, for helping me verify facts about Pop Hollinger.

I am grateful to all the people who agreed to interviews. I want to single out Jim Hanley, whose sharp memory and wit has helped enrich this story. Also, Bud Plant was a great help to me, generous with his time and eager to help me get in touch with some of his many old friends and colleagues. Many people shared photographs, including Jackie Estrada, David Miller, and Mike Zeck, who gave me access to their large photo collections.

Gillian Berchowitz, the director of Ohio University Press/Swallow Press, saw promise in this idea and made it happen. Also, thanks to Nancy Basmajian, Sebastian Biot, Rick Huard, Jeff Kallet, Beth Pratt, Sally Welch, and everyone else at the press.

Several people read versions of the manuscript and provided help with fact-checking and editing. Michelle Nolan and Jordan Kurella both gave me thorough notes and sound advice. Other readers included Vivian Witkind Davis, Josh Davis, and David Ploskonka.

Since I moved to Columbus in 2008, the city's comics scene has come into its own. Thanks to the people who make it great, a very long list that includes, but is not limited to, Lucy Caswell, Bob Corby, Rebecca Perry Damsen, Ken Eppstein, Vijaya Iyer, Susan Liberator, Laurenn McCubbin, Caitlin McGurk, James Moore, Jenny Robb, Tracie Santos, Jeff Smith, and Tom Spurgeon. One of my favorite things about Columbus is the Billy Ireland Cartoon Library and Museum at Ohio State University, whose staff members were there to help me examine old price guides and convention programs, among many other rare items.

And last, I want to thank my family. My father, Walt Gearino, took me to comic shops when I was a kid, and died while I was working on this book. I think you would have liked it, Dad. Thanks also to my mother, Maureen, and my brothers, Adam and Jon. Adam was with me during a day of interviews in his city, Chicago, and was a superb tour guide. My wife, Samara Rafert, is my most trusted editor, and helped make time for writing and research by wrangling our energetic daughters, Eliza and Norah.

Notes

NOTE ON SOURCES

Unless I specify otherwise, all quotations are from interviews I conducted. Also, I want to recognize two sources that I do not cite in the text but that were essential. First is Michael Dean, "Fine Young Cannibals: How Phil Seuling and a Generation of Teenage Entrepreneurs Created the Direct Market and Changed the Face of Comics," *Comics Journal,* no. 277 (July 2006). This magazine feature was the most substantial exploration of the origins of the direct market I had seen to that point, and it left me wanting to know more. Next is Robert Beerbohm, "Secret Origins of the Direct Market," *Comic Book Artist,* no. 6 (Fall 1999), no. 7 (February 2000). Beerbohm, himself a former retailer, knows more about the origins of the direct market that just about anyone.

CHAPTER 1: MAGICAL POWERS

1. The number of shops was provided by Milton Griepp of ICv2.com, who got it from Diamond Comics Distributors.

2. Heidi MacDonald, "Scott Pilgrim's Finest Sales Chart," ComicsBeat.com, September 17, 2010, http://www.comicsbeat.com/scott-pilgrims-finest-sales-chart-1 -million-in-print/.

3. Jim Milliot, "With No Buyer, Bankrupt Hastings Will Close All Stores," PublishersWeekly.com, July 21, 2016, http://www.publishersweekly.com/pw/by-topic /industry-news/bookselling/article/70982-hastings-will-close-all-stores.html.

4. John Jackson Miller, "Comics and Graphic Novel Sales Top $1 Billion in 2015," Comichron.com, July 12, 2016, http://blog.comichron.com/2016/07/comics-and -graphic-novel-sales-top-1.html.

5. "Digital Comic Sales Declined in 2015," news release, ICv2.com, July 11, 2016, http://icv2.com/articles/markets/view/34923/digital-comic-sales-declined-2015.

CHAPTER 2: THIS BOLD GUY (1968–73)

1. The origins of DC Comics can be found in many places, including Ron Goulart, *Ron Goulart's Great History of Comic Books* (Chicago: Contemporary Books, 1986).

2. Tim Hessee, "The Pop Hollinger Story," in *The Comic Book Price Guide*, 12th ed., by Robert M. Overstreet (New York: Harmony Books, 1982), A58–A66. Since almost all writing about Pop Hollinger refers back to this article, I sought to verify the main points, which I did by contacting the exceedingly pleasant people at the Cloud County Historical Society Museum in Concordia, Kansas.

3. Information about Claude Held and other early comics retailers, except for Pop Hollinger, is from Bill Schelly, *Founders of Comic Fandom: Profiles of 90 Publishers, Dealers, Collectors, Writers, Artists, and Other Luminaries of the 1950s and 1960s* (Jefferson, NC: McFarland, 2010).

4. The photo is posted with the credit "photo courtesy of Gary Groth" at http://www.fantucchio.com/fandom_reunion_comic-con_2011/1969_ny_comic_art_convention_luncheon_photo.html.

5. The few sentences here don't do justice to the fascinating history of underground comics, which can be found in several good books, including Patrick Rosenkranz, *Rebel Visions: The Underground Comix Revolution, 1963–1975* (Seattle: Fantagraphics Books, 2003).

6. Details on Phil Seuling's youth and young adulthood are from Carole Seuling.

7. Information about After Hours Bookstore is from Jonni Levas, who later was Seuling's business partner, and John Michael Cozzoli, who grew up in the neighborhood and was a customer at the store.

8. Eisner interviewed Seuling on October 27, 1983, and a transcript later was printed several times, including in Will Eisner, *Will Eisner's Shop Talk* (Milwaukie, OR: Dark Horse, 1991).

9. Details about the end of Seuling's marriage came from interviews, including with Bud Plant, Ron Forman, Michelle Nolan, and Carole Seuling.

10. Background on the censorship campaign came from Jonni Levas, among others.

CHAPTER 3: NONRETURNABLE (1973–80)

1. "A Guest Editorial by Phil Seuling," *Vampirella* #25 (June 1973): 3.

2. News of the legal settlement and commentary about the changes to Seuling's shows comes from NOW WHAT?, a column by Murray Bischoff, in *The Buyer's Guide for Comics Fandom*, no. 40 (1973): 26.

3. The description of the downturn in comic sales was based on an account in Seuling's interview with Eisner from *Shop Talk,* and on my interviews with others, such as former Marvel editor in chief Jim Shooter and retailer Chuck Rozanski.

4. There were about two hundred comic shops in 1977, according to Melchior Thompson, a longtime consultant to comic shops. This estimate is in line with what retailers tell me.

5. This information is based on comments from Levas, who was part of the business, and Jim Hanley, who was active in comics fandom at the time.

6. Seuling spoke of the immediate success of the distribution business in the *Shop Talk* interview.

7. Material about Donahoe Brothers comes from my interviews with Jim Friel, who worked for the company, and Richard Pini, who, along with his wife Wendy, later had a story published by Tim Donahoe.

8. Bill Schanes, formerly of Pacific, and Steve Geppi, a former customer of Irjax, informed me that those companies did not have contracts.

9. Cover date verified by the Grand Comics Database, http://www.comics.org.

10. This paragraph uses material from interviews with Friel and Milton Griepp.

11. Background on Irjax comes from Mike Friedrich and Steve Geppi and from court documents from the company's lawsuit against Sea Gate.

12. From court documents in the Sea Gate case, which were obtained from the National Archives. The files are from the U.S. District Court for the District of Maryland, civil case number 78–1884.

13. The concerns about subdistributors were described to me by Chuck Rozanski.

14. Seuling's newsletter was part of the court file in the case. Additional details about the case, such as names of parties and dates of events, also came from the file.

15. Friedrich told me that Marvel's lawyers insisted the company set up uniform terms of service for distributors, and he said DC would later have its version of the same process.

16. Rozanski later reprinted the letter in his column for *Comics Buyer's Guide,* and he has the text from the letter posted at http://www.milehighcomics.com/tales /cbg102.html. He gave permission for me to reprint it here.

CHAPTER 5: SECRET CONVERGENCE

1. Information on sales is based on annual sales figures compiled at http://www .comichron.com.

2. DC's relocation and the reasons for *Convergence* were widely covered at the time. One example: Jevon Phillips, "DC Comics Move to Burbank: It's All about Convergence," *Los Angeles Times,* June 3, 2015, http://www.latimes.com/entertainment /herocomplex/la-et-hc-dc-comics-publishers-20150604-story.html.

3. Laura Hudson, "What Is Going on with DC's Super-Confusing *Convergence*?," Wired .com, November 19, 2014, https://www.wired.com/2014/11/dc-comics-convergence/.

4. Alexander Jones, "Surprising No One, the End of Marvel's *Secret Wars* Is Delayed into 2016," ComicsBeat.com, November 30, 2015, http://www.comicsbeat .com/surprising-no-one-the-end-of-marvels-secret-wars-is-delayed-into-2016/.

5. Vaneta Rogers, "Just How Much Is Frank Miller Involved with *Dark Knight III: The Master Race?*," Newsarama.com, November 18, 2015, http://www.newsarama .com/26853-how-much-is-frank-miller-involed-with-dark-knight-iii-the-master -race.html.

CHAPTER 6: THE VALKYRIES

1. Kate Leth tells about the origins of the Valkyries in Arielle Yarwood, "Female Comic Shop Workers Create Their Own Group: Beware the Valkyries," BitchMe-dia.org, September 23, 2013, https://bitchmedia.org/post/interview-with-kate -leth-about-beyond-the-valkyries-comics.

2. Neil Gaiman, in *HOW TO GET GIRLS (into your stores),* a 1997 handbook for retailers published by Friends of Lulu, an organization for women in comics.

CHAPTER 7: HEYDAY (1980–84)

1. The description of Big Rapids' sales pitch is from Milton Griepp and Greg Ketter.

2. Jonni Levas said Sea Gate continued to be the industry leader for a few years after the Irjax lawsuit.

3. Griepp provided details on WIND and Big Rapids. Friel spoke about Big Rapids, and told me about the Lenin poster.

4. The marketing and distribution of *Elfquest* was described to me by Richard Pini. Dave Sim spoke about his early days selling *Cerebus* in several interviews with the *Comics Journal,* including in issue no. 130 (July 1989).

5. "Direct Sales Boom," *Comics Journal,* no. 64 (July 1981): 7.

6. Percentages are from Jim Shooter.

7. "Pacific Comics," in *Comics Between the Panels*, by Steve Duin and Mike Richardson (Milwaukie, OR: Dark Horse Comics, 1998).

8. The timing, location, and names of attendees at the meeting mainly came from Chuck Rozanski.

9. "The International Association of Direct Distributors," an article by Rozanski that originally appeared in *Comics Buyer's Guide* (June 2004). I saw it at MileHigh-Comics.com, http://www.milehighcomics.com/tales/cbg121.html.

10. Obituary of Jack Shuster, accessed at the website of Kraft Sussman Funeral Services, kraftsussman.com. http://kraftsussman.com/tribute/details/1021/Jack -Shuster/obituary.html,

11. The context for Kalish's hiring, including comments about the comics market at the time, was from Mike Friedrich.

12. I heard versions of this anecdote from Joe Field, Jim Hanley, and Melchior Thompson.

CHAPER 8: TURTLES, MICE, AND FISH (1984–88)

1. Background on *Turtles* mainly comes from Gary Groth's interview with Kevin Eastman in the *Comics Journal*, no. 202 (March 1998). Some details are from retailers, such as Jim Hanley.

2. Gary Groth, "Black and White and Dead All Over," *Comics Journal*, no. 116 (July 1987).

CHAPTER 9: COLLECTORS VS. READERS

1. References in this chapter to the Overstreet guide are to the 2016–17 edition. Robert M. Overstreet, *The Overstreet Comic Book Price Guide*, 46th ed. (Timonium, MD: Gemstone, 2016).

2. Ibid., referring to ads on page 289, and the back cover.

3. Information on Comics Guaranty Company, including pricing, taken from the company's website, CGCComics.com.

4. The effect of high CGC scores on pricing was described to me by Chuck Rozanski, and can be seen in records of sales of high-grade comics.

5. Details on eligibility for *Dark Knight III* variant covers come from the Diamond Comics Distributors order form for November 2015 releases.

CHAPTER 10: RAINA'S WORLD

1. Telgemeier's background details from Jennifer Maloney, "The New Wave of Graphic Novels," *Wall Street Journal*, December 31, 2014, https://www.wsj.com/articles/the-new-wave-of-graphic-novels-1420048910.

2. "Paperback Graphic Books," *New York Times*, May 17, 2015, https://www.nytimes.com/books/best-sellers/2015/05/17/paperback-graphic-books/.

3. "Remembering Rory—Photos and Stories," posted at http://flyingcolorscomics.blogspot.com/2008/05/remembering-rory-photos-stories.html, May 23, 2008.

CHAPTER 11: RE-REBIRTH

1. DC sales estimates are from David Carter, "DC Comics Month-to-Month Sales December 2015: And Lo, There Shall Be a Rebirth," ComicsBeat.com, February 2, 2016, http://www.comicsbeat.com/dc-comics-month-to-month-sales-december-2015-and-lo-there-shall-be-a-rebirth/. The article uses sales figures obtained from Milton Griepp of ICv2.com.

2. Johns's comments are from "Exclusive: DC Comics Rebirth Official Announcement," posted by ComicBookResources.com on YouTube.com, February 19, 2016, https://www.youtube.com/watch?v=JN_r_-OB42M.

3. Details on DC Rebirth pricing and scheduling were revealed in a panel at WonderCon in Anaheim, California, March 26, 2016, and covered in the comics and entertainment media, such as Borys Kit, "WonderCon: DC Relaunching Comics with Rebirth, Dropping Price of Comics," HollywoodReporter.com, March 26, 2016, http://www.hollywoodreporter.com/heat-vision/wondercon-dc-relaunching -comics-rebirth-878493. The fact that many titles would be returnable was reported in several outlets, including "DC Comics to Make 141 of Their Rebirth Titles Returnable," BleedingCool.com, April 14, 2016, http://www.bleedingcool .com/2016/04/14/dc-comics-to-make-141-of-their-rebirth-titles-returnable/.

4. DC's market share success in 2011 was covered by Comichron.com, including John Jackson Miller, "September 2011 Comic Book Sales Figures," http://www .comichron.com/monthlycomicssales/2011/2011-09.html.

5. June and July 2016 sales information from John Jackson Miller, monthly reports on Comichron.com, accompanied by blog entries about sales, http://www .comichron.com/monthlycomicssales/2016/2016-06.html and http://www .comichron.com/monthlycomicssales/2016/2016-07.html.

6. *Captain America* publication history was cobbled together from the Comics .org website.

CHAPTER 12: DEATHMATE (1988–94)

1. Background on the trading card business came from interviews with Steve Geppi, Milton Griepp, and others.

2. The two million sales figure for *Spider-Man* #1 is widely stated, and was said to come from Marvel at the time, but I couldn't locate the original source. Details about the book and its sales can be found in Patrick A. Reed, "25 Years Ago: Todd McFarlane's *Spider-Man* #1 Changed the Industry," ComicsAlliance.com, June 19, 2015, http://comicsalliance.com/tribute-todd-mcfarlane-spider-man/.

3. Sales figures for *X-Force* #1 and *X-Men* #1 were publicized at the time by Marvel. As is true with nearly all sales figures for comics in the direct market, there is no publicly available way to verify the numbers.

4. Store counts are from Melchior Thompson, "Estimated Direct Market Size in North America 1977–2016," a summary of his market research that Thompson provided to me.

5. Image's formation was covered in "Bye Bye Marvel; Here Comes Image," Newswatch, *Comics Journal*, no. 148 (February 1992).

6. Background on *Deathmate* is from retailers, and also is nicely summarized and skewered in Brent Chittenden, "It Came from the Long Box: *Deathmate*," ComicBookDaily.com, December 8, 2011.

7. Jeff Smith was reluctant to name the retailers that helped him when he launched *Bone,* for fear of accidentally leaving someone out. When I threw out some names, he confirmed that Field, Hanley, and Root were among the early supporters, but asked that I specify that this is not a complete list.

CHAPTER 13: THE MAILMAN (1994-2016)

1. Store counts, including the dramatic drop in the number of stores, are from material provided by Melchior Thompson.

2. Description of the market players comes from interviews with Steve Geppi, Milton Griepp, and others.

3. Sean Howe, *Marvel Comics: The Untold Story* (New York: Harper Perennial), 361.

4. The Perelman years at Marvel are described by Howe, "Boom and Bust," in *Marvel Comics: The Untold Story*.

5. Ivan Snyder, "Welcome . . . ," in *Mega Business: The Marvel Comics June 1995 Catalog*, 9.

6. Milton Griepp, "Four Fridays," *Internal Correspondence* (June 1995): 80.

7. "The Wonderful World of Dave Sim," *Internal Correspondence* (June 1995): 11.

8. Howe, *Marvel Comics: The Untold Story*, 387.

9. Diamond confirmed in a press release in November 2000 that the government probe had concluded; text from Comic Book Resources (cbr.com) archived at http://archive.li/sU6cL.

10. Figures are from the table "Estimated Overall North American Market Size" in "Comic Book Sales by Year," Comichron.com, http://www.comichron.com/yearlycomicssales.html.

CHAPTER 15: "ALL OF THE ABOVE" STORES

1. Comicopia ranked number 6 in the reader poll, which appeared in the *Comics Journal*, no. 151 (July 1992): 96.

2. Brian Hibbs, "Ethics and the Comics Industry" *Comics Buyer's Guide*, September 20, 1991. The text for this column and others is posted at the website for his store, http://www.comixexperience.com/tilting-at-windmills.html.

3. Brian Hibbs, "ComicsPro's Astoundingly Useful Annual Meeting," CBR.com, March 21, 2016, http://www.cbr.com/comicspros-astoundingly-useful-annual-meeting/.

CHAPTER 17: OLD SCHOOL

1. Neil Gaiman, "Psst. DreamHaven. Pass it on . . . ," NeilGaiman.com, February 13, 2007, http://journal.neilgaiman.com/2007/02/psst-dreamhaven-pass-it-on.html.

CHAPTER 19: COMICS AND . . .

1. Charles Brownstein, "RIP Dominic Postiglione," CBLDF.org, August 11, 2014, http://cbldf.org/2014/08/rip-dominic-postiglione/.

CHAPTER 20: BEST OF THE BEST

1. "Retailers Speak Out: A Forum," a partial transcript of a panel from a Toronto comics convention, *Comics Journal*, no. 151 (July 1992): 101.

EPILOGUE: A GOLDEN AGE OF ART AND ANXIETY

1. Kieran Shiach, "Marvel's Controversial Secret Empire Event Is Over. Was It Worth It?," Polygon, September 14, 2017, https://www.polygon.com/comics/2017/9/14/16307304/secret-empire-ending-explained.

2. Sales figures from Comichron.com.

3. Milton Griepp, "Marvel's David Gabriel on the 2016 Market Shift," ICv2, March 30, 2017, https://icv2.com/articles/news/view/37152/marvels-david-gabriel-2016-market-shift.

4. Ibid.

5. "Comics and Graphic Novel Sales Down 6.5% in 2017," Comichron.com, http://www.comichron.com/yearlycomicssales/industrywide/2017-industrywide.html.

6. Dominguez-Letelier's blog post was reprinted by Dan Casey, "Meltdown Comics, and LS Landmark, to Close after 25 Years, Nerdist.com, March 21, 2018, https://nerdist.com/meltdown-comics-closing-nerdmelt-showroom-los-angeles/.

7. "Zanadu Comics Has Evolved—Visit Our Online Storefront," February 2018, http://www.zanaducomics.com/.

8. Milton Griepp, "ICv2 Interview: Perry Plush on the End of His 42-Year Run as Comic Store Owner," ICv2, November 20, 2017, https://icv2.com/articles/news/view/38977/icv2-interview-perry-plush-end-his-42-year-run-comic-store-owner.

9. Jazmine Joyner, "How White Feminism Drove Me Out of the Valkyries," The MNT, August 29, 2018, https://www.comicsmnt.com/?p=1134.

10. Andrea Ayres, "Statement: The Valkyries Disbands Citing Failure to Serve Its Community," The Beat, September 6, 2018, http://www.comicsbeat.com/the-valkyries-disbands-citing-failure-to-serve-marginalized-communities/.

11. Chicago Humanities Festival, "My Favorite Thing Is Monsters," YouTube, November 7, 2017, https://www.youtube.com/watch?v=B9Pvk1l-_Lo.

12. Heidi MacDonald, "My Favorite Thing Is Monsters Gets 30,000 Second Printing," The Beat, March 14, 2017, http://www.comicsbeat.com/my-favorite-thing-is-monsters-gets-30000-second-printing/.

13. George Gene Gustines, "It Just Wasn't Meant to Be, Batman," *New York Times,* July 1, 2018, https://www.nytimes.com/2018/07/01/fashion/weddings/it-just-wasnt-meant-to-be-batman.html.

14. Brian Hibbs, Facebook post, July 1, 2018.

Index